Capital, Expectations, and the Market Process

Capital, Expectations, and the Market Process

Essays on the Theory of the Market Economy

By Ludwig M. Lachmann

Edited with an Introduction by
Walter E. Grinder

SHEED ANDREWS AND McMEEL, INC.
Subsidiary of Universal Press Syndicate
Kansas City

This edition is cosponsored by the Institute for
Humane Studies, Inc., Menlo Park, California, and
Cato Institute, San Francisco.

Capital, Expectations, and the Market Process copyright
© 1977 by the Institute for Humane Studies, Inc.,
Menlo Park, California.

Library of Congress
Cataloging in Publication Data
Lachmann, Ludwig M
    Capital, expectations, and the market process

    (Studies in economic theory)
    Bibliography: p.
    Includes index.
    1. Austrian school of economics—Addresses,
essays, lectures. 2. Economics—Addresses, essays,
lectures. 3. Capital—Addresses, essays, lectures.
I. Title. II. Series.
HB98.L3   330.15   77-1357
ISBN 0-8362-0678-9
ISBN 0-8362-0682-7 pbk.

CONTENTS

Acknowledgments

It has been a privilege and an honor to help assemble and bring to publication this collection of Professor Ludwig M. Lachmann's essays. Professor Lachmann is a delightful person to work with. He is a scholar whose wisdom matches his years, but whose energy and sense of intellectual excitement is that of a far younger man. He is a veritable fountain of knowledge, a never-ending stream of economic insight, which is always offered in his unique and curiously wonderful style. The Lachmann style combines a magisterial gusto with an omnipresent and delightfully amused twinkle in his eye.

There is no end of those to whom I should like to offer my thanks. First, there is the memory of Ludwig von Mises, an intellectual giant from whom we all have learned so much.

Second, there are the Institute for Humane Studies and, more important, the memory of its founder and guiding spirit, F. A. "Baldy" Harper. Without the support of the Institute none of this would have been possible. Thanks here must also go to all of those now associated with the Institute, especially to Charles G. Koch, George H. Pearson, and Kenneth S. Templeton.

Next I must thank my other Austrian mentors: Israel M. Kirzner, Murray N. Rothbard, and Hans F. Sennholz. Professors Kirzner and Rothbard especially lent their support and encouragement throughout the project. A very special thanks must go to Professor F. A. Hayek, whose works have influenced both Professor Lachmann and myself.

Thanks, too, are in order for Robert F. Ambacher, who helped to translate into English the two originally German articles included in this collection, and for Walter Block, who helped during the early stages of preparation of this volume.

A special thanks goes to the hard-working general editor of

this series of Austrian works, Laurence S. Moss. Last, but certainly not least, I would like to thank my patient wife, Mary Jane Grinder, for her help in typing the manuscript.

I wish to thank the following publications and publishers for reprint permission: *Zeitschrift für Nationalökonomie, Economica, Metroeconomica, Ordo, South African Journal of Economics*, Routledge and Kegan Paul, Augustus M. Kelley, Institute for Humane Studies, and D. Van Nostrand.

Walter E. Grinder
New York City

PART ONE
INTRODUCTION

In Pursuit of
the Subjective Paradigm
Walter E. Grinder

1.

For more than fifty years Ludwig M. Lachmann has been participating in scholarly debates on the development and application of economic theory; yet he is relatively unknown to professional economists and the intellectual community at large. Most mainstream economists find no comfort in his work because as a member of the Austrian school he opposes the direction taken by modern economic analysis. An intellectual descendant of Carl Menger (1840-1921), the founder of the Austrian school, Ludwig von Mises (1881-1973) and Friedrich A. Hayek (b. 1899), the Austrian school's most important twentieth-century representatives, Lachmann remains an outsider. It is hoped that this selection of his essays will introduce his thought to a wide and receptive audience.

What distinguishes Lachmann from other economists is his total devotion to subjectivism in economics. In fact, the evolution of his understanding and application of subjective concepts over the past four decades is a coordinating theme for these otherwise disparate essays and lectures. Lachmann's position today is that of a radical subjectivist.

According to Lachmann, economic phenomena cannot be explained unless they are related, either directly or indirectly, to subjective states of valuation as manifested either in choice or in expectations about the market. The implication is not that Lachmann opposes macroeconomic concepts per se. On the contrary, he has done some of his most important work in macroeconomics. His argument is that macroconcepts must be

3

traced to their microeconomic roots in the minds of valuing individuals in the market. In this respect, he is within the Austrian tradition as established by Menger, Mises, and Hayek.

Lachmann agreed with Erich Streissler that the importance of the Austrians and the subjective revolution that took place during the 1870s lies not so much in the development of the notion of marginalism as in the subjectivism established by Menger and his followers ("To What Extent Was the Austrian School Marginalist?" *History of Political Economy* 4 [Fall 1972]: 426–41; see also "The Significance of the Austrian School" [references to articles included in this volume are in abbreviated form]). Lachmann did not deny the historical importance of Menger's contributions to the technical development of marginal economics, although, Léon Walras's concept of "rareté," and William Stanley Jevons's notion of "final degree of utility" were in the air during the late 1860s and early 1870s. According to both Streissler and Lachmann the Austrian contribution was unique in its insistence on the thoroughly subjective character of utility, on the impossibility of finding an objective measure of utility for comparing or adding together levels of subjective welfare among individuals.

It is the thoroughgoing subjectivism of Menger, Mises, and, interestingly enough, Max Weber that Lachmann identified as the true heritage of the Austrian school (*The Legacy of Max Weber* [London: Heinemann, 1970]). Whether in defining "cost" in terms of privately perceived forgone opportunities, or in defining the market rate of interest as an expression of the individual time preferences of the members of the community, or—as is most important in Lachmann's work—in emphasizing the importance to the economy of private expectations about market conditions, subjectivism distinguishes the Austrian school.

Subjectivism as understood and articulated by the Austrians never became part of neoclassical economics after the marginal revolution of the 1870s, although several historians of economic thought, including Mises, maintained just the opposite (Joseph A. Schumpeter, *History of Economic Analysis* [New York: Oxford

University Press, 1954], pp. 849–50). Fritz Machlup stated that all essential insights of the early Austrian school had been incorporated into mainstream economics by the 1920s [lecture before the Austrian Club of New York City in 1968]; and Ludwig von Mises wrote that "all the essential ideas of the Austrian School were by and large accepted as an integral part of economic theory" (*The Historical Setting of the Austrian School of Economics* [New Rochelle, N.Y.: Arlington House, 1969], p. 41). While subjectivism dominated the early work of Jevons and Philip Wicksteed in England (in this regard philosophically more "Austrian" than other British economists), the Austrian emphasis on the subjective character of economics had almost been forgotten by the time Alfred Marshall's *Principles of Economics* had become the leading textbook among English-speaking economists during the 1890s and well into the first quarter of the twentieth century. English utilitarianism with its impossible program of "adding up" utilities to get a monetary measure of social or individual welfare eventually became the methodological underpinning of neoclassical economics.

The Lausanne school, which included Walras and Vilfredo Pareto, took the mathematical-functionalist rather than the philosophical approach to the discipline of economics (Emil Kauder, "The Intellectual and Political Roots of the Older Austrian School," *Zeitschrift für Nationalökonomie* 17 [December 1957]: 411–25). Individuals were viewed, not as actors pursuing ends susceptible to alteration and adjustment, but as pegs on which static indifference curves could be hung. The meaning of acts to the actors was disregarded in the methodology of the Lausanne school. Rather it was the desire to reduce economics to an "exact" science that led Walras and later Pareto to adopt the quantitative and graphical methods of the physical sciences in presenting the basic insights of marginalism. When subjective notions did enter the analysis of the Lausanne school, it was in the form of "tastes" that were regarded as basic and immutable. In fact, according to Lachmann, time and change—essential ingredients of the economic world—were subtly excluded in the Lausanne school's reliance on the technique of general equilibrium analysis. An individual free to change his mind is excluded by the assumptions of the timeless artificial world of general equilibrium.

As the concepts of neoclassical economics were developed, especially in J. R. Hicks's *Value and Capital* (Oxford: Clarendon Press, 1939), the subtle fusion of the Cambridge and Lausanne schools was completed. The subjective valuations of the individual and his task of choosing among *unequal* alternatives—notions considered basic discoveries of the early Austrian writers—were supposedly incorporated into neoclassical economics. But the truth is that the Austrian tradition was buried in a plethora of curves, models, and other quantitative abstractions.

The evolution of Lachmann's thought may be divided into three fairly distinct periods, which coincide with his experience in three different countries. First, there is Lachmann the young student, who is introduced to subjective economics in Germany. Second, there is the journeyman Lachmann maturing within the vibrant intellectual atmosphere of the London School of Economics during the 1930s and 1940s. Finally, there is the mature scholar at the University of the Witwatersrand in South Africa during the 1950s and 1960s. Unlike many who become less active as they get older, Lachmann has continued to search out new issues and push his thought in new directions to become one of the most vigorous and resolute advocates of the subjectivist position in the entire discipline of economics.

For a long time, however, Lachmann was unaware of the width of the gulf that separated his position from that of his neoclassical colleagues. For several decades he believed that almost all economists (with the exception of the Marxists) were part of one big, sometime feuding, but ultimately compatible family. In order to understand his failure to appreciate the gulf between his Austrian approach and the neoclassical school, it is necessary to trace his intellectual odyssey. This volume of essays is not only a positive contribution to an understanding of the market but also constitutes a single document about one man's intellectual development. Lachmann's work over almost five decades amounts to a forceful reassertion of the precious Mengerian insight that economic phenomena are essentially subjective.

2.

In 1924 Ludwig Lachmann entered the University of Berlin to study economics. The formal teaching of economics had deteriorated during the Weimar Republic, and there was little interest in theoretical economics in the aftermath of the *Methodenstreit* (Mises, *The Historical Setting*). Among the economic historians only Max Weber was held in academic esteem, and he was not a technically trained economic theorist. The one theoretical economist known in Germany was Joseph Schumpeter, and the name of Pareto was beginning to be heard on the fringes of German economic discussion. Only in monetary theory were German economists accomplishing anything amounting to a breakthrough, mainly due to the efforts of Albert Hahn and Siegfried Budge (H. S. Ellis, *German Monetary Theory 1905*–1933 [Cambridge: Harvard University Press, 1934]).

During the summer of 1926 Lachmann went to the University of Zurich, where Manuel Saitzew (the Russian-born economic historian) provided him with an overview of Ricardian economics and the marginal revolution. That summer in Zurich marked Lachmann's first, if brief, introduction to the subjectivist position in economics. Already he was attracted to the subjectivism of Carl Menger. In a comparison of the marginal and classical schools not only did the marginalists outshine the Ricardians, but in Lachmann's opinion Menger's accomplishment was the most impressive among the three codiscoverers of marginal utility.

After he returned to Berlin, Lachmann studied the then-current monetary theories, which included business cycle analysis, and concentrated on the work of A. L. Hahn, whose ideas paralleled those of R. G. Hawtrey in England. At this time he also had his first encounter with the Wicksell-Mises theory of the trade cycle, which was beginning to attract attention through the writings of both Mises and Hayek (Friedrich A. Hayek, *Geldtheorie und Konjunkturtheorie* [Vienna; 1929]; English edition, *Monetary Theory and the Trade Cycle,* trans. N. Kaldor and H. M. Croome [London: Jonathan Cape, 1933]).

A common practice among students at German universities at that time was to hire a tutor for independent study. Lachmann's choice of a tutor was young Emil Kauder—a stroke of good fortune for both of them, for they shared an interest in the Austrian school. Werner Sombart, Lachmann's mentor and dissertation sponsor at Berlin, advised Lachmann to read Schumpeter and Pareto but discouraged him from spending time on the writings of the Austrian school. Here again the prejudices of the lingering *Methodenstreit* may clearly be seen. Kauder and Lachmann concentrated on the work of Pareto, and although through this study Lachmann mastered Walrasian general equilibrium analysis well enough to earn his doctorate in 1930, both he and Kauder became convinced that the functional analysis of the Lausanne school was unsatisfactory.

As is often true, Lachmann's real economic education—his detailed inquiry into the problems of the discipline—began after he met the requirements for his doctorate. In addition to the study of Pareto he and Kauder began work on Hayek's *Monetary Theory and the Trade Cycle* (London: Jonathan Cape, 1933) and *Prices and Production* (London: George Routledge, 1931). During these sessions Kauder stressed the importance of subjectivism, especially subjective opportunity cost as the key concept in economic analysis. Lachmann also returned to the study of genetic-causal economics, the term of Werner Sombart and Hans Mayer (Hans Mayer, *Der Erkenntniswert der funktionellen Preistheorien* [Vienna: 1932]) for the Austrian method of reducing aggregates to statements about individual choices.

By this time, Lachmann's basic theoretical formulation, with the possible exception of the role of changing expectations in economic life, had been worked out. The foundations of Lachmann's theoretical structure were (1) a firm belief in the subjective theory of value and the related concept that the economic cost of an action always refers to a forgone opportunity; (2) a preference for the genetic-causal method of inquiry in contrast to the mathematical-functional approach of the Lausanne school, (3) a familiarity with the *verstehende methode* as espoused by Max Weber (an aspect of Lachmann's work that lay dormant for the next twenty years), and (4) an acceptance of the Mises-Hayek theory as a cogent explanation of the trade cycle.

3.

In early 1933 Lachmann left Germany and settled in England, where he discovered the difference in the intellectual climate, especially in the attitude toward economic theory, to be striking. Cambridge University as well as the more cosmopolitan London School of Economics was teeming with sophisticated ideas. These were, indeed, what G.L.S. Shackle termed "the years of high theory" (*The Years of High Theory,* 1926-1939 [Cambridge: Cambridge University Press, 1967]).

At the London School the neoclassical synthesis reigned supreme. This synthesis included elements of the Walrasian, Austrian, and classical traditions and, owing to Hayek's influence, a major emphasis on the Austrian theory of the trade cycle. At Cambridge University, on the other hand, the heritage in economic theory began with Marshall, and all contact with the Austrian tradition was avoided. When Lachmann arrived at the London School, Hayek was at the peak of his academic influence. The "big four"—John Hicks, Nicholas Kaldor, Abba P. Lerner, and Lionel Robbins—all adhered to the "new view" of production and its structure. This was definitely a period notable for the convergence of economic doctrines, as described by Lachmann in "Austrian Economics in the Present Crisis." Other important economists of Hayek's persuasion included Gottfried Haberler (Harvard University), Alvin Hansen (Harvard University), Fritz Machlup (Princeton University), Hans Mayer (University of Vienna), Richard von Strigl (University of Vienna), and, of course, Ludwig von Mises (University of Vienna).

During the 1930s the Hayekian view of the business cycle dominated the newly emerging orthodoxy (besides Hayek's writing cited above, see G. Haberler, "Money and the Business Cycle," in *Gold and Monetary Stabilization,* ed. Quincey Wright [Chicago: University of Chicago Press, 1932]; and Lionel Robbins, "Consumption and the Trade Cycle," *Economica* 12 [November 1932]: 413–30). Moreover, the trade cycle theory of Mises and Hayek suggested explanations for macrophenomena through the use of conceptual devices that in effect reduce them to microeconomic phenomena (Gerald P. O'Driscoll, *Economics as a Coordination Problem* [Kansas City: Sheed Andrews and McMeel, forthcoming]).

Another theoretical development at the London School that Lachmann found congenial was the notion of "opportunity cost." Lionel Robbins among others claimed that costs were necessarily subjective and accessible only to the private decision maker (James Buchanan and G. F. Thirlby, *L.S.E. Essays on Cost* [London: London School of Economics and Political Science, 1973]). Elsewhere the original objective interpretation of opportunity cost prevailed, and eventually the London School accepted the neoclassical practice of grafting a monetary measure of opportunity cost onto the existing body of microeconomic analysis. Subsequently, James Buchanan tried to revive interest in the subjective interpretation of opportunity cost and the early London School tradition (*L.S.E. Essays;* and *Cost and Choice* [Chicago: Markham, 1969]).

Unable to secure an academic position in Britain, Lachmann became a student of Hayek, as were Helen Makower and G. L. S. Shackle. During his first year at the London School Lachmann made the acquaintance of Paul Rosenstein-Rodan, who before leaving Austria had assisted Hans Mayer, holder of Menger's chair at the University of Vienna. From Rosenstein-Rodan Lachmann gained insight into the importance of expectations in economic activity and hence in economic theory.

During those early years of the Great Depression, when the theory of the business cycle was of central concern, the Austrian school economists focused on the factor of changing expectations. Ludwig von Mises had examined the influence of price expectations on the demand for money (*Theory of Money and Credit* [New Haven: Yale University Press, 1959]) and undertook to integrate expectations into the Austrian account of the business cycle. In 1933 Hayek presented his famous Copenhagen lecture, "Price Expectations, Monetary Disturbances, and Malinvestments," in which he systematically explored the relationship between expectations and the business cycle (*Profits, Interest, and Investment* [New York: Augustus M. Kelley, 1969], pp. 135–156). Also from this time the role of expectations became a central theme in Lachmann's writings.

Lachmann's first important article in this vein appeared in 1937 (*Economica* 4 [August 1937]: 295–308) under the title "Uncertainty and Liquidity Preference." Here Lachmann explored the relationship between price expectations and the demand for money. In 1943 expectations received central attention in "The Role of Expectations in Economics as a Social Science." Here Lachmann described how changing expectations alter plans of economic agents and upset the alleged tendency toward equilibrium. For Lachmann, the theory of expectations represents the second wave of subjectivist economics after Menger's breakthrough in the theory of value. According to Lachmann, economic theories that ignore the role of changing expectations are incomplete and misleading.

4.

Hayek's criticism of John Maynard Keynes's *Treatise on Money* appeared in 1930 and was of a theoretical nature and analytical in form ("Reflections on the Pure Theory of Money of Mr. J. M. Keynes," *Economica* 11 [August 1931]: 270–95; 12 [February 1932]: 22–44). Then the magnitude of the "secondary depression" that gripped the Western nations after the fall of the Kredit Anstalt in Vienna in May 1931 caught the Austrians by surprise. In 1936, when Keynes's *General Theory of Employment, Interest, and Money* appeared with its argument that a deficient aggregate demand accounts for the general collapse in business and employment, the Austrian theory began to lose adherents.

During the winter of 1935–36, Abba Lerner spent a semester at Cambridge and participated in Keynes's seminar where the soon-to-be-published *General Theory* was discussed at length. Lerner returned to the London School convinced that Keynes was correct and Hayek wrong. During that same year, Lachmann prepared a paper under Hayek's sponsorship in which he examined Keynes's explanation of "secondary depression." Since the Austrian theory of the business cycle was developed to explain the "primary depressions" typical in the nineteenth century, it needed to be supplemented by a theory of secondary depressions to account for the massive downturn in all sectors of the economy that immobilized the industrialized nations of the world. In Lachmann's view the cause of the primary depression was credit expansion by the banking system leading to malinvestment and later liquidation. But once in the throes of a primary depression, there was something to be said for Keynes's theory as an explanation of the secondary depression. On this point, Lachmann was closer to Gottfried Haberler ("Some Reflections on the Present Situation of Business Cycle Theory," *Review of Economic Statistics* 18 [February 1936]: 1–7; and Wilhelm Roepke, *Crisis and Cycles* [London: W. Hedge & Company, 1937]) than he was to Mises and his disciples. Lionel Robbins defended the Mises-Hayek theory (*The Great Depression* [New York: The Macmillan Co., 1934]) as did Murray N. Rothbard at a later date (*America's Great Depression* [Kansas City: Sheed & Ward, 1975]). Thus in 1936 Keynes presented a challenge on which some Austrians find themselves divided.

By 1938 the Hayekian position was ignored in the enthusiasm for the new Keynesian analysis. As has been said, "[The] voices [of the Austrians] were drowned in the fanfare of the Keynesian orchestra" (John Hicks, *Capital and Growth* [Oxford: Oxford University Press, 1965], p. 185).

In brief the Austrian theory of the business cycle was never refuted or even rejected at the London School, but simply forgotten despite the efforts of Hayek and subsequently Lachmann (as noted below) to improve the theory (Hayek, *Profits, Interest, and Investment* [1939; reprint, New York: Augustus M. Kelley, 1969]). With the Keynesian revolution, macroentities had replaced the action of individuals. Subjectivism and individual causation had been superseded by functional relations among objectified aggregates, which had few if any real world referents in the actions of economizing individuals. A whole tradition transplanted to British soil vanished. When Lachmann had arrived in London during the early 1930s, everybody was a Hayekian, but by the beginning of World War II the only consistent and thoroughgoing Hayekians left were Lachmann and Hayek himself.

5.

Lachmann spent the next decade trying to piece together what had gone wrong. In 1938 he was appointed Leon Fellow of the University of London to examine economic theory on the causes and phenomena of the Great Depression. He traveled extensively in the United States, where he did research at Columbia University, Harvard University, and the University of Chicago. While at Chicago he participated in Frank H. Knight's famous seminar in economics. Knight, though one of the great defenders of subjectivism in economics, had little sympathy with Austrian capital theory and the theory of the business cycle erected on those foundations. Perhaps after being stimulated by Knight's seminar, Lachmann wrote two articles—"On Crisis and Adjustment" and "A Reconsideration of the Austrian Theory of Industrial Fluctuations"—in which he tried to reestablish the validity of the Austrian position. However, as World War II grew in intensity and the economies of the industrialized countries began to mobilize for the war effort, Lachmann's work failed to attract attention. The same was true of Hayek's *Profits, Interest, and Investment* (1939), another restatement of the Austrian theory. Keynesian theory was better suited to the direction of a command economy mobilizing for war, and perhaps for this reason the Austrian analysis was ignored.

In a final effort to familiarize English readers with Austrian capital theory, Hayek published *The Pure Theory of Capital* (London: Routledge & Kegan Paul, 1941). This important work systematically developed the main points of his own investigations in neoclassical terminology. Hayek's treatise did not attract the scholarly attention it deserved, and Hayek, somewhat discouraged, turned his attention to political philosophy and the philosophy of science. Hayek's brilliant *Counter-Revolution of Science* (London: Free Press, 1955) and the essays included in *Individualism and Economic Order* (London: Routledge & Kegan Paul 1949) largely date from this period and document the gradual shift in his research interests from pure economics toward social philosophy.

Although there were many areas of intellectual agreement between Lachmann and Hayek, Lachmann was not really satisfied with Hayek's *Pure Theory of Capital.* Hayek based a large part of his 1941 analysis on Böhm-Bawerkian foundations, and Lachmann considered Hayek's work to possess many of the disadvantages of the current macroeconomic approach. Lachmann considered himself a follower of Menger's subjectivism, and he, like Menger, criticized the work of Eugen von Böhm-Bawerk as a deviation from the main line of development of Austrian economics, in that Böhm-Bawerk's analysis lost sight of the individual and built a model of capital accumulation based on the older Ricardian notion that capital was a "subsistence fund."

In 1941 Lachmann was appointed a lecturer at the University of London and later moved to Aberystwyth, Wales. In 1943 he received an appointment at the University of Hull, where he remained until 1948. In Wales and later at Hull he perfected his subjectivist position. His work on expectations continued ("The Role of Expectations"). In reaction to Hayek's *Pure Theory of Capital* and also in response to the general character of modern capital theory, he began a project that was to occupy him for the next ten years. He believed that by analyzing defects in capital theory, he could expose misconceptions in other areas of macroeconomic analysis.

Building on the essential insights of Hayek's classic 1935

paper, "The Maintenance of Capital" (*Economica* 2 [August 1935]: 241–76), Lachmann attacked the assumption that capital is a homogeneous and measurable aggregate in his article "On the Measurement of Capital" (*Economica* 8 [November 1941]: 361–77). His later paper "Complementarity and Substitution" is a detailed presentation of the view that capital is not a homogeneous aggregate but rather a complex interdependent *structure* of heterogeneous producer's goods. This line of inquiry culminated in the publication of his book *Capital and Its Structure* in 1956 (2d ed., Kansas City: Sheed Andrews and McMeel, forthcoming).

Despite his differences with Hayek on certain aspects of capital theory, Lachmann found Hayek's work on methodology both a guide and an inspiration. The key to a proper understanding of the discipline of economics is the realization that there is more to economic analysis than the pure logic of choice. This criticism was implicit in Hayek's methodological writings. Still it was not clear what that something "more" was. Not until after Lachmann became head of the department of economics at the University of the Witwatersrand in Johannesburg did he succeed in settling the problem to his own satisfaction.

6.

In 1947 Paul Samuelson attempted to fuse the ideas of Keynes and general equilibrium analysis into a new neoclassical synthesis. Lachmann read Samuelson's *Foundations of Economic Analysis* (Cambridge: Harvard University Press, 1947) and, not surprisingly, found the synthesis unconvincing. Although Keynesian economics had some relevance to extreme situations such as the Great Depression and the command economies of World War II, its prescriptions were unsound for an economy functioning under normal conditions.

By the time Lachmann reviewed Ludwig von Mises's *Human Action* (1949) in 1951 ("The Science of Human Action") he had become reacquainted with the writings of Max Weber. The combined influence of Mises and Weber prompted Lachmann to censure Samuelson and others for trying to graft new concepts onto old ideas until economic theory had lost all proportion. To Lachmann there were basically two distinct and mutually exclusive ways of analyzing complex economic phenomena. The Samuelson-Keynes synthesis in positing quantitative relationships between fictitious entities represented the failure of modern economics. The Mises-Weber approach, on the other hand, belonged to a tradition that endeavored to *understand* the essence of economic action. It embodied and introduced the subjective, or interpretive, economic analysis.

In his inaugural lecture at the University of the Witwatersrand ("Economics as a Social Science") Lachmann presented a synthesis of his views with those of Mises and Weber. In agreement with Mises, he conceived human action to be more than automatic reaction within a given economic environment; therefore any theory professing to *interpret* economic activity must refer to the purposive actions of individuals. Since choice is an activity of the human mind, it is impossible to divorce choice from the larger notion of purpose. Economics is therefore a discipline that promotes understanding of economic activity, and not a discipline that uses the methodology of the natural sciences to predict the outcome of economic activity.

Lachmann's work during the 1950s may be described as a fusion of (1) his concept of the role of expectations in capital theory, (2) the Misesian view of human action as purposive, and (3) the *verstehende* sociology of Max Weber. Since thought and action are identical categories, an understanding of thought will also furnish an understanding of action. To understand action is to comprehend the thought that sets that action in motion. Interpretive economics relates complex economic phenomena to the individual plans and purposes that set them in motion, and this analysis requires constant reference to the plans, preferences, values, and expectations of acting individuals.

7.

In assessing the evolution of economic theory during the

decades 1933–1953 ("Some Notes on Economic Thought"), Lachmann attached great significance to the use made of expectations in economic analysis. He took issue with the basic premise of Keynesian analysis that the market economy requires constant stimulation by the state to avoid general stagnation. He also criticized microeconomists who view competition as a state of affairs (that is, "when the demand curve facing the firm is perfectly elastic") rather than as a process. In "Ludwig von Mises and the Market Process" Lachmann found the neoclassical view of competition not only defective but totally misleading as a standard for judging the efficacy of real world market conditions. He concluded that both micro and macroeconomics had led contemporary economists down dead-end streets.

In his 1956 article "The Market Economy and the Distribution of Wealth" Lachmann applied the Misesian notion of market process to the distribution of social income. Here he attacked the concept that the distribution of wealth should be taken as a datum rather than a result of the market process. The market economy constantly adapts to changing historical conditions and alterations in the plans of acting individuals. As conditions change, Lachmann pointed out, the mode of distribution of wealth changes also. These views led Lachmann to join with Mises in a critique of neoclassical economists' use of equilibrium analysis as a blueprint for reordering the social world. This point of view is expressed in "Methodological Individualism and the Market Economy."

8.

In his review of Joan Robinson's *Accumulation of Capital* (1956) Lachmann sought to place the book within the traditional framework of economics. Because she was interested in long-run equilibrium questions, not the mainstay of early Keynesian analysis, Robinson could not be called a Keynesian. In his review "Mrs. Robinson and the Accumulation of Capital" Lachmann dubbed her a "latter-day Ricardian" and thus classified her and her followers as counterrevolutionaries to the subjectivist revolution that Menger has initiated in reaction to Ricardo and the adherents of classical analysis.

The counterrevolutionary character of a growing body of current economic thought deeply disturbed Lachmann. Throughout the next decade he worked out a counterattack against the neo-Ricardians. A most insightful article in this vein first appeared in German (translated under the title "The Significance of the Austrian School in the History of Ideas").

At this same time Lachmann was becoming increasingly disenchanted with the neo-Keynesian model builders, or "neoclassical formalists" as he called them. He questioned the value, either for understanding the economy or for formulating policy, of elegant models without a base in the microeconomic realities of the market. Once again he deplored the rejection of the subjective springs of economic phenomena for mathematical formulations and misleading equilibrium models. He singled out for criticism the work of the post-Keynesian theorists J. R. Hicks, Paul Samuelson, and Robert Solow (translated under the title "Model Constructions and the Market Economy") in an article that originally appeared in German.

In *Macro-economic Thinking and the Market Economy* (London: Institute of Economic Affairs, 1973), Lachmann found fault with both the neo-Keynesians and the neo-Ricardians for ignoring the real issues in their disputations. He also sketched the subjectivist, or Austrian, answers to such important questions as the nature of techniques of construction to profit relationships in a market economy. In short, the controversy over "reswitching," as it came to be known, is largely due, in Lachmann's estimation, to a confusion about the nature and source of profit. Profit is a result of adjustment to unexpected change, and therefore the magnitude of profit is constantly changing. Moreover unexpected change cannot be integrated within an equilibrium model of the economy. In equilibrium profit cannot exist.

9.

During the 1950s and 1960s Lachmann continued to work on

two lifelong interests, that is, the role of changing expectations in the economy and the theory of capital. His advanced concepts about expectations are formulated in "Professor Shackle on the Significance of Time." Static equilibrium models are misleading because they ignore the importance of unanticipated change. Is there any reason to believe a tendency toward equilibrium really exists? Static equilibrium analysis and the models distilled from it assume that equilibrium can be attained automatically. To the contrary, in any real world market situation whether individual plans diverge or converge depends on the way expectations adjust. But inasmuch as expectations are conjectures about the future, it is presumptuous to graft expectations onto equilibrium models where the final position is predetermined by conditions stated at the outset.

Lachmann's concepts of expectations are both novel and intriguing. The future is unknowable but not unimaginable. Persons differ in their mental projections, since it is improbable that any large number of persons will ever anticipate the future exactly, expectations will always diverge. According to Lachmann (following G. L. S. Shackle), the forces for the divergence of plans are likely to be stronger than those for their convergence.

Fluctuations in economic life continuously alter the basic constellation of knowledge; and this fluidity is, after all, the essence of the economic problem and the reason why efficient central planning is impossible (see, for example, Hayek, "The Use of Knowledge in Society," in *Individualism and Economic Order*, pp. 77–91). In his review of Shackle's *Time in Economics* ("Professor Shackle"), Lachmann pushed the logic of Hayek's insight to the conclusion that any attempt at economic prediction is futile: "The impossibility of prediction in economics follows from the fact that economic change is knowledge, and future knowledge cannot be gained before its time." In a review of one of Shackle's later works, Kenneth Boulding called this stand on prediction and knowledge "Lachmann's Law" ("A Review of *Epistemics and Economics* by G. L. S. Shackle," *Journal of Economic Literature* 11 [December 1973]: 1373–74). Thus after Mises and Hayek,

Shackle was the economist whose thought had a tremendous impact on Lachmann's intellectual development.

As noted, the Lachmann-Shackle position that forces of divergence tend to outweigh forces of convergence makes a general market equilibrium unlikely. According to Lachmann, the strength of the forces of convergence depends almost entirely on the activities of entrepreneurs. If entrepreneurs take advantage of the price-cost discrepancies attending changing circumstances, the entrepreneurial function of using resources in search of profit (the process of innovation and imitation) will, as most Austrian economists agree, lead to a convergence of the plans of individuals in markets. However, because change is ever present and unpredictable, individuals have different expectations about the character and extent of change. It is this factor more than any other that precludes anything approaching a macroeconomic general equilibrium in the uncertain world of market activity.

10.

Lachmann's policy positions are consistent with his basic approach to economic analysis. Although a determined opponent of interventionism in the market, his opposition is less philosophically founded than that of either Mises or Hayek. In many ways he is the perfect example of the traditional "classical liberal" economist. His defense of the market economy derives mostly from a deep concern for the historical development of Western civilization. All interference with the entrepreneurial process of adjustment and the market's consequent diffusion of knowledge weakens the forces of equilibrium and impedes rapid market clearing. Either piecemeal or planned market intervention inevitably creates dislocations that lead in turn to more extensive market interventions—a spiral that eventually cripples the market economy without providing a satisfactory substitute.

From the twelfth century onward Western civilization and the market economy developed side by side. During the nineteenth century the market economy experienced an accelerated development to the material advantage of the expanding populations of the Western world. During this century, and especially after World War I, both economic theory and economic policy have deteriorated to the point that the survival of the market economy is threatened. For the greater part of the twentieth century Western society has been sustained by the past accomplishments of the relatively unhampered market economy of the nineteenth century; however, such capital consumption cannot go on forever.

Interventionism in one form or another has become the stated policy of Western governments. Planners profess the ability to coordinate economic affairs better than the freely operating market process, which they often characterize as "chaotic" or "anarchistic." In one form or another central governments cooperate with the private sector in programs to "rationalize" or "improve upon" the market system by cultivating "balanced growth" ("Cultivated Growth and the Market Economy"). However, intervention, no matter how well intentioned, leads to secondary economic dislocations that further hamper the market process and set the stage for more severe maladjustment.

Perhaps the most alluring and ultimately most pernicious of planned interventions are the expansionary, or "easy money," policies of the central banks. It is monetary or credit expansion, causing a system-wide distortion of the price structure and the entrepreneurial process, that makes economic calculation difficult and sometimes impossible. Why do central banks inflate their currencies, and why do the Austrian economists see the consequences of this inflation to be so economically and socially disastrous?

Originally the money supply is increased with the object of artificially lowering market rates of interest in order to stimulate investment, production, and employment. However, along with the massive infusions of new money into the various banking networks is the ominous development of powerful and government-favored labor unions. Faced with the political-economic power of organized labor and the knowledge that monetary deflation would create labor unrest, governments resort to expansion of the money supply as a method of temporarily achieving full employment. In their privileged position, unions force a continued upward movement in money wages that can only be sustained by resorting to further increases in the money supply. Therefore the twin causes of the Western monetary malaise are monetary expansionism and powerful labor unions that prevent downward movements in wages and prices ("Causes and Consequences of Inflation in Our Time").

To Lachmann the significance of inflation among the Western nations is not simply the continual rise in prices or the consequent redistribution of income from creditors to debtors. Equally important is that the artificial booms and consequent slumps caused by the infusion of money into the loan market make the market economy appear inherently unstable. This encourages the clamor for further intervention, such as planning for "investment stabilization" and the related call for "indicative planning." With wages not permitted to fall because of the threat of union unrest and prices and wages moving upward at an accelerating pace, the planners opt for wage and price controls. At this point the market process cannot operate effectively, and if the wage and price controls are enforced, the market system comes to a halt. For these reasons government intervention in economic affairs should be minimal. The role of government should be as circumscribed as possible and conform to the classical liberal ideal of supporting the free market by strengthening the institutions of private property and voluntary business contract.

11.

The roots of Lachmann's subjectivism date from his student days in the 1920s and his discovery of Menger's writings. However, while the subjectivist position in economics including the views that utility, cost, and market phenomena are rooted in the private plans of individuals was never dominant during the 1920s, it was considered a respectable position. By 1960 all had changed. Lachmann viewed with alarm the trend to ignore the Austrian, or subjective, contribution to the discipline. While to some observers Lachmann's subjectivism appeared increasingly uncompromising, his basic position was that, in Hayek's words, "every important advance in economic theory during the last hundred years was a further step in the consistent application of subjectivism" (*The Counter-Revolution of Science* [New York: Free Press, 1955], p. 31). Consequently, as subjectivism lost favor in academic circles, Lachmann defended it with greater intensity. The form of Lac mann's defense was heavily influenced by the work of Alfred Schütz.

In 1935 Felix Kaufmann lectured at the London School on the recent writings of the Austrian philosopher and sociologist Alfred Schütz (A. Schütz, *Der sinnhafte Aufbau der sozialen Welt* [Vienna: Julius Springer, 1932; translated as *The Phenomenology of the Social World* [Evanston: Northwestern University Press, 1967]). In synthesizing the philosophy of Edmund Husserl and the sociology of Max Weber. Schütz presented a forceful anti-positivist defense of the subjective foundations of the social sciences. While the Kaufmann lecture did not create much of a stir among the London School economists, Lachmann found it meaningful. Several years later he read an account of Schütz's *Der Aufbau* that appeared in *Economica* (A. Stonier and K. Bode, "A New Approach to the Methodology of the Social Sciences," *Economica* 4 [November 1937]: 406–24) but was not motivated to study Schütz in depth. Not until the midfifties when the subjectivist position was badly in need of defense did Lachmann begin a systematic analysis of Schütz's philosophy.

According to Lachmann, if the methods of the social sciences are to elucidate social phenomena, they must be based on the concept that the social world contains not only objective measurable facts but the "perceptions" of these facts by social actors, each of whom plans on the basis of his unique perceptions. If the social sciences are to mature, they must follow the course laid out by Mises, Hayek, and Schütz. Lachmann's work in this area is contained in "The Historical Significance" and his full-length study of Max Weber's thought, *The Legacy of Max Weber.*

12.

In 1975 Ludwig Lachmann was named Visiting Professor of Economics at New York University and spends the academic year in New York City and the summer months at his home in Johannesburg, South Africa. He remains an active teacher and scholar, and a listing of his most recent publications appears at the end of this volume.

Austrian Economics in the Present Crisis of Economic Thought

1.

In the present confused state of thinking on fundamental economic issues the time may have come to set forth a succinct outline of a position that we may with some justification denote as "Austrian." This has to be done in a situation of considerable turmoil. While the Ricardian counterrevolution of our days has thus far failed to present any new insights that are either novel or compelling, the neoclassical forces called upon to resist it already seem to be in some disarray.[1] Perhaps this is a temporary phenomenon due merely to the sheer dash and verve with which the attackers have conducted their forays; perhaps it betrays a sense of insecurity, reflecting an awareness of the weakness of their position. Elsewhere we learn, less than three decades after Keynes's death, of a crisis in Keynesian economics. And if as perspicacious a thinker as Professor G. L. S. Shackle chooses to give his most mature work, *Epistemics and Economics*, the subtitle *A Critique of Economic Doctrines* (Cambridge: Cambridge University Press, 1972), the implication that all is not well with more than one doctrine is noteworthy.

The main reason for an Austrian pronouncement is that otherwise a possibly interesting contribution to the discussion of some of the issues currently in dispute may go by default. But there are other reasons, with some of which we shall have to deal later on. One of them arises from the fact that, while a certain strand of Austrian thought has, over the last few decades, be-

---

This essay was prepared by the author especially for this volume and appears in print for the first time.

come fused with, and embedded in, what has come to be called
the *neoclassical synthesis*, some Austrians have refused to regard
this as a happy union. They and their heirs may feel that the case
for a divorce is now strong.

There is, however, also a case against such an Austrian pronouncement. It derives its strength from a distaste for what
many will regard as a factious enterprise. The view is widely held
that "schools of thought" belong to the adolescent stage of a
discipline. We have heard it said that there is only good and bad
economics, hence no place for Austrian economics. A mature
discipline, we are told, continues to fuse what is best in the
contributions of various schools and to discard the rest. Such a
synthesis may not be easy to achieve, but we must do nothing to
jeopardize it.

It seems to us, however, that the validity of such views depends
on the epoch in which one is living. There are, in the history of
economic thought, ages of convergence and ages of divergence.[2]
The period from about 1890 to 1914, the age of Fisher, Marshall, Pareto, and Wicksell, in which the neoclassical synthesis
was born, was an age of convergence in which rivers flowing
from many diverse sources merged into one broad stream. Ours,
by contrast, is an age of divergence. We have already described
the scene on which high-level debates in economic theory are
pursued today as one of considerable turmoil. When factions are
already in existence, who can be blamed for being factious?
Where the air is full of the clamor of rivals, who can be re-
proached for raising a voice of dissent? In an age of convergence
an enterprise such as ours may be frowned upon; in an age of
divergence it can hardly be condemned.

2.

The fact that Sir John Hicks gave his recent book *Capital and
Time* the subtitle *A Neo-Austrian Theory* [Oxford: Clarendon
Press, 1973] adds to the confusion reigning on our methodological scene. While it constitutes an obstacle, at the same time it
provides us with an opportunity to exhibit certain aspects of

Austrian thought by contrasting them with the well-articulated thought of a great contemporary. For in confronting this book the "Austrian" economist of our days is compelled to state that he is not a neo-Austrian in the Hicksian sense; and of course he has to explain why he is not before he can proceed to make his own positive contribution. But the very fact that he has to justify his refusal to follow Hicks enables him to make his reader gradually familiar (in a way that otherwise might not seem called for) with some Austrian ideas, at first by showing that they do not fit into the Hicksian mold, later on by displaying their positive uses in understanding a dynamic world. It thus becomes possible to examine the same object successively from various angles.

This is not the place to review Sir John's remarkable book.[3] We are not even called upon to do justice to it as an attempt to clarify some of our contemporary confusions. All we are concerned to show here is that a good deal of what is offered to us as neo-Austrian is at variance with what we must regard as fundamental Austrian tenets. It was not for nothing that Menger regarded Böhm-Bawerk's theory "as one of the greatest errors ever committed."[4] Böhm-Bawerk was, at least in his theory of capital and interest, a Ricardian, interested in capital only as a receptacle of the flow of interest, who asked the Ricardian question why and how the owners of "intermediate products" contrived to draw a permanent income from their wealth as if they were factor owners. He found a Ricardian answer to this question.

Hicks follows Böhm-Bawerk in stressing the time dimension of production, but also employs a kind of sequence analysis as providing causal chains to trace the gradual unfolding of the effects of technological innovation on income distribution and growth. We are shown how, with the lapse of time, these effects gradually show themselves at successive stages of production. Time is here both the dimension of production and the dimension in which the effects of change show themselves.

In order to accomplish this sequence analysis and formulate a theory of the "traverse" from one equilibrium path to another, Hicks has to make two assumptions, static expectations and the existence of only one good. The former means that the actors in his model always expect the future to be exactly like the present. The Austrian objection to this assumption rests not merely on its lack of realism, striking though this is. Can we really imagine employers who, though experiencing continually rising wage rates, nonetheless always expect their future wage costs to be the same as their present? Much worse is that this assumption effectively prevents what from the Austrian standpoint are some of the more important problems concomitant to change from ever coming into view.

Austrian economics reflects a "subjectivist" view of the world. The subjective nature of human preferences is its root. But in a world of change the subjectivism of expectations is perhaps even more important than the subjectivism of preferences. The assumption of "static expectations," however, means not merely that expectations as autonomous forces causing economic change are ignored so that a mechanism of other forces may be exhibited in its "pure form" but also that the *diversity of expectations,* the pattern of inconsistent expectations held by different individuals at the same time, which we find in the real world, cannot even come into sight. Static expectations mean no less than that the minds of all actors at the same moment work in identical fashion. One of the achievements of the subjectivist revolution is blandly nullified.

Hicks's other assumption, the one-commodity world, is no less open to objection from an Austrian point of view. But as criticism of it has also played a prominent part in the neo-Ricardian counterrevolution, at least at one stage, it will be more conveniently dealt with in our next section.

Since the label "neo-Austrian" has now been preempted by Hicks for his own brand of theory, we are unable to dub the point of view to be elucidated here "neo-Austrian." We might perhaps call it neo-Mengerian, or Mises-type, or even palaeo-Austrian. Each of these would be an awkward label. We trust that if in what follows we simply call it Austrian without qualifying epithet the reader will understand what we mean by it.

3.

Since Sraffa in 1960 gave the signal, the attack on the Walras-Paretian general equilibrium theory has steadily gained ground.[5] From an Austrian point of view the strong antisubjectivist bias of this neo-Ricardian movement is naturally reason enough to oppose it. A style of economic thinking in which there is no place for human preferences, let alone time preferences, is hardly acceptable to the heirs of Menger. But some of the weapons the neo-Ricardians have used in their attack on the neoclassical citadel are of great intrinsic interest to the student of intellectual warfare. They might turn out to be useful for other purposes. It will be worth our while to have a close look at them and see what we can learn from them.

From a common source in Wicksell's work two broad streams of capital theory have emerged over the last fifty years. One is the distinctly Austrian stream we find manifested in Professor Hayek's work, in *Prices and Production* (London: George Routledge, 1931); in "The Maintenance of Capital" (*Economica* 2 [August 1935]: 141–276); and in *The Pure Theory of Capital* (London: Routledge & Kegan Paul, 1941). Here emphasis is on the importance of relative price movements and the impossibility of measuring investment without a criterion for the maintenance of a heterogeneous capital stock. The other stream found prominent expression in Professor Joan Robinson's well-known critique of neoclassical capital theory. Here the problems stressed by Hayek are ignored. The fact that in all these years there has been, with one exception noted below, virtually no contact between these two streams is of course just another reflection of the present crisis of economic thought.

In what follows we attempt to show that a keen pursuit of the implications of some of the more successful critical arguments used in the course of the neo-Ricardian counterrevolution will take us far afield, away from the mountain fastness of macroeconomics and into fields in which what happens depends on individual action and expectations, which of course need not be consistent; and that in the course of this pursuit one of the main sources of Keynesian inspiration becomes rather tarnished. Three examples will serve our purpose.

1. Ever since Professor Joan Robinson proclaimed "the generalization of the General Theory" as her aim, Cambridge economists fond of being described as "neo-Keynesians" have taken an interest in growth theory. In these endeavors the notion of investment, the famous Keynesian $I = S$, naturally plays a prominent part. How can its use be reconciled with the now-accepted fact that outside long-run equilibrium a measurable capital stock does not exist? The usual answer is that investment is a flow, not a stock, and thus exempt from such objections. But this answer applies only to gross investment, not to that part of it which concerns growth. Can we isolate this latter element without having to concern ourselves with the maintenance of the capital stock?

Keynes defined "the *investment* of the period" as "the addition to capital equipment as a result of the productive activities of the period."[6] But if we cannot measure this capital equipment, how do we know what constitutes an addition to it? To hold that in the short period capital is *by definition* constant and thus provides a firm floor for our adding activity would be to ignore the pre-Wicksellian innocence of the Marshallian definition. The awkward fact remains that the supposedly measurable macroeconomic magnitude I has to be measured by means of another magnitude based on subjective evaluation.

Keynes was well aware of the problem. He explicitly agreed with Professor Hayek "that the concepts of saving and investment suffer from a corresponding vagueness,"[7] but added that this applies only to net saving and net investment since they depend on subjective evaluation. By contrast "The *saving* and the *investment*, which are relevant to the theory of employment, are clear of this defect, and are capable of objective definition."[8]

In fact we soon learn that this is not so. For Keynes's own notion of investment, by contrast to the contaminated "net investment," is defined as gross investment minus user cost, as $A_1 - U$. In the "Appendix on User Cost" Keynes admitted that "user cost partly depends on expectations as to the future level of wages" and that "it is the expected sacrifice of future benefit involved in present use which determines the amount of user cost."[9] Thus Keynesian investment, affected by user cost, is by no means "capable of objective definition." User cost depends on expectations, which are as subjective as preferences. Investment is no more "objective" than the stock of capital.

2. From Ricardo to Professor Pasinetti the difference between a "classical corn economy" and a multicommodity world has often been used as a basis for critical arguments of all kinds. It has been a standard criticism of Böhm-Bawerk's theory that, in order to demonstrate the higher productivity of roundabout production, we need as a yardstick a price system invariant to those changes in interest and wages that are the necessary result of roundabout production. Furthermore, in a multicommodity world the subsistence fund must consist of wage goods in precisely that proportion in which wage earners wish to spend their incomes on them, otherwise there will be capital gains and losses. Pasinetti's main criticism of Irving Fisher's "rate of return over costs" has been that the price system of a multicommodity world entails a uniform rate of profit, and that to "explain" the rate of return on capital in terms of opportunities for profit inherent in such a price system is no explanation at all.

It seems to us, however, that the argument may be turned around and used to disclose, not just the inconsistency of certain conclusions within the framework of equilibrium theory, or even of a heuristic device such as Fisher's "rate of return over costs," but also the weakness of the notion of a "price system" in a world of change. In a world in which prices depend on supply and demand in a multitude of markets, a constant price system is almost inconceivable. Relative prices change every day for one reason or another, for instance, changes in knowledge that may occur on both sides of the market. A Ricardian might say that these are daily fluctuations around an equilibrium level determined by "underlying forces" like technology and the wage level, but, apart from changing technology, he can say that only if he regards demand as an ephemeral force. As soon as we regard demand as a "datum," daily price changes reflect changed data.

We conclude that a price system implying a uniform rate of profit and wage rate cannot exist. The forces tending to bring it about will always be weaker than the forces of change. For the explanation of phenomena observed in a market economy it is useless. The market is a continuous process, not a "given" state of affairs. Divergent rates of profit in a multicommodity world are both a result of change and a cause of further change.

3. In a one-commodity world the stock of capital is homogeneous and physically measurable. In a multicommodity world it loses this property and becomes heterogeneous. Here, as we saw in the case of Böhm-Bawerk's subsistence fund, there arises the problem of its composition or structure. Where many capital goods are durable and specific, the stock will never have its "equilibrium composition." Some capital goods, when worn out, will not be replaced by replicas. This fact of course presents an obstacle to the construction of any equilibrium theory of capital such as would fit into a general equilibrium model. It is hardly surprising that most neoclassical economists choose to ignore this inconvenient fact. Some have brought themselves to imagine that they have found a substitute for the missing theory of capital structure in a theory of intertemporal consumption—a capital theory without capital.

For the neo-Ricardians the problem at least seems to exist. In Pasinetti's writings we find occasional references to it. "Two techniques may well be as near as one likes on the scale of variation of the rate of profit and yet the physical capital goods they require may be completely different."[10] In his reply to Dr. Dougherty he explicitly describes this as "one of the important results of the reswitching-of-technique debate."[11] In his altercation with Professor Solow he writes, "The two situations a and b that Solow compares differ not only by the single consumption good he has hypothesized but also by *the whole structure of capital goods*."[12]

A capital structure is an ordered whole. How does it come into existence? What maintains it in the face of change, in particular, unexpected change? These are questions that now claim our attention. A capital structure is composed of the capital combinations of various firms, none of which is a simple miniature replica of the whole structure. What makes them fit into this structure? Wherever we might hope to find answers to these questions, it must be clear that they cannot be found within the realm of macroeconomics. Capital combinations, the elements of the capital structure, are formed by entrepreneurs. Under pressure of market forces entrepreneurs have to reshuffle capital combinations at intervals, just as they have to vary their input and output streams. Change in income distribution is just one such force. "Capital reswitching" in a world of heterogeneous capital is merely one instance of the reshuffling of existing capital combinations.

In the field of capital theory the crisis of economic thought has given rise to a situation full of irony. The neo-Ricardians have discovered a range of problems they are unable to tackle since this can only be done on a microlevel, a level to which their macroeconomic commitment does not permit them to descend. Their neoclassical opponents meanwhile, while irked by no such scruples, prefer to ignore these problems altogether and are turning to a capital theory without capital instead.

4.

To substantiate Austrian dissent from neoclassical economics is no easy task. As we pointed out above, some Austrian strands of thought have merged into the main stream of what we may call the neoclassical synthesis. Some Austrian thinkers were quite content to see their school lose its identity within this broader union. Others felt less happy about it.

One reason, less superficial than might appear, why our task is difficult lies in the need to make the reader see the present neoclassical establishment and its main doctrines in a perspective that is not its own, one in which pupils in the best schools are not taught to view the economic world, not to mention the products of the textbook industry, and that must therefore be unfamiliar to the reader. By now most economists have learnt that the world

seen in a Ricardian perspective is different from the world seen
in, say, a Samuelsonian perspective. But other perspectives are
just as possible. We may, for example, view both the perspectives
mentioned as mere variants of a style of thought we might
describe as *late classical formalism*. It is a characteristic of this
mode of thought that for it the manifestations of spontaneous
human action appear in the guise of formal entities, the continuous existence of which can only be assured by imposing con-
straints on spontaneity.

In order to sustain Austrian objections to neoclassical doctrines we must thus elucidate a "third perspective" rooted in
subjectivism. But when we say that the central issue here stems
from a different approach to the problem of knowledge and its
relevance to economic action, many readers might refuse to
follow us into what they might regard as a field of philosophy.

In these circumstances it will be best to start by indicating two
areas which are not in dispute, despite what has sometimes been
said in the past. Professor Jaffé, in reviewing the volume *Carl
Menger and the Austrian School of Economics* (ed. J. R. Hicks and W.
Weber [Oxford: Oxford University Press, 1973]), speaks of "the
Austrians, who were not interested in the mathematical pin-
point determination of equilibrium price à la Walras, but looked
rather for the interval within which any price is advantageous to
trading parties on both sides."[13] Suffice it to say that the introduction of the notion of the *core* in recent neoclassical writings
has removed this point of dispute. Secondly, the difference has
sometimes been traced to a preference for process analysis by the
Austrians and for equilibrium analysis by the neoclassical
economists, a difference between "genetic-causal" and "functional" analysis.[14] But this difference is not essential in any way
that concerns style of thought. A type of equilibrium theory that
employs process analysis to show how various equilibria are
attained is quite conceivable. Sir John Hicks's "traverse" comes
readily to mind. Forging chains of causation is not beyond the
power of the neoclassical mind. We see no reason why the attempts now made in such quarters "to require of our equilibrium
notion that it should reflect the sequential character of actual

economics" might not succeed.[15] If they do, the issue falls away.

The real issue lies much deeper. We catch a first glimpse of it when, with a critical mind and an air of innocence, we follow the usual introduction to general equilibrium theory. We are presented with three classes of "data," tastes, resources, and knowledge, which are to serve as our "independent variables." This is, surely, rather embarrassing, as knowledge "exists" in a way different from that in which rivers and typewriters do. How are we to determine that change in knowledge that would just offset a change in resources in such a way as to preserve an existing equilibrium situation? And what is the economic significance of tastes and resources nobody knows?

Closer reflection shows of course that what is meant here by knowledge as a "datum" is merely technical knowledge about the use of resources, while tastes and resources as such are known to every participant in the market. When they change, the fact is at once known throughout the market, and this does not constitute a separate change of datum. Such universal market knowledge by every participant is simply taken for granted. Neoclassical economics, then, operates with two kinds of knowledge; one appears as an independent variable and the other does not. In neoclassical writings, from presidential addresses to textbooks, this fact is never mentioned. By contrast, Austrian economics takes no form of knowledge for granted. The market appears to it as a continuous process, in the course of which the knowledge possessed by some participants becomes diffused to many, while new knowledge is acquired by some, and some earlier knowledge becomes obsolete. The reader will now understand why we said that the problem of knowledge is at the bottom of the dispute.

It goes without saying that it is possible to modify the rigor of the assumption about universal market knowledge, and this has been done recently. The pattern of limited market knowledge then becomes a new "datum." But such an assumption in no way affects the real weakness of the equilibrium model, which is that knowledge of whatever kind is here treated as an external datum and not as, at least partly, a product of the market process. Can market knowledge exist irrespective of what happens in the market? Some aspects of the problem are best elucidated by reference to two statements made by Professor Hahn in his recent inaugural lecture: "I shall want to say that an agent is *learning* if his theory is not independent of the date t. It will be a condition of the agent being in equilibrium that he is not learning."[16] It is difficult to know the range of implications here envisaged. Strictly speaking, it means that point-of-time equilibrium is the only equilibrium possible since it involves no learning. We may doubt, however, whether this is what was meant. For if so, how can such an equilibrium ever "reflect the sequential character of actual economies?" So we must assume that Professor Hahn envisages some time sequences in which nothing is learned by any participant and others in which something is learned. Needless to say, the former variety cannot exist. Time and knowledge belong together. As soon as we permit time to elapse, we must permit knowledge to change. The pattern of knowledge never stands still.

We are also told that "practical men and ill-trained theorists everywhere in the world do not understand what they are claiming to be the case when they claim a beneficent and coherent role for the invisible hand."[17] Here Hahn regrettably does not know that those he criticizes conceive of the market in terms very different from his own.

What Hahn means is that only in a market system with perfect intertemporal markets, including "contingent futures markets," could a Pareto optimum be attained; in the real world in which there are only a few forward markets, and virtually none for industrial goods, no such optimum can be reached. "Ill-trained," alias "Austrian," economists are not entitled to claim Pareto optimality for the market economy of the real world.[18]

But the Austrians are making no such claim, and Hahn simply misunderstood their position. He tacitly assumes that everybody, like his well-trained disciples, identifies the market economy with a general equilibrium model. But to Austrians the market is a competitive process, not a given state of affairs. No general equilibrium model, however large the number of intertemporal markets it includes, can serve as a simile for the market processes of reality, and the Pareto optimum is at best an irrelevant fiction. The markets of the real world, by contrast, while at no time constituting an ordered whole, invariably give rise to coordinating forces, reflecting and, over time, generating changes in the pattern of knowledge. In a market economy, as Professor Kirzner stated, "at any given time, an enormous amount of ignorance stands in the way of the complete coordination of the actions and decisions of the many market participants. Innumerable opportunities for mutually beneficial exchange . . . are likely to exist unperceived. . . . The normative question raised by Hayek is how well the market succeeds in bringing together those uncoordinated bits of information scattered throughout the economy. Successful coordination of these bits of information cannot fail to produce coordinated activity—exchange—benefiting both parties."[19]

In their defense of the market economy the "ill-trained" economists may have a strong or a weak case. It cannot be refuted by reference to a fictitious optimum irrelevant to it. Evidently the market processes of reality require closer study than they have thus far received. All Hahn has to offer his well-trained disciples is an argument insinuating to others a utopia that is very much his own. The formalistic mind, we may note, incapable of conceiving of a market otherwise than as a set of determinate relationships, is helpless when confronted with a set of forces the interaction of which yields no determinate outcome.

The Austrian objection does not apply to the use of the notion of equilibrium as such. It applies to its indiscriminate misuse at the three different levels of the individual, the market, and the economic system. Equilibrium of the individual, household or firm, as an expression of consistent action, is indeed an indispensable tool of analysis. Equilibrium involving action planned by different minds involves altogether new problems. Equilibrium on a simple market, such as a Marshallian corn market, still has its uses. "Equilibrium of the industry" is already harder to handle. When we speak of "general equilibrium," we are simply hypothesizing that among the forces of interaction between markets the equilibrating forces are of overwhelming power and will prevail over all obstacles. Also, they must be able to do their work quickly, before any changes in data can take place. General equilibrium is thus possible in a stationary world. Equilibrium in a world of change requires peculiar hypotheses.

In neoclassical writings we look in vain for arguments sustaining such strong hypotheses. For it is characteristic of the style of formalistic thought that a concept found useful in one context is often torn out of its natural habitat and indiscriminately transplanted to alien soil. Such are the uses of abstraction to careless thinkers.

5.

The reader may feel that, instead of the promised outline of the Austrian position, he has been presented with a series of critical comments directed against non-Austrian views. He may demand to be told, in particular, what is to take the place of the general equilibrium model as the central paradigm of economic theory.

It was necessary, however, to prepare by extensive criticism the fundament on which to erect our structure. Our constructive task will be so much the easier. Our positive proposals simply follow the direction of our critical comments. As regards equilibrium in particular, all we need to do is let our thoughts roam freely along the lines indicated at the end of the previous section.

What would happen, we may now ask ourselves, if we were to reverse the order of significance assigned to equilibrating and disequilibrating forces respectively in neoclassical thought? If we were to assume that all equilibrating forces, so far from being of overwhelming strength, must sooner or later succumb to obstacles of various kinds before having reached their "destination"? In a world in which unexpected change is likely to overtake equilibrating forces, in which new knowledge is continually coming into existence as old knowledge becomes obsolete, this appears to us the more plausible hypothesis. This reversal of the order of significance attributed to the various forces of interaction cannot but affect the perspective in which we view the course of market processes.[20]

For neoclassical thought equilibrium is central; processes that may or may not lead to it are subsidiary to its main objective. For us, by contrast, market processes reflecting the interplay between equilibrating forces are the essence of the matter, while equilibrium itself, as Mises put it, is nothing but "an auxiliary notion employed in its context and devoid of any sense when used outside of this context."[21] We refuse to believe that the equilibrating forces are always overwhelming strength.

Not all market action is consistent action. The actions of competitors are an obvious example. The notion of a "state of competition," perfect or otherwise, in which they are *made* consistent, is not merely useless as a tool of analysis; it presents an obstacle to our understanding of competition as a process. In a market economy, at all times, as Professor Kirzner says, "an enormous amount of ignorance stands in the way of the complete coordination of the actions and decisions of the many market participants. Innumerable opportunities for mutually beneficial exchange . . . are likely to exist unperceived." Market processes, to be sure, will reduce such ignorance. But during the very same period in which old knowledge becomes more widely diffused, much of it becomes obsolete, and new ignorance emerges simultaneously with the new knowledge gained by some.

Economists have learnt that some technical progress is absorbed by means of "learning by doing." But different men learn different lessons from doing the same work and embody what they have learned in differentiated products. The same applies to market knowledge. While the competitive market process leads to the erosion of profit margins, it also inspires some producers to seek safety in product differentiation. The market process is not a one-way street.

The image of economic action that emerges from our reflections is thus that of the *market as a continuous process without beginning or end.* Marshallian markets for individual goods may, for a time, find their respective equilibria. *The economic system never does.* This process is propelled by equilibrating forces of intermarket interaction which are, again and again, thwarted by changes in the pattern of the distribution of knowledge. These changes in turn result in part from the impact of exogenous forces, such as the progress of science and technology; in part from human reaction to market events; and also in part from the spontaneous action of the alert minds of participants inspired, but not compelled, by what they witness on the market scene around them.

NOTES

1. For a somewhat blurred reflection of this state of affairs, see K. J. Arrow, "Limited Knowledge and Economic Analysis," *American Economic Review* 64 (March 1974): 1–10; see also F. H. Hahn, "The Winter of Our Discontent," *Economica* 40 (August 1973): 322–30. For as faithful a mirror image as the situation permits, we have to turn to John Hicks, *Capital and Time* (Oxford: Oxford University Press, 1973).

2. "The young economists of the 1920s were not spellbound, like those of earlier decades, by the great glow from a great focus of convergent thought where all the world's economists seemed to pour in their blending illuminations" (G. L. S. Shackle, *The Years of High Theory* [Cambridge: Cambridge University Press, 1967], p. 291).

3. L. M. Lachmann, "Sir John Hicks as a Neo-Austrian," *South African Journal of Economics* 3 (September 1973): 195–207.

4. J. A. Schumpeter, *History of Economic Analysis* (Oxford: Oxford University Press, 1954), p. 847.

5. Piero Sraffa, *Production of Commodities by Means of Commodities: Prelude to a Critique of Economic Theory* (Cambridge: Cambridge University Press, 1960).

6. J. M. Keynes, *The General Theory of Employment, Interest, and Money* (New York: Harcourt, Brace & World, 1936), pp. 62–63.

7. Ibid., p. 60.

8. Ibid. Here, for once, the two streams of capital theory mentioned above were in contact. The encounter produced little but confusion.

9. Ibid., pp. 69–70; esp. 69n.

10. Luigi Pasinetti, "Switches of Technique and the 'Rate of Return' in Capital Theory," *Economic Journal* 79 (September 1969): 523.

11. Luigi Pasinetti, "Reply to Mr. Dougherty," *Economic Journal* 82 (December 1972): 1352.

12. Robert Solow, "On the Rate of Return: Reply to Pasinetti," *Economic Journal* 80 (June 1970): 429.

13. William Jaffé, "Review of *Carl Menger and the Austrian School of Economics*," *Economic Journal* 84 (June 1974): 401.

14. This distinction was drawn by Hans Mayer in "Der Erkenntnis-wert der funktionellen Preistheorien," in *Die Wirtschaftstheorie der Gegenwart*, 4 vols. (Vienna, 1932), 2:148–50. The expression *causal-genetic* was introduced by Sombart (Werner Sombart, *Die drei Natio-nalökonomien* [Munich, 1930], p. 220).

15. F. H. Hahn, *On the Notion of Equilibrium in Economics* (Cambridge: Cambridge University Press, 1973), p. 16.

16. Ibid., p. 19.

17. Ibid., p. 14.

18. We find the same argument in K. J. Arrow's presidential address before the American Economic Association: "Even as a graduate student I was somewhat surprised at the emphasis on static allocative efficiency by market socialists, when the nonexistence of markets for future goods under capitalism seemed to me a much more obvious target" (Arrow, "Limited Knowledge," pp. 5–6). In the absence of intertemporal markets men will pursue inconsistent plans, some of which must fail. So do the plans of all competitors. What the argument really shows is the incompatibility of intertemporal equilibrium with competition and not the vulnerability of "capitalism."

19. Israel M. Kirzner, *Competition and Entrepreneurship* (Chicago: University of Chicago Press, 1973), p. 217.

20. "It will be a *kaleidic* society, interspersing its moments or intervals of order, assurance and beauty with sudden disintegration and a cascade into a new pattern. . . . It invites the analyst to consider the society as consisting of a skein of *potentiae*, and to ask himself, not what *will* be its course, but what the course is capable of being in case of the ascendancy of this or that ambition entertained by this or that interest" (G. L. S. Shackle, *Epistemics and Economics* [Cambridge: Cambridge University Press, 1972], p. 76).

21. Ludwig von Mises, *Human Action: A Treatise on Economics* (New Haven: Yale University Press, 1949), p. 352.

PART TWO
SETTING THE STAGE

The Significance of the Austrian School of Economics in the History of Ideas

1.

To speak of the spirit and its history in our age is a precarious undertaking. Even though one escapes the suspicion of having sat at the feet of a metaphysician such as Hegel, one still may face an indictment of "essentialism." Fortunately, the authors of this *Festschrift* need harbor no such fears. Neither the celebrant of this anniversary nor the readers of this journal will be in any doubt as to what is meant by the spirit of the Austrian school in economic theory.

It is almost a century since Menger wrote the *Grundsätze* and founded the Austrian school.[1] In this century there have been decades of triumph and decades of neglect. The favorable and unfavorable climate of the times has had much to do with the successes and failures of the school. At the end of the first century of its existence, we may expect a number of critical assessments of its ideas and their development. It is not my intention, however, to deal with problems of the history of ideas in the narrower sense.

In what follows I shall attempt to indicate the cognitive aim,

This essay, "Die geistesgeschichtliche Bedeutung der österreichischen Schule in der Volkswirtschaftslehre," *Zeitschrift für Nationalökonomie* 26 (February 1966): 152–67, was translated by Robert F. Ambacher of Millersville State College and Walter E. Grinder.

intellectual trend, and typical methodology of the Austrian
school in the light of some of its major achievements, and to
contrast them with those of other economic schools. I maintain
that there is a characteristic and demonstrable "intellectual style"
of the Austrian school and that this style is geared to the interpretation of cultural facts, as will have to be shown. This
posture is of course in opposition to the currently dominant
methodological monism of positivism, which proclaims that
there is only one truly "scientific" mode of thought, namely, that
of the modern natural sciences. In contrast, I shall attempt to
show that the ideas and aims of the representatives of the Austrian school, perhaps unconsciously, were always directed not
only toward the discovery of quantitative relationships among
economic phenomena but also toward an *understanding* of the
meaning of economic actions.

It is curious that two thinkers, so different in descent, temperament, and intellectual interests as Schumpeter and Sombart,
agreed in their judgment of the work of the Austrian school at
least insofar as they saw in the teachings of the Viennese an
imperfect preliminary to the general equilibrium theory of the
Lausanne school. Schumpeter's position followed naturally
from his view that Walras's accomplishment represented the
very apex of the history of economic thought. He ascribed to the
"defective technique" of the Viennese their failure to ascend to
the true height of Walras's accomplishment after having discovered the ladder.[2]

Sombart's aim, on the other hand, was apparently to be able to
deny any intellectual affiliation with the Austrians. For him, they
belong to "taxonomic economics" (*ordnende Nationalökonomie*)
but fare poorly compared with the Lausanners. "If there is to be
any taxonomic economics, let it be Pareto's" appears to have
been his verdict.[3] I believe that both were mistaken because they
misunderstood the cognitive aim and intellectual trend of the
Austrian school.

2.

Characteristic of the trend of thinking of the Austrian school is, in our view, *Verstehen* (understanding), introduced as a method into the theoretical social sciences. This statement in no way diminishes the significance of the concept of marginal utility, but only indicates that in the creation of this fundamental concept the Austrians had predecessors like Dupuit and Gossen, as well as contemporaries like Jevons and Walras, who, however—as we shall see—developed their own methodologies.

On the other hand, *Verstehen* as a method in the social sciences has, as is well known, a long and glorious history. Not only in the interpretation of texts, as in theology, jurisprudence, and philology, but also in the interpretation of the meaning of human actions, as in all history, this method has always found application. There is, however, a significant difference between *understanding* as *historical method,* as it found its systematic expression, for example, in Droysen's *Historik,* and *understanding* as a *theoretical method,* that is, as a method for the interpretation of *typical courses of action with the aid of thought designs,* for example, economic plans.[4] The characteristic accomplishment of the Austrian school was, in our view, the gradual development of understanding as a method in the second sense. For them the thought design, the economic calculation or economic plan of the individual, always stands in the foreground of theoretical interest.

Before substantiating my thesis by contrasting the essential characteristics of Austrian thought with those of the classical and the Lausanne school, I must meet two obvious objections. It may seem that my interpretation of Austrian thinking cannot be reconciled with the methodological views of two thinkers like Menger and Mises.

One objection might be that in Menger's *Untersuchungen,* for decades considered the methodological catechism of the school, understanding as a method of the theoretical social sciences, and especially of economics, is never mentioned.[5] On the contrary,

Menger declared again and again that the task of the social sciences, as of the natural sciences, is to find "exact laws." Sombart thus appears to be correct when he characterized the *Untersuchungen* as the "most significant methodological work dealing with economics in the manner of the natural sciences."[6]

We must, however, take into account the intellectual climate of the years in which Menger's work originated. In the first place, understanding as a method of theoretical culture study was scarcely known in 1883, the year in which both Dilthey's *Einleitung in die Geisteswissenschaften* [*Introduction to the Social Sciences*] and Menger's *Untersuchungen* were published. Secondly, with the publication of Menger's work the *Methodenstreit* began. Menger, in particular, attacked the attempts of Schmoller and his friends to impose *historical understanding* on the theoretical social sciences, for example, economics, as the only legitimate method. Hence, one could hardly expect much sympathy from Menger for variants of the same methodology still awaiting elucidation even if he had known them. But he did not.

Third, and probably most important, the real theoreticial work of the Austrian school had scarcely begun in 1883. Neither Wieser nor Böhm-Bawerk had appeared on the scene. Paradoxical as it may seem, the method defended by Menger in his *Untersuchungen* was neither his own nor the one followed by his disciples, but really that of the classical school. Mises correctly observed: "The transition from the classical to the modern system was not completed all at once, but gradually: it took considerable time until it became effective in all areas of economic thought, and a still longer time had to elapse before one became aware of the full significance of the completed change."[7] Hence I might say that what later on became the characteristic method of the school had scarcely made an impact in 1883.

Fourth, the day came when even Menger saw himself compelled to oppose the methods of the natural sciences in economics. In two letters to Walras, of June 1883 and February 1884, he insisted that we are dealing not only with quantitative relationships but also with the "essence" of economic phenomena. He also asked how with the aid of mathematics one could ascertain the essence, for example, of value, rent, or the entrepreneur's profit.[8] However, since mathematics is essential to the modern natural sciences, Menger's attack was directed just as much against the latter as against the former. And if it is permissible to equate the "comprehension of essence" with the "interpretation of meaning," we may conclude that Menger's intention in both letters was to defend the possibility of an economic theory designed to interpret meaning. It is of particular interest that both letters were written almost immediately after the completion of the *Untersuchungen*.

Another objection might be that Mises ascribed understanding as a method peculiar to the historical sciences, and that our formulation is incompatible with his distinction between *Begreifen* and *Verstehen*. The apparent contradiction, however, is purely verbal. Mises admitted explicitly: *"In itself, it would be conceivable to define as understanding any procedure directed toward the comprehension of the meaning of things,"* and that is precisely our standpoint. He continued, *"As things are today, we must resign ourselves to contemporary language usage. We want, therefore, within the procedure directed toward the comprehension of the meaning of things, a procedure of which the sciences of human conduct make use to separate 'Begreifen' and 'Verstehen.' 'Begreifen' seeks to comprehend the meaning of things by discursive thought; 'Verstehen' seeks the meaning through a total empathy with the total situation under consideration."*[9]

I do not believe that today's usage demands this distinction. It is nevertheless clear, I hope, that the method here ascribed to the Austrian school is the same as the one Mises labeled *"Begreifen."* This method, which aims at discovering the *meaning* of things, apparently conflicts with most methods used in and suitable to the natural sciences.

3.

I shall now investigate in detail the characteristics peculiar to Austrian thinking. Let us first contrast it with that of the classical school. I shall, however, disregard Adam Smith, who is too

firmly rooted in the eighteenth century for our problems to
concern him. For to the mentality of his time natural law and the
"natural economic order" were each "a piece of nature," and
conceptual distinctions such as we shall have to make were completely foreign to it.

With Ricardo and his disciples it was different. They consciously emulated natural science. The cognitive aim was the
ordering of economic processes in terms of quantities. Such
theory could be called successful insofar as it was able to determine quantitative relationships. Typical of the classical intellectual style are three characteristics.

First, the central problem: the distribution of income among
the three factors of production: labor, land, and capital. This
distribution is determined by two "laws," which are regarded as
empirical laws of nature (and they would be, if they really generally applied!), namely, the Malthusian law of population and the
law of diminishing returns to land.

Secondly, the central concept: value. This is a concept denoting
"substance," which bears the typical traits of an older natural
science. It is the measure of all economic things, as well as the
fundamental norm of all exchange processes. But why exchange
takes place at all is never discussed. In business the measure of all
things is the monetary unit. The economist, knowing that the
value of money fluctuates, distrusts this standard. Ricardo believed that he had found a measure free from this defect in the
quantity of work necessary for the production of each good.
Gradually, and almost without his noticing it, the measure became for him the substance of all economic processes, if not their
cause. For us all that matters is that the classical "objective"
theory of value is based on a concept denoting "substance."

Third, economic man appears in classical theory only in his
capacity as a factor of production. This means not merely that
the consumer is not an economic subject, but that *homo oeconomicus*
is always a producer. It means, moreover, that the only transactions of economic interest are those one performs in one's capacity as a factor of production: as a worker, as a landowner, or as a
capitalist. Within these three classes, all members are regarded

as equal. This assumption of homogeneity of the factors of production has odd consequences for the realism of classical theory.[10] All capitalists, whether they invest wisely or unwisely, receive the average rate of profit on their invested capital. Malinvestments, capital losses, and bankruptcies do not exist. The assumed homogeneity of the factors of production makes it impossible to evaluate the success of any economic activity. Fundamentally, we cannot really speak of economic activity here. As in nature, people *react* to the current external conditions of their economic existence: they *do not act*.

It is only against this background of the classical thought that the specific accomplishment of the Austrian school becomes transparent. It can perhaps best be characterized in the following manner: Here, too, one strives to discover laws. But, no matter what Menger might originally have believed, the laws of catallactics are logical laws, *vérités de raison*. From the law of marginal utility there gradually developed an economic calculus, that is, a "logic of choice." How this logic is related to reality, so that real processes can be interpreted with its help, is an important question and will be discussed later on.

The significance of the Austrian school in the history of ideas perhaps finds its most pregnant expression in the statement that here man *as an actor* stands at the center of economic events. Certainly, manifold quantitative economic relationships are also for the Austrian school in the first place the cognitive object of economic inquiry. But the determination of these quantitative relationships is not the ultimate objective. One does not stop there; for these relationships flow from acts of the mind that have to be "understood," that is, their origin, their significance, and their effects must be explained within the framework of our "common experience" of human action.

Also important for understanding the Austrian school is that here, in contrast to the classical school, men are viewed as *highly unequal*. Each one has different needs and abilities. The quantities and prices of goods sold in the market depend on these individual needs and abilities. This fact is exactly what the subjective theory of value stresses. Each economic agent through his action imprints his individuality on economic events. Man as a consumer cannot be squeezed into any homogeneous class. The same may be said of man as a producer. The concept of opportunity costs disrupts the homogeneity of the cost factors and broadens the area of subjectivity, which now also embraces the theory of production.

Finally, in the work of the Viennese school the classical concept of value undergoes a fundamental change. Value is no longer a "substance" inherent in goods. The central concept of Viennese theory is *evaluation,* an act of the mind. The value of a good now consists in a relationship to an appraising mind. Owing to the heterogeneity of needs, it is highly improbable that the same good will be given the same appraisal by different economic agents.[11] Out of the Ricardian concept of quasi-substance has emerged a concept of mental relationships.

4.

My next task is to differentiate the specific characteristics of the Viennese school from those of the Lausanne school. It has been maintained that there are no fundamental differences between the two schools, that it is only a question of variations on the same theme, namely, of modern subjective value theory. I consider this view misleading and will attempt to show which fundamental differences do in fact exist here. Above all, this view ignores the fact that Austrian thinkers go far beyond the mere ordering of quantitative relationships, an activity much cultivated in Lausanne and elsewhere.

In the last eighty years, prominent Austrian thinkers in each generation have found it necessary to draw a dividing line between their mode of analysis and that of the school of Lausanne. I have already mentioned Menger's two letters to Walras. Almost three decades later Wieser himself was impelled to defend the "psychological" method adopted by him and his colleagues against the "mechanistic" method Schumpeter had borrowed from the Lausanners and his teacher Mach.[12] Twenty years later, H. Mayer attacked the "cognitive value of functional price theories" and subjected it to a sharp and thorough criticism.[13] And as late as 1948, Leo Illy, in a chapter in *Das Gesetz des Grenznutzens* [*The Law of Marginal Utility*],[14] rightly criticized the defects of certain price theories that merely order price phenomena without explaining them. So the differences existed, and they still do. It is for us to determine those characteristics of the Austrian style of thought to which formalistic analysis cannot do justice.

Now it is not to be denied that Austrian theorists have not always adroitly defended their position. The "occasional blunders and unfortunate formulations in the application of their method of research," which Hans Mayer justifiably criticized, have often impaired the effectiveness of their arguments.[15] For example, Wieser always spoke of the Austrian as the "psychological" school, although he admitted that "perhaps our method would be exposed to fewer misunderstandings, if one had called it not the psychological but the psychical, although this name as well would still be open to misunderstanding. Our object is, simply, the consciousness of economic man with its wealth of general experience, i.e., that experience which every practical man possesses and which, therefore, every theoretician as a practical man finds in himself, without the need first to acquire such experience by means of special scientific methods."[16] But Max Weber had already made clear, three years before Wieser, that the alleged "psychological" foundation of the Viennese theory was based on a misconception: "The rational theory of price formation not only has nothing to do with the concepts of experimental psychology, but has nothing to do with a psychology of any kind, which desires to be a 'science' going beyond everyday experience. . . . The theory of marginal utility and every other subjective value theory are not psychologically, but—if one desires a methodological term—'pragmatically' based, i.e., involve the use of the categories 'ends' and 'means.' "[17]

In other respects, too, the methodological defense of the Austrian school was not always successful. To speak of "the cause of value" is obviously questionable. One lays oneself open to the objection that the economic system constitutes a general nexus of relationships within which "causes" can only be ordered as a class and, as such, have to be dealt with as "data." The distinction between "genetic-causal" and "functional" price theories, which, as we shall see, positively strikes at the heart of the matter, met with the same objection.[18] The opponents maintained that, with a general interdependence of all quantities and prices, each individual quantity and price is, at the same time, the effect and cause of others. Against the distinction between "price forma- tion theory" and "price change theory," the latter valid only within the framework of comparative statics, the argument was advanced that in disequilibrium the same forces must influence price, whether or not equilibrium existed before. In the timeless statics of the Lausanne theory this argument is certainly valid, but otherwise it is not.

The difference between the Vienna and the Lausanne school is already reflected in the assumptions made by both. Among these, the role of time is of special significance. It is certainly not overstating the case if we say that the real disagreement con- cerns, in the first place, the significance attributed to the element of time. Lausanne theory is meaningful within the framework of timeless statics; the world of the Austrian school, on the other hand, requires time for its full meaning. This is not just a matter of the level of abstraction; it is much more than that.

Austrian theory needs the dimension of time, since all human action is only possible in time. The Lausanne theory of equilib- rium not only does not require time; it requires time's exclusion. From the very beginning, Edgeworth and Walras clearly saw that any passage of time before the state of equilibrium is reached renders that state itself indeterminate, since all data-changing events happening on the path to a state of equilibrium help to determine that state. Lausanne theory requires, then, that all transactions undertaken on the path to equilibrium can be nul- lified, whether by "recontract" or by other means. This is the essence of timeless statics. For the Austrians, however, it is exactly these transactions, undertaken in the course of time, that are their real objects of interest, since conscious human action is bound to plans, and all plans require a time dimension.

I described how, in the course of the development of the Austrian theory, a theory of economic calculus gradually unfolded as a corollary of the law of marginal utility. Economic plans depend on the economic calculations of each agent. The interplay of economic plans accounts for the market phenomena. Now, there is certainly a general nexus of all market phenomena, and the Austrians by no means denied this fact. However, they took relatively little interest in the forces that operate in this connection, since these could operate only in a timeless world, that is, in a world without change. What appeared to them much more urgent was to take into account the continual need, in a constantly changing world, to adapt economic plans to these changes. For in such a world a general condition of equilibrium cannot be achieved. We thus see why economic plans occupy a central place in Austrian theory, while the general nexus of market phenomena is neglected. One takes one's orientation from reality.

It might be held, however, that Lausanne theory also takes account of the economic plans of individuals since they enter into its system as "data." But the utility—and supply—functions in the work of Walras, and indifference curves in the work of Pareto, do not reflect real economic plans as we know them from our own experience. They must provide for every possible situation if the state of equilibrium is to be determinate. In fact they are comprehensive lists of alternative plans, comprehensive enough for unlimited application. Obviously, this requirement is quite beyond the capacity of the human mind. "No person will be in a position to indicate, truthfully and with mathematical accuracy, an infinite number of combinations of goods which would all be equally important to him. The expression 'experiment,' used here by Pareto, is completely unsuitable: we have here simply the figment of an experiment."[19]

For the general theory of equilibrium, such functions are certainly an essential logical foundation. The difference between a taxonomic *(ordnende)* and a *verstehende* economics becomes quite apparent here. What is a logical necessity for the former must be considered as an absurdity by the latter. Here, the two schools part company for good.[20]

The methodology borrowed from the natural sciences may eschew concern with the alien—and dangerous!—theme of the construction of economic plans. However, it can do so only by assuming that all conceivable plans are already "given" from the start!

Pareto saw much more clearly than his predecessor Walras that genuine economic plans do not really fit into the model of the Lausanne school, and that to use them as "data" one must first divest them of their nature as mental acts. This is the true meaning of the famous sentence: *"L'individu peut disparaitre, pourvu qu'il nous laisse cette photographie de ses goûts."*[21] Here plainly man as economic agent does not stand at the center of economic life. This statement of course makes sense only in a timeless stationary world in which these photographs would retain permanent validity. Everyday human acts shape the real world anew. Accordingly, all attempts to attach a time dimension to the timeless theory of equilibrium and thus to make it "dynamic" must fail.

It is probably unnecessary to discuss in detail a criticism once marshalled against the Austrian school regarding the so-called "circle of economic determination." Viennese economists were charged with becoming entangled in circular reasoning since, on the one hand, market prices were derived from the valuations of the economic agents, and, on the other hand, the determination of these very valuations required prices already given. Illy showed that the reasoning in reality was not circular and that the criticism confused prices expected and prices actually paid.[22] Economic agents must certainly orient themselves to prices they expect, but they by no means have to be the prices then formed in the market. In the system of equations of the Lausanne school, it is of course impossible to distinguish between expected and paid prices. This is again a necessary consequence of timeless statics.

5.

We saw that the methodology of the Austrian school evolved gradually, for a long time without the members of the school being aware of it. It sometimes happened that the methodological pronouncements of some of its most prominent members lacked programmatic validity—often even for the time in which they were expressed. This was true, for example, of Menger's *Untersuchungen*. Moreover, Menger, concerned with establishing "exact laws," never clearly distinguished between logical laws and empirical laws, between *vérités de raison* and *vérités de fait*.

As mentioned above, during its development marginal utility theory became a theory of economic calculus and of economic plans, and thereby a genuine "logic of choice." But as late as 1911, Wieser referred to "common experience" as the ultimate basis of economic knowledge. It is to Mises that we owe the clear formulation of the logic of choice. However, as regards the actual relevance of this logic to human action, it will be seen that common experience is still indispensable to us.

In Hayek's work are to be found penetrating discussions of the "scientistic" style of thought and its inadequacy for the problems of the social sciences,[23] but also the first indication of problems of economic theory lying beyond the pure logic of choice.[24] What matters here is, above all, the state of knowledge as a spring of human action and the process of its changes in time.

I now come to the main question of this section: how can a system of pure logic, like that of the logic of choice, provide factual knowledge? The answer follows from the essence of my thesis: the distinction between logic and factual knowledge is justified in the realm of nature, where no meaning is directly accessible to us, and in which care must thus constantly be taken to distinguish between our concepts and reality. In the realm of human action it is different. Here such a distinction seems unjustified. On the one hand we are unable to verify or falsify our schemes of thought as hypotheses by predicting concrete events. Scientific tests are not available to us since they require a complete description of that concrete "starting position" in which the test is to take place. Every human action, however, depends on the state of knowledge of the actors. A verification test therefore would require an exhaustive description of the state of knowledge of all actors, also according to the mode of distribution—an

obvious impossibility. Otherwise, however, the starting position
is not exactly defined, and no real test is possible.

In economics this means that every concrete transaction depends, among other things, on the expectations of the participants. To test an economic theory *in concreto,* we must, then, be
able, at the point of time of theory formulation, to predict the
expectations of economic agents at the (future) point of time of
the verification test. It is easy to see why the representatives of a
taxonomic economics are eager to keep the problem of expectations at arm's length as far as possible.

For "understanding" in economics, on the other hand, some
methods are available that, though closed to the natural sciences, lend themselves for interpreting human actions. The
historian inquires into the meaning and significance of concrete
actions of individuals and groups. This whole method is in-
applicable in the natural sciences. The history of science shows
that research is confined to the ordering of quantitative relationships. In the theoretical cultural sciences, on the other hand, the
significance of typical courses of action is interpreted with the
aid of schemes of thought, such as the logic of choice. The
approach is justified by the fact that all human action, at least
insofar as it is of scientific interest, is oriented to plans. Plans are
logical constructs immanent to the course of action. A plan
serves the economic agent as a guideline; he orients himself to it.
The social sciences can thus use plans as means of interpretation.
Actions certainly are events in space and time and, as such, are
observable. But observation alone cannot reveal meaning; for
this, methods of interpretation are needed.

Why exactly is the logic of choice the scheme needed for
interpreting economic actions? The logic of choice is a "logic of
success"; its categories are means and ends. Why should we opt
for precisely this method in interpreting economic transactions?
Common experience gives us the answer: in economic life most
people seek success. The striving for success as the meaning of
economic action warrants the validity of the logic of choice.

Thus Mises was correct when he asserted that only logic, and
not experience, can warrant the validity of economic theories—

as opposed to Wieser, who in his critique of Schumpeter invoked common experience.[25] And logic certainly is immanent in all human action. But this alone does not mean that the logic of success, which depends upon means and ends, is also the logic governing all action. Conceivably another kind of logic, one employing other categories, might be applicable here. In order to claim the validity of just this logic of success for economic life, we have to invoke common experience.

Finally we have to remember that, in a dynamic world there are economic problems that the logic of choice by itself cannot master. While it explains the designing of economic plans under given conditions, the revision of economic plans in the course of time, as well as the entire range of the problems of expectations, are outside the realm of logic. At best, we may say that in a stationary world economic plans will be adapted more and more to real conditions. It is exactly on this fact that the theory of general equilibrium of the Lausanne school rests.

6.

I do not wish to conclude these observations without taking a brief look at the *future tasks of "verstehende," or "interpretative," economics.*

Our main aim, naturally, must be to preserve and defend in all directions the methodological independence of the theoretical social sciences in general, and of economics in particular. This certainly does not mean that methods may never be borrowed from other disciplines. The relevant question, however, always is whether these methods, however successful they may be outside the realm of economics, are able to serve our purposes, namely, the interpretation of human action.

If we keep this question in mind, we shall continue the work of Menger under the altered circumstances of our own time. In this we need only follow precedents already given in the work of the Austrian school. According to one of its most perceptive thinkers, E. Schams, we must always distinguish, in accepting mathematical methods, between "the mathematical form of the statement" (*ansetzendes Denken*) and the "material constants" to which it refers; only the uncritical acceptance of the latter into economic science is inadmissible.[26]

No doubt the task outlined here is not simple, especially in our time. In recent decades, especially in Anglo-Saxon countries, an unbelievable narrowing and impoverishment of the philosophical outlook has taken place. Today, innumerable economists everywhere, some in responsible positions, who have never learned of the existence of our problems, naively believe that the scientific method is the only legitimate one in all fields of knowledge.

How should we approach our task? First of all, we must continuously stress the inadequacy of the products of intellectual inquiry that ignores the meaning of actions. We must always be prepared to ask our opponents the following questions: Whence? By what means? To what end? When, for example, the designers of macroeconomic models present to us their creations, we may certainly admire their elegance: we may not, however, neglect to ask from which actions of the economic agents these models spring. We must also always ask what expectations guide these actions, and what would occur if these expectations were altered. When, moreover, such model builders attempt to include technical progress in their models, for example, in the form of a "technical progress function," they must be shown that they are attempting to grasp meaningful action by an intellectual method to which meaning is alien, and that a significant discussion of these interesting problems is thereby made impossible. But we must not rest content with criticism of a method of inquiry that defies meaning; we must show the fruitfulness of the *verstehende* method in its various applications. There are, we may show, alternatives to equilibrium analysis. Certainly, in the analysis of a state of disequilibrium, we cannot dispense with an account of the equilibrating forces, but that does not mean that we must describe in its entirety a state of equilibrium, which is never really attained, decorated with formulas and equations. We can save ourselves that endeavor. All that is important is that every state of disequilibrium presents possibilities for profitable activity—be it income, capital gains, or even only the avoidance of losses. Each disequilibrium stimulates alert minds, but by no means all minds, to profitable action, and this action will reduce the chances for further profit. That is all that may be said. The cumbersome pedantry of the usual market models, with their alleged "precision," is an obstacle rather than a help to understanding. What has happened to "perfect competition" should be enough of a warning.

Even outside the special field of economic theory, the need for the defense of the methods of inquiry specific to the cultural disciplines presents tasks that are as pressing as they are difficult. Here it is most important to put the methodological independence of the social sciences on a firm epistemological basis.

Since the Renaissance the theory of knowledge has taken its orientation almost exclusively from the methods of the natural sciences. For these sciences, which deal with apparently "meaningless" events, there is no alternative, in the absence of other criteria of comparison, but to attempt to make their theories and observable events agree in such a manner that predictions concerning these events may be made, and then "verified." With human activity, however, this is impossible, since every action depends on the state of knowledge of the agent *at the point in time of the action*, which is not predictable *at the point in time of the formulation of the theory*. What, then, must the social scientist do to distinguish useful from useless theories? Which criteria of valid knowledge are at his disposal?

Since we lack successful prediction as a means of evidence, we must of course devote special care to the validity of our theoretical assumptions. The Austrian school has always done so, as, for example, we saw above in the criticism of the Lausanne theory. Also, in the theoretical social sciences a gap between scheme of thought and reality may have a different significance than in the natural sciences. For their task is essentially the comparative study of schemes of the agents, on the one hand, and typical courses of action, on the other. Here the significant and meaningful character of both can serve as *tertium comparationis*. In such comparative studies deviations from the planned schedule are often more interesting than a smooth course proceeding according to plan would have been. An economic plan as an observed fact does not lose its significance for us when it fails. On the contrary, we owe to such a plan our criterion of success, which alone allows us to speak of failure. A coherent plan of action that no one applies often allows us to draw interesting conclusions concerning the character of the situation, including the expectations entertained by the agents.

In these reflections I have taken the economic plan of an individual as the prototype of the scheme of thought lying at the base of action, mainly on account of its central significance for economic theory of Austrian character. Economic agents orient themselves to plans. There is no parallel for this in the study of the physical world. But to what facts do the planners orient themselves when making their plans? Partly to natural data, and partly to the actual or expected actions of other people. But there also are certain superindividual schemes of thought, namely, *institutions,* to which the schemes of thought of the first order, the plans, must be oriented, and which serve therefore, to some extent, the coordination of individual plans. They constitute, we may say, "interpersonal orientation tables," schemes of thought of the second order. To them praxeology, for which until now the plan and its structure have understandably occupied the foreground of interest, will increasingly have to turn in time to come.

NOTES

1. *Grundsätze der Volkswirtschaftslehre* [Foundations of Political Economy] (Vienna, 1871); 2d ed. by Karl Menger, Jr. (1923); translated as *Principles of Economics* (Glencoe, Ill., 1950).

2. J. A. Schumpeter, *History of Economic Analysis* (New York, 1954), p. 918. "They [the Austrians], too, found the ladder. Defective technique only prevented them from climbing to the top of it. But they did climb as high as their technique permitted. In other words: we must see in the Jevons-Menger utility theory an embryonic theory of general equilibrium or, at all events, a particular form of the unifying principle

that is at the bottom of any general-equilibrium system. Though they did not make it fully articulate, mainly because they did not understand the meaning of a set of simultaneous equations, and though they saw in marginal utility the essence of their innovation instead of seeing in it a heuristically useful methodological device, they are nonetheless, just like Walras, among the founding fathers of modern theory."

3. W. Sombart, *Die drei Nationalökonomien* (Munich, 1930), pp. 136–37. "The result of our investigations is clearly established. . . . We could observe that the majority carried out its work with unclear and incomplete concepts of the essence of the scientific method. Only the relationists or functionalists, i.e., the adherents of the 'mathematical' school, have thought the problems through and arrived at a clear and consistent method. Every friend of lucid thought must therefore feel some sympathy for these economists. They alone, also, have earned the respected title of 'exact' researchers, which so many other adherents of the scientific method in economics have most unjustly arrogated to themselves." (The last sentence is, of course, a sideswipe at Menger.)

4. J. G. Droysen, "Historik," in *Vorlesungen über Enzyklopädie und Methodologie der Geschichte* (Munich: Hrsg. von Rudolf Hübner, 1937).

5. Carl Menger, *Untersuchungen über die Methode der Sozialwissenschaften und der politischen Ökonomie insbesondere.* [Inquiries into the Method of Social Sciences and Particularly Political Economy] (Leipzig, 1883); translated as *Problems of Economics and Sociology* (Urbana, Ill., 1963).

6. W. Sombart, op. cit., p. 159.

7. Ludwig von Mises, *Grundprobleme der Nationalökonomie* (Jena, 1933), p. 67n; translated as *Epistemological Problems of Economics* (Princeton, 1960).

8. W. Jaffe, "Unpublished Papers and Letters of Léon Walras," *Journal of Political Economy,* 1935, p. 200.

9. L. Mises, op. cit., p. 125.

10. Only for land is this not valid. Ricardo's rent theory rests on the heterogeneity of land.

11. H. Mayer, "Zur Frage der Rechenbarkeit des subjektiven Wertes," in *Festschrift für Alfred Amonn* (Bern, 1953), p. 76, n. 6. "The exact conception of the process by itself and the feel for language should have made it clear that to speak of subjective values as though they were a property of goods, is an elliptical and at bottom misleading way of expression: we are dealing with the process of evaluation, and this takes place not according to 'larger' or 'smaller,' but according to a higher or lower position within a hierarchy."

12. F. v. Wieser, "Das Wesen und der Hauptinhalt der theoretischen Nationalökonomie," in *Gesammelte Abhandlungen* (Tübingen, 1929), pp. 10–34.

13. H. Mayer, "Der Erkenntniswert der Funktionellen Preistheorien," in *Die Wirtschaftstheorie der Gegenwart,* 2 vol. (Vienna, 1932) 2: 147–239.

14. L. Illy, *Das Gesetz des Grenznutzens* (Vienna, 1948).

15. H. Mayer, loc. cit., p. 150.

16. F. v. Wieser, loc. cit., p. 16.

17. M. Weber, "Die Grenznutzlehre und das psychophysische Grundgesetz," in *Gesammelte Aufsätze zur Wissenschaftslehre,* 2d ed., 1951, p. 396.

18. H. Mayer, loc. cit., p. 148.

19. A. Mahr, "Indifferenzkurven und Grenznutzenniveau," *Zeitschrift für Nationalökonomie* 14 (1954): 325 SS.

20. Pareto saw very well how absurd it is to ask a poor peasant woman how many diamonds she would buy at a given price if she were a millionairess, but the logic of his system forced such assumptions upon him. Cf. V. Pareto, *Manuel d'Économie Politique,* 2d ed. (Paris, 1927), p. 260.

21. V. Pareto, ibid., p. 170.

22. Leo Illy, *Das Gesetz des Grenznutzens* (Vienna, 1948), ch. 6, pp. 183–238.

23. F. A. Hayek, "Scientism and the Study of Society," *Economica* 9 (1942): 267; 10 (1943): 34 ff.; 11 (1944): 27 ff.

24. F. A. Hayek, "Economics and Knowledge," in *Individualism and Economic Order* (London, 1949), pp. 33–56.

25. L. Mises, loc. cit., pp. 21–22.

26. Cf. E. Schams, "Die zweite Nationalökonomie," *Archiv für Sozialwissenschaft* 64 (1930): 453 ff.; and "Wirtschaftslogik," *Schmollers Jahrbuch* 58 (1934): 513 ff.

The Role of Expectations in Economics as a Social Science

1.

In modern theory the introduction of expectations has opened new vistas to the economist and, at the same time, set him a new problem. It has made him realise that economic action concerned with the future, so far from being strictly determined by a set of objective "data," is often decided upon in a penumbra of doubt and uncertainty, vague hopes and inarticulate fears, in which ultimate decision may well depend on mental alertness, ability to read the signs of a changing world, and readiness to face the unknown. But it has also compelled him to reflect on the causal explanation of expectations, to ask himself why they are what they are. This problem bristles with difficulties.

Given this fact and the natural proclivity of every science to become more limited in scope as it grows more conscious of its premises, it was perhaps inevitable that economists confronted with this problem should have attempted to dispose of it by relegating expectations to the category of "data" alongside with wants, resources, and the technical facts of production. This line was in fact taken by Lord Keynes,[1] Dr. Morgenstern,[2] Professor Myrdal,[3] and Dr. Rosenstein-Rodan.[4] But it is readily seen that expectations must feel ill at ease in this company. What entitles us to treat wants and resources as data and disinterest ourselves in their causal derivation is the simple fact that *qua economists* we have nothing to say about them. Why the geographical distribution of mineral resources is what it is, why the cinema-going public of the 1930s preferred moving pictures directed by René Clair to moving pictures directed by Ernst Lubitsch, are in themselves interesting questions, but the economist has no answer to

Reprinted from *Economica* 10 (February 1943).

them. Expectations, on the other hand, are on a somewhat different plane as they are, while wants and resources are not, largely the result of the experience of economic processes. It is therefore hardly surprising that the treatment of expectations as data, the explanation of which is not the task of the economist, should have given rise to strong protests. Outstanding among the critics are Dr. Lundberg and Professor Schumpeter.

"It is sensible to link actions with expectations," states Dr. Lundberg, "only if the latter can be explained on the basis of past and present economic events. Total lack of correlation here would mean the complete liquidation of economics as a science. Not even an assumption of certain anticipations as given and an analysis of consequent plans and actions on the basis just mentioned would have the slightest interest. . . . In every process of economic reasoning we therefore have to make certain assumptions, often not specified, concerning the relations between expectations on the one hand and current or past prices, profits, etc., on the other."[5]

"Expectations cannot be used as part of our ultimate data in the same way as taste for tobacco can," writes Professor Schumpeter. "Unless we know why people expect what they expect, any argument is completely valueless which appeals to them as *causae efficientes*. Such appeals enter into the class of pseudo-explanations which already amused Molière."[6] "If we discontinue the practice of treating expectations as if they were ultimate data, and treat them as what they are—variables which it is our task to explain—properly linking them up with the business situations that give rise to them, we shall succeed in restricting expectations to those which we actually observe and not only reduce their influence to its proper proportions but also understand how the course of events moulds them and at certain times so turns them as to make them work toward equilibrium."[7]

Unfortunately, however much we may agree with the point of view of these authors, it is not easy to carry out their proposals which are by no means unambiguous. In order to link up expectations "with the business situations that give rise to them" we must first of all define a "business situation." If we define it in

objective terms (as a combination of prices paid, quantities produced and sold, etc.) we soon find that the relationship between
business situations and expectations is not uniquely determined
as the same "business situation" may give rise to various kinds of
expectations. A price rise, for instance, may lead to expectations
either of a future fall, if the people in the market have some kind
of "normal level" at the back of their minds, or of a future rise, if
inflationary forces are suspected to be at work. If, on the other
hand, we define "business situation" in subjective terms, viz. as
the interpretation which the people give to the objective facts,
there will be as many "business situations" as there are different
interpretations of the same facts, and they will all exist alongside
each other.

The absence of a uniform relationship between a set of observable events which might be described as a *situation* on the one
hand, and expectations on the other hand, is thus seen to be the
crux of the whole matter. Expectations, it is true, are largely a
response to events experienced in the past, but the *modus
operandi* of the response is not the same in all cases even of the
same experience. This experience, before being transformed
into expectations, has, so to speak, to pass through a "filter" in
the human mind, and the undefinable character of this process
makes the outcome of it unpredictable. We provisionally conclude that expectations are the result of a variety of factors only
some of which are observable events, and only some of which are
of an economic nature. It follows that they have to be regarded as
economically indeterminate and cannot be treated as "variables
which it is our task to explain."

Under these circumstances, what can the economist do but
construct various hypothetical types of expectations conceived as
responses to various hypothetical situations, and then leave the
process of selection to empirical verification in the light of
economic history? Several such "ideal types" either of expectations, like Lord Keynes' "long-term" and "short-term" expectations, or of the holders of expectations, like Professor Schumpeter's "static producer" and "dynamic entrepreneur" or Professor
Hicks's "sensitive" and "insensitive" traders, have already been

evolved and served to elucidate important dynamic problems. This is a most promising field of research and much progress can be achieved along this line. It seems to us, however, that it is possible to carry the general theory of expectations a stage farther, and to the demonstration of this possibility the present paper is devoted.

The next step in the study of expectations, to be sure, has to consist in evolving hypothetical "ideal types" and testing them in the light of economic history. But it cannot be emphasised too strongly that if these efforts were to be confined to the study of relations between objective facts and expectations they would be quite useless. The Social World consists not of facts but of our interpretations of the facts. Nothing will be achieved in the way of an inductive study of expectations until people's expectational responses to the facts of a situation are made *intelligible* to us, until we are able to understand *why* the acting and expecting individuals interpreted a set of facts in the way they actually did. From this point of view we need not deplore unduly the indeterminateness of expectations, for it is *intelligibility* and not *determinateness* that social science should strive to achieve.

We have now reached a point at which it must be evident that we are here facing a fundamental issue in the methodology of economics, and of social science in general. The intricacy of our problem is derived from the inadequacy of the traditional methods of analysis in a case of indeterminateness. Before we can pursue our study of expectations any further we shall have to reconsider some of the first principles of economic analysis.

2.

All human action is directed towards purposes. Hence, as Professor Knight has repeatedly reminded us in recent years, all human activity is problem-solving. Man, before setting out on his course of action, has to make a plan embodying the means at his disposal and the obstacles he is likely to encounter, otherwise his action is not (rational) conduct but (non-rational) mere behaviour. Before starting on his way he tries to chart the path leading to the achievement of his purpose in the topography of his mind. If we say that we wish to "explain" an action, what we mean is not merely that we wish to know its purpose, but also that we wish to see the plan behind the action. Plan, a product of the mind, *is* both the common denominator of all human action and its mental pattern, and it is by reducing "action" to "plan" that we "understand" the actions of individuals. Plan is the *tertium comparationis* between our mind and the mind of the person who acts.

In economic action the problem to be solved is to devise a plan for the allocation of scarce resources to alternative wants in such a way as to maximize satisfaction. Equilibrium theory, which studies the problem and its implications, teaches us that, for each individual at least, the problem has a determinate solution. And since the elements of the plan are quantifiable, if not measurable, the problem and its solution can be illustrated *more mathematico*. However, that a problem has a determinate solution does not entail that those attempting its solution will actually succeed, otherwise there would be no failures in examinations or in business. A plan may fail, of course, for almost any number of reasons. For instance, it may have been faulty from the beginning because of lack of consistency between its various elements; or, while it was perfectly consistent, unexpected obstacles may have been encountered in the course of its execution of which it had failed to take account; or the planner may have misjudged the extent and efficiency of the resources at his disposal. It will be noted that in the second and third instance, but not in the first, failure is due to wrong expectations. Expectations therefore take a prominent place in the theory of economic action; but thus far such a theory does not exist.

It has to be admitted that hitherto the scope of economic theory has been unduly restricted to the formal characteristics of the economic problem and its implications. Equilibrium economics (what Professor Hayek has termed "The Pure Logic of Choice") studies the full implications of a set of data, the "conditions of equilibrium"; it does not study the ways in which these logical implications are translated into human action, which is thus conceived as a quasi-automatic response to an external "stimulus." But in the theory of economic action no such mechanistic preconception is admissible, a point which the introduction of expectations brings out with all necessary clarity. Unfortunately, the Pure Logic of Choice has filled the minds of economists to such an extent that the study of the actual means and ways by which men try to realise their aims has come to be sadly neglected.[8] Economists, not unnaturally, prefer to do their field-work in a pleasant green valley where the population register is exhaustive and everybody known to live on either the right or the left side of an equation. Only on rare occasions—and scarcely ever of their own free will—do they embark on excursions into the rough uplands of the World of Change to chart the country and to record the folkways of its savage inhabitants; whence they return with grim tales of horror and frustration. Traces of such folklore can be found in the touching Swedish saga of the unhappy partnership of Ex Ante (the plan) and Ex Post (the outcome of action).

Needless to say, if our attention is thus confined to the formal characteristics of the economic problem, if our approach remains "functional" rather than "causal-genetic," we shall not only be unable to find explanations for failure to solve the problem, but also be in no way equipped to deal with characteristic instances of failure, like crises and misinvestment; hence, the peculiar helplessness of equilibrium theory in front of trade cycle problems. Whenever confronted with such problems, we shall almost inevitably be biased in favour of an explanation which runs in terms of initial inconsistency of, at least some, plans, for consistency is precisely one of those formal characteristics which we are best trained to investigate. A typical example of this is the explanation of industrial fluctuations which is currently in fashion. Such fluctuations are regarded solely as variations in the degree of utilisation of the resources of Society, and underutilisation is explained by inconsistency between the plans of investment planners and of saver-consumers. We cannot therefore be surprised to learn that such theories have no real explanation for malinvestment and capital losses in investment goods industries, and that one of their favourite assumptions is that all such goods (tin, copper!) are made "to order!"

In the light of these considerations we are now able to view the indeterminateness of expectations in its proper perspective. In a world of imperfect foresight in which no plan can meet all contingencies all human activity is bound to be indeterminate; in this respect expectations are simply on a par with everything else. What may (and in the case of economic activity happens to) be determinate is the problem which this activity seeks to solve, but it does not follow that in this it will succeed; there is, after all, a difference between a problem tackled and a problem solved. Determinateness, we realise, is a possible property of problems; it is not a possible property of human action.

The reader will not, we hope, infer from all this that the Pure Logic of Choice with its equations and its indifference curves is altogether useless. On the contrary, it serves a most useful purpose by making economic activity *intelligible* to our problem-solving mind. For it is only by reducing the apparently chaotic World of Action to a mental pattern of relative simplicity that our problem-solving mind can comprehend it. All we have to remember is that to describe an action in terms of a problem is, of course, not to say that it will succeed in solving it.

After this long digression we may now return to our study of expectations. It is evident that if so often we fail to solve our problems, in a world of imperfect foresight the chief reason has to be sought in our being misguided by wrong expectations. More particularly will this be so in the economic field, in which the theoretical interest in expectations arose, not by accident, from the study of crises and depressions, the classical instances of failure to solve the problem of the optimum allocation of resources. That expectations are germane to failure is plain enough, but what precisely is the character of their relationship?

We have seen that we need not deplore the indeterminateness of expectations because this quality they share with all other forms of human activity. But, we said, it is the task of social science to make them intelligible. To make an action intelligible means to show not only its purpose, but also the general design of the plan behind it. What, then, are expectations? We saw that all human conduct (as distinct from mere behaviour) presupposes a plan. We now have to realise that, as a prerequisite to making a plan, we have to draw a mental picture of the situation in which we are going to act, and that the formation of expectations is incidental to the drawing of this picture. Such a picture of the situation will be drawn differently by different individuals confronted with the same observable events in accordance with psychic differences such as temperament, but the degree of variation between them does not entirely depend on psychic factors. In a stationary world in which the same observable events continually recur this degree of variation would be small although, owing to the psychic factors, it probably never would reach zero. But in a World in Motion it must be large, chiefly among other reasons because here every view of a situation necessarily implies a judgment on the character of the forces producing and governing motion. Two farmers confronted with the same observable event, a rise in apple prices, will yet take different views of the situation and react differently if one interprets it as a symptom of inflation and the other as indicating a shift in demand under the influence of vegetarianism.

The upshot of all this is, of course, the familiar proposition that observable events as such have no significance except with reference to a framework of interpretation which is logically prior to them. From this there follow two conclusions, a narrower one concerning expectations, and a broader one pertaining to the formulation of the economic problem in a dynamic World.

As to the first, our argument appears to shed some light on the nature of the "filter" which, as we learned, forms the link between observable events and expectations. We now know that, while it remains true that our expectations for the future are a response to our experience of the past, the mode of our response is largely governed by our interpretation of this experience. In a World of Change this interpretation is bound to reflect strongly what we believe to be the major forces operating in this World, causing and governing change. We now realise that ultimately it is the *subjective* nature of these beliefs which imparts indeterminateness to expectations as it is their *mental* nature which renders them capable of explanation.

Our second conclusion points to the desirability of a dynamic revision of the formulation of the economic problem. The problem is usually stated in terms of (objective) "resources" and (subjective) "wants." In a stationary World these terms may have an unambiguous meaning, but in a dynamic World what is a resource depends on expectation, and so does what constitutes a want worth satisfying. In a properly dynamic formulation of the economic problem all elements have to be subjective, but there are two layers of subjectivism, rooted in different spheres of the mind, which must not be confused, viz. the subjectivism of want and the subjectivism of interpretation.

3.

We have now reached a point at which we may pause and look around for an opportunity to test the efficacy of our newly forged analytical tools. Ultimately, of course, the only satisfactory test of any theoretical construction is the light it sheds on some segment of reality, its making an otherwise incomprehensible set of facts intelligible to us. Such a test will be applied in the concluding section, but prior to it we shall embark on another one of a somewhat different nature. In the light of the knowledge thus far gained we shall examine Professor Hicks's concept of "elasticity of expectations." Considering the prominent place which this notion has come to occupy in the analytical apparatus of up-to-date economic theory, it should provide us with a suitable starting-point from which to measure whatever further progress it may be possible to make by the help of other devices. The purpose of our test is to see whether the lamp we have constructed is capable of throwing light on corners of the problem of expectations which the lighting apparatus hitherto in use had left dark.

In dealing with expectations Professor Hicks wisely refrains from seeking determinateness. He distinguishes between the influence of current prices on expectations and, on the other hand, all other influences the effects of which are labelled "autonomous changes." Neglecting the latter he concentrates on the former type of influence. But seeing that "that influence may have various degrees of intensity, and work in various different ways"[9] we realise that we need a criterion of classification, and it is for this rôle that the "elasticity of expectations" is cast.[10] Its great merit is that by making it unnecessary to postulate a once-and-for-all uniform relationship between changes in current prices and expectations it enables us to deal with variable forms of this relationship. Its defect, we believe, is that, being a measure, it cannot tell us *why* this relation should take these variable forms any more than the most elaborate thermometer can tell us the causes of the fever from which the patient is suffering. However, for the greater part of his study of dynamic equilibrium Professor Hicks is content to make less than full use of the potentialities of his weapon and to assume the elasticity to be unity; he is in fact assuming a uniform relationship, and as long as he does this the defect mentioned does not cause much harm. But as soon as, in his discussion of wage rigidity, he abandons this restrictive assumption and allows for variations in this relationship, he apparently becomes conscious of the defect and feels compelled to give some kind of causal explanation of the forms which these variations may take. Unfortunately, however, the study of these variations is immediately restricted to those existing simultaneously between different groups of persons, after which it is not surprising that the causal explanation runs in terms of a spurious brand of "group psychology." It is sought in the greater or smaller "sensitivity" with which different people react to identical present changes.[11]

It is not easy to attach any precise meaning to these terms. Does Professor Hicks seriously maintain that the same individual confronted with the same kind of change will invariably react in an identical—and incidentally, predictable—manner? Only such invariability of reaction would entitle us to use intensity of reaction as a criterion of classification. If, on the other hand, we allow for changes over time in the "sensitivity" of individuals, and thus for changes in the composition of the two groups, is it not precisely our task to explain these changes? Since there can be little doubt that in fact men's expectational reactions to change are subject to wide fluctuations, we have to find a principle informing us in accordance with what these reactions vary. There may be numerous reasons, but it would seem that they can all be reduced to the simple fact that men's reactions to identical observable events will vary if for any reason these come to have a different meaning to them. The conclusion suggests itself that whether a given price change—or, for that matter, any other observable event—will at different times give rise to identical expectations will largely depend on the way in which people interpret it. Interpreting an event means to fit it into a picture of the "situation," a concept of a structure which serves as framework of reference. It follows that the "elasticity of expectations," if it is not to lead us into having to accept absurdities like an invariant "sensitivity," itself requires interpretation in the light of our argument.

4.

By now the reader will probably have grown impatient to see our theory of economic action go into action. We said above that ultimately the only satisfactory test of a theoretical construction is its capability of throwing light on what otherwise must remain dark corners of reality. We now propose to test the method we advocate by showing its usefulness in elucidating a problem which has loomed large in recent controversies on the rate of interest; we shall thus be concerned with interest-expectations, not with price-expectations. But before testing it let us briefly summarise the position we defend.

All human action is directed towards purposes and therefore requires a plan. Plans are not made *in vacuo,* and the planner has therefore to draw a mental picture of the situation in which he will have to act, of the constellation of circumstances which he cannot, or at least thinks he cannot, change and which to him are "data." We assert that the formation of expectations is incidental to, and derives its meaning from, this activity of the mind, and we therefore conclude that expectations have to be interpreted with reference to the situation as a whole *as the expecting individual sees it.*

The problem we shall discuss refers to the influence of expectations on the rate of interest. It is not our intention to take part in any of the numerous and fierce controversies which have of late raged on the theory of interest. On the contrary, we take as our starting-point a proposition which we believe to be entirely beyond controversy: that interest-expectations are one of the factors influencing the rate of interest. It is perhaps not unprofitable to insert here a brief sketch of the evolution of this idea in modern economic thought. It was introduced by Lord Keynes who used it as the main pillar to give shape and concreteness to his liquidity preference curve the negative slope of which could not otherwise be convincingly demonstrated.[12] It was further elucidated by Mr. Durbin, who pointed out that "large stocks of securities, just as much as large stocks of commodities, constitute a continuous and serious threat to monetary equilibrium, and the existence of stocks of securities is inevitable in a way that stocks of commodities are not,"[13] for the larger stocks are relative to current output the wider the scope for speculative price fluctuations and the smaller the influence of long-run supply on market price. Mr. Harrod drew the important practical conclusion that in a capital market which has a very definite expectation about the future rate of interest "it seems improbable that banking policy, however inspired and well informed, could secure a sufficient fluctuation in long-term interest rates to ensure a steady advance,"[14] as at rates lower than the expected the supply of securities would tend to become almost infinitely elastic. Professor Hicks does "not believe that we can count upon anything more than a small elasticity of interest-expectations."[15] "When the rate of interest (any rate of interest) rises or falls very far, there is a real presumption that it will come back to a 'normal' level. This consideration would seem to prevent interest-expectations from being very elastic."[16] But to the extent to which expectations are inelastic other influences on the current rate will grow correspondingly weaker. In Dr. Thomas Wilson, its latest exponent, the idea that the long-term rate of interest is largely fixed by "speculation" in the capital market has almost assumed the character of a major economic principle and been made the cornerstone of a trade cycle theory.[17]

We do not question the occurrence of inelastic interest-expectations, but it is a corollary of our argument that we have to insist on an *explanation* of such occurrences. It is already a little surprising that while what in common parlance are described as "speculative markets" are mostly characterised by wide and frequent price fluctuations, "speculation" is here held responsible for price inflexibility. But so far this merely goes to show that "speculation" may be a misnomer for the phenomenon under discussion. More significant is that, almost under our hands, the proposition that expectations are *one* of the factors influencing the rate of interest has changed into the proposition that if expectations are inelastic none of the other factors will have a chance to influence the result, because with a highly elastic supply of securities the other factors may influence the volume of sales but cannot affect price. This already suggests that unless the rate of interest is to be "left hanging by its own bootstraps" the other factors must somehow already be taken into account by the expectations. Furthermore, if the case of inelastic interest-expectations has such far-reaching consequences it clearly is our task to investigate what causes such expectations.

A little reflection will show that if in a market a strong increase in demand does not lead to any appreciable rise in price, not only must supply be extremely elastic, but where large stocks are the cause of this elasticity, holders of stocks must have a reason for selling out. They clearly will do it only if they have reasons to believe that the present strong demand is not only of an exceptional but of a transitory nature, and that for this very reason price will in the long run not be affected by it. If we apply this reasoning to the capital market we find that interest-expectations are most likely to be inelastic in a situation in which the capital market, that is to say, the majority of holders of securities, does not believe in the permanence of the forces exerting pressure on the market and hopes later on to be able to "re-stock" cheaply. It follows that if we find a case in which increased savings do not cause any appreciable fall in the rate of interest this indicates that the capital market has its suspicions—which may turn out to be entirely unjustified— about the permanent character of this sudden increase in the demand for securities. We are now able to understand the meaning of the "normal level" in the minds of people whose expectations are inelastic: this is a level determined by what are believed to be permanently operative forces. A market will exhibit inelastic expectations only if it believes that price is ultimately governed by long-run forces, and if it has a fairly definite conception of what these forces are. A capital market with inelastic interest-expectations is then a market which refuses to be impressed by present-day demand for securities which it believes to be short-lived. If therefore in a depression we find the long-term rate of interest remaining relatively inflexible this indicates that, rightly or wrongly, the capital market believes in the continued existence of investment opportunities yielding marginal profit at the former level, investment opportunities which the depression may have obscured but which it has not obliterated. For the same reason, in such a case, as Mr. Harrod predicted, an attempt to put the bond market under pressure by means of open-market operations is likely to prove a failure.

Finally, we always have to remember that whenever we observe large transactions taking place at little price change this indicates a case of conflicting expectations. It is scarcely necessary to remind the reader that we are here concerned solely with explaining a certain class of expectations, not with judging them in the light of *ex post* knowledge which the expecting individuals did not possess. It is indeed fairly obvious that in a dynamic economy with rapid technical progress and wide and frequent income fluctuations all expectations based on the prevalence of long-run trends must be of a somewhat problematical character, but to our present problem this is strictly irrelevant.

If inelastic expectations are really as frequent and important as some writers would have us believe, an interesting problem arises with regard to the interpretation of Wicksellian theory, more particularly in its Austrian version. According to this doctrine booms and slumps are engineered by banks lowering the "money rate of interest" below its "natural level," or raising it above it. Whatever the precise meaning of these terms, we now know that if banks are to succeed in altering the long-term rate of interest, expectations have to be very elastic. Seen from this angle, the Wicksellian theory appears to be based on a very special assumption, viz. of a capital market without a very strong mind of its own, always ready to follow a lead on the spur of the moment, and easily led into mistaking an ephemeral phenomenon for a symptom of a change in the economic structure. Without fairly elastic expectations there can therefore be no crisis of the Austro-Wicksellian type. But again, before we can accept this theory we are entitled to hear an explanation why elastic expectations should be prevalent. Such a gullible capital market we should expect to find in an economy the structure of which is still highly fluid and in which long-run forces have not yet had time to take shape. We tentatively suggest that such a state of expectations may be typical of an economy in the early stages of industrialisation, or of an economy undergoing "rejuvenation" owing to rapid technical progress.

In reality, of course, expectations of greatly varying degrees of elasticity are met with. It may be possible to reconcile apparently irreconcilable theories by reducing their differences to different assumptions about the prevailing type of expectation. But the story does not end here. In a World of Change no one type of expectation can be relied upon to provide stability. Neither a gullible capital market nor an obstinate one, nor, we may add, any intermediate variety is in itself a bulwark against crises of every kind. They each provide us with protection against some afflictions while leaving us unprotected against others. To investigate in what conditions what type of expectations is likely to have a stabilising or destabilising influence is no doubt one of the next tasks of dynamic theory. We submit that it cannot be successfully tackled unless expectations are made the subject of causal explanation.

NOTES

1. At least for the "state of long-term expectation," *General Theory of Employment, Interest, and Money* (New York: Harcourt, Brace & World, 1936), pp. 147–49.

2. "Vollkommene Voraussicht und wirtschaftliches Gleichgewicht," *Zeitschrift für Nationalökonomie* 6 (September 1935): 337–57.

3. *Monetary Equilibrium* (London: W. Hodge & Company, 1939).

4. "The Coordination of the General Theories of Money and Price," *Economica* 3 (August, 1936): 257–80.

5. Erik Lundberg, *Studies in the Theory of Economic Expansion* (Stockholm and London: P. S. King & Son, 1937), p. 175.

6. J. A. Schumpeter, *Business Cycles*, 2 vols. (New York: McGraw-Hill, 1939), 1:140.

7. Ibid., p. 55.

8. Fortunately not without exception. While, for instance, equilibrium theory takes the shape of production functions for granted. Professor Schumpeter's theory of Innovation, which is really a theory of entrepreneurial action, explains how in the course of economic development one production function comes to supersede another.

9. J. R. Hicks, *Value and Capital* (Oxford: Clarendon Press, 1959), p. 205.

10. "I define the elasticity of a particular person's expectations of the price of commodity X as the ratio of the proportional rise in expected future prices of X to the proportional rise in its current price." Ibid., p. 205.

11. "Some people's expectations do usually seem to be in fact fairly steady; they do not easily lose confidence in the maintenance of a steady level in the prices with which they are concerned; so that, when these prices vary, their natural interpretation of the situation is that the current price has become abnormally low, or abnormally high. But there are other people whose expectations are much more sensitive, who easily persuade themselves that any change in prices which they experience is a permanent change, or even that prices will go on changing in the same direction." Ibid., p. 271.

12. *General Theory*, pp. 168–72.

13. E. F. M. Durbin, *The Problem of Credit Policy* (London: Chapman & Hall, 1935), p. 103.

14. R. F. Harrod, *The Trade Cycle* (Oxford: Clarendon Press, 1936), pp. 124–25.

15. J. R. Hicks, op. cit., p. 282.

16. Ibid., p. 262.

17. Th. Wilson, *Fluctuations in Income and Employment* (London: I. Pitman, 1948), Ch. II, pp. 16–26.

Professor Shackle on the Economic Significance of Time

1.

In the first of the De Vries Lectures, delivered in Amsterdam in 1957,[1] Professor Shackle has further developed those ideas on the rôle of time in economic theory which students of his work know from his article on "The complex nature of Time as a concept in Economics."[2] These ideas are important for at least three reasons,

1) As Professor Shackle explains at the end of his first lecture, they embody the presuppositions on which his whole work on expectations rests. In order to discuss *Decision and Uncertainty* (the subjects of his second lecture) we must assume, he tells us, a world in which meaningful decisions, which are not merely mechanical responses to a given situation, or as he puts it, "decisions having content and interest" are possible. In his first lecture, Professor Shackle argues the case for our belief in such a world and against determinism in human action.

2) These ideas have an obvious bearing on the possibility of dynamic theory in Economics, in particular of models of micro- and macro-economic type. In fact Professor Shackle goes even farther and appears to deny the possibility, in a dynamic setting, of anything more than an equilibrium theory of the isolated decision-making individual, such as he gave us in *Expectations in Economics*.

3) The approach has very far-reaching implications for the methodology of Economics and the social sciences in general. For Professor Shackle argues in fact that the notion of Time as a

Reprinted from *Metroeconomica* 11 (April/August 1959).

"space," a homogeneous continuum, as the natural sciences use it, cannot be applied to the phenomena of human action because to the individual acting at a given moment, time is not homogeneous. This therefore is an issue which concerns all the social sciences.

In this paper we shall confine ourselves to a discussion of the problems listed under 2) and 3). No significance attaches to our neglect of issue 1). We shall simply take it for granted, that what Professor Shackle says about the logical structure and presuppositions of his own work is correct.

But all important work, such as the present, points beyond itself. It is in the implications of Professor Shackle's views for the progress of economic science that we are mainly interested.

This paper therefore falls into two parts. In the first, we shall examine Professor Shackle's views on the economic character of Time. In the second we shall consider some wider implications, for the methodology of Economics and the social sciences, of the inapplicability of certain concepts which the natural sciences can and do take for granted.

The natural starting point for both is our author's critique of the naturalistic time concept as applied to the phenomena of human action.

"In the classical dynamics of the physicist, time is merely and purely a mathematical variable. The essence of his scheme of thought is the fully abstract idea of function, the idea of some working rule or coded procedure which, applied to any particular and specified value or set of values of one or more independent variables, generates a value of a dependent variable. For the independent variable in a mental construction of this kind, *time* is a misnomer. Time as we seem to experience it has a character profoundly and radically different from that of a mere algebraic abstraction capable of being adequately represented by the symbol of a scalar quantity" (p. 23). How, then, do we experience time?

"In the experience of human individuals each of these moments is in a certain sense *solitary*. There is for us a *moment-in-*

being, which is the locus of every actual sense-experience, every thought, feeling, decision and action" (p. 13).

"The moment-in-being rolls, as it were, along the calendar-axis, and thus ever transports us willy-nilly to fresh temporal viewpoints. This I shall call dynamic movement in time" (p. 15).

The human mind can, it is true, transcend the present moment in imagination and memory, but the moment-in-being remains nevertheless always *self-contained* and *solitary.*

"Any point of the calendar-axis within most of the supposed lifespan of the individual can by expectation or by memory be brought into relation with each successive station of the moment-in-being. But each such relation, in another sense, subsists wholly inside the moment-in-being. Expectation and memory do not provide a means of comparing the actuality of the moment-in-being at one of its stations with that at another, they do not enable two moments, distinct in location on the calendar-axis, to be in being together, for the nature of 'the present,' the essence of the moment-in-being, is an impregnable self-contained isolation" (p. 16).

It follows that it is impossible to compare human actions undertaken at different moments in time. For no two moments can be "in being" together, "the actuality of one denies and excludes the actuality of the other, there is no 'common ground' on which they can be brought face to face. The attempt to compare the individual's actual feelings at t_0 with his actual feelings at t_2 is for him impossible and does not make sense" (pp. 18-19).

In other words, in describing the phenomena of human action, time cannot be used as a co-ordinate because we lack an identifiable object which "passes through time." Man with his "feelings," preferences, and the content of his consciousness changes in unpredictable fashion. Our author holds that this implies the impossibility of any intertemporal or interpersonal dynamics. His dynamics "seeks to show the internal structure of a single moment," it is "private and subjective." It is valid for an individual at a point of time. Is he right in thus confining the scope of dynamic theory?

2.

He is certainly right in questioning the usefulness of the naturalistic notion of time (as a continuum) for economic analysis. The natural sciences deal with changes in the properties of objects which are predictable because they are uniformly linked to changes in other variables, e.g. to motion in space, the passing of time, or forces emanating from other objects. But there is no way of telling in what way the preferences of a given individual will change over time, even when it is exposed to certain given conditions.

But if we were to take Professor Shackle's thesis literally, there could be no testing the success of plans, no plan revision, no comparison between *ex ante* and *ex post*. In fact planned action would make no sense whatever. Nor could there be a market in which the "private and subjective dynamics" of the individuals trading become socially objectified in the form of market prices and quantities of goods exchanged. Common experience tells us that these phenomena do exist. What, then, has gone wrong with our author's thesis?

It seems to us that while his thesis applies to human ends, of which we are unable to postulate any continuous existence in time, it does not apply to our knowledge of the adequacy of means to ends. But economic action is concerned with both, means and ends. The discontinuity of human ends, stressed by Professor Shackle, does not entail that there are no continuities at all in human action.

If no intertemporal comparison of the states of a man's knowledge were possible, most examinations would be pointless. Certainly in medicine and applied science all examinations involve intertemporal comparisons concerning knowledge of the adequacy of means to ends. We can, and occasionally do, learn from experience. Whatever may be discontinuous in us, the human mind is continuous. The acts of the mind of which our conscious life consists, follow each other ceaselessly. Bergson and Husserl have shown that the content of our consciousness is best regarded as a continuous stream of thought and experience.

No doubt Professor Shackle would not wish to deny all this. It would be ironic indeed if he, who set out to defend free will and the autonomy of the human mind, should in the end have to deny the continuity of mind. But on occasion he comes perilously close to holding such a position.

In our view he is going too far in one direction and not far enough in another. He is going too far when for discontinuity, which is a property merely of our ends, he wrongly claims the status of a universal category of human action.

But we can at least imagine a world in which the preferences of the individuals do not change for a time, and over longer periods change with almost imperceptible slowness. For such a world a dynamic theory would, even on Professor Shackle's showing, be possible. The continuity of ends would warrant it. But even in such a world Professor Shackle's general thesis about the creative power of the mind and our inability to predict its acts would still hold, because men would still be interpreting experiences, acquiring knowledge, planning and revising plans. We are able to imagine a world in which tastes do not change but unable to imagine one in which knowledge does not spread from some minds to others. Even continuity of ends does not entail an invariant means-end pattern; men would still be eager to make better use of the means at their disposal. *Time* and *Knowledge* belong together. The creative acts of the mind need not be reflected in changing preferences, but they cannot but be reflected in acts grasping experience and constituting objects of knowledge and plans of action. All such acts bear the stamp of the individuality of the actor.

Professor Shackle's strong emphasis on the subjective nature of economic action thus deserves every support, but our preferences and our interpretation of the world around us belong to different layers of experience. Our author fails to distinguish adequately between the subjectivism of utility and the subjectivism of interpretation.[3]

Intertemporal comparisons are thus possible except in cases where fundamental changes take place in an individual's system of preferences. But even the possibility of such intertemporal comparison does not of course mean that we can predict the future. While we may be able to say that a certain plan has so far succeeded we never can tell whether it will be further pursued. New ways of using the resources employed, or new and better ways of gaining the objective of the plan may in the meantime have been discovered, and may make it inadvisable to go on with the original plan, successful though it has been.

3.

The model Professor Shackle set forth in *Expectations in Economics,* and for which he has now provided a methodological basis, is a Robinson Crusoe model. It is concerned with the equilibrium of the isolated individual and with the mental acts by which it is reached. It tells us nothing about market processes, nothing about the exchange and transmission of knowledge. But must we stop there? Is there no bridge from the solitary dynamics of Robinson Crusoe to a dynamic market theory?

The central problem of such a theory can be stated briefly. It concerns the distribution and transmission of knowledge in a market economy. Men make use of one another's resources and satisfy one another's wants. How, in a changing world, do they acquire the requisite knowledge about these changing wants and resources? There is no simple answer since today's knowledge may or may not have become obsolete by to-morrow. But common experience suggests that "keeping track" of these changes is possible and requires a continuous sequence of such acts of interpretation as we mentioned above. Different men will not be equally good at it.

Professor Shackle admits that besides his kind of dynamics, the private and subjective dynamics of the isolated individual, there may be others, e.g. the public and objective dynamics of the econometric model builders. "Between these two kinds of dynamics we can perhaps imagine a third kind, in which we should suppose an outside observer to be simultaneously informed by everyone of the individuals composing the whole economic system about the knowledge, thoughts, desires, expectations and decisions making up the content of each individual's mind in some one moment, a moment located at the same point of the calendar-axis for every individual" (pp. 25–26).

In the market, however, we have such an outside agency which, moreover, not merely registers decisions but also informs the individuals participating in it about them. How far a concrete market serves this function depends of course on a number of factors, such as its extent and degree of perfection. The markets for the services of the factors of production provide as a rule fairly good information about production plans.

Markets for products, on the other hand, provide it only where forward sales are possible. A perfect intertemporal market on which all producers sold their products before they were produced would provide complete information about all production plans. But of course, while a perfect forward market can provide information and bring production plans into consistency with each other and with the plans of consumers, it cannot predict the future. Here Professor Shackle is quite right in saying of his "outside observer," "But even if he could do this, he would not be able, on our assumption that each individual is a decision-maker in the real sense, to go beyond this very first and immediate interplay of decisions and foresee the further evolution of the system. For he could not predict what would be the next *decisions*" (p. 26).

Thus, a dynamic market theory which shows how the expectations and plans of various individuals are brought into consistency with each other, is possible. It is possible to transcend the "private and subjective" dynamics of the individual and to reach the "socially objective" dynamics of the market, provided that our market is a forward market. Interpersonal and intertemporal dynamics belong together. The theory of equilibrium of the isolated individual is not necessarily the last word in dynamics.

4.

We must now turn to the wider implications of Professor Shackle's ideas for the methodology of Economics and the social sciences in general. Our starting point is, again, his demonstration that the naturalistic concept of *Time* as a homogeneous continuum cannot be applied to an individual making his plans. We also have to consider the implications of his thesis that in economics prediction is impossible.

There can, of course, be no question of doubting the status of Economics as a science. Like other scientists, economists attempt to formulate systematic generalisations about observable phenomena. Like other scientists they frame hypotheses which are meant to reflect certain features of reality, and which stand or fall by this test.

If by "scientific method" we mean nothing more than this, no methodological problem arises. But it now appears that we must be on our guard against the uncritical adoption of certain auxiliary axioms and notions which may be useful to natural scientists but less so to us, like "time" as a continuum or "the closed system" within which alone determinism and prediction are possible.[4]

This means that economics needs a methodology *sui generis,* at least insofar as it has to deal with creative acts of the mind, with the setting of objectives and the interpretation of experience, which have no counterpart in nature. There can of course be no question of our setting forth here even an outline of such a methodology. But a few hints may be dropped and a few points made.

On the subject of prediction Professor Shackle's conclusions are quite definite and, in our view, cogent. "Complete prediction would require the predictor to know in complete detail at the moment of making his prediction, first, all 'future' advances of knowledge and inventions, and secondly, all 'future' decisions. To know in advance what an invention will consist of is evidently to make that invention in advance" (pp. 103-104).

"Predictability of the world's future history implies predictability of decisions, and this is either a contradiction in terms or an abolition of the concept of decision except in a perfectly empty sense" (p. 104). And "*Predicted man* is less than human, *predicting man* is more than human."

But of what use, it may be asked, is economics if economists are unable to predict? The answer, we think, is that the systematic generalizations of the economists enable us to understand better certain predicaments of the past and present. The main social function of the economist is to provide the historian and the student of contemporary events with an arsenal of schemes of interpretation. Moreover, there is such a thing as "negative prediction." It is often possible for the economist to predict that a certain policy will fail because of its inherent contradictions, e.g. a policy designed to increase deficit-financed investment and at the same time to stop an inflation. But in this case his prediction is based on a purely logical argument, not on any knowledge of specific circumstances, present or future. This possibility of making negative predictions is therefore quite consistent with Professor Shackle's conclusions.

Economists should, in our view, openly admit that they are unable to make positive predictions about the world. In this respect they are inferior to the natural scientists. But, on the other hand, in certain other respects the social sciences are actually superior, since they can, as the natural sciences cannot, give an intelligible account of the world with which they are dealing. We have to remember that the natural sciences, in the centuries of their evolution, have discarded a number of questions to which their methods can provide no answers, e.g. questions concerned with purpose and cause.

Why men have two legs and dogs have four, why the velocities of light and sound are what they are, why a certain flower emanates a certain smell, are questions with which modern natural sciences do not concern themselves. But why modern economies have evolved a certain type of money and credit system, or the institutions of the "Welfare State," are relevant and meaningful questions to which answers can be provided.

The essence of the matter is that human action is planned, though of course few plans may ever succeed. It is always possible to compare the outcome with the plan, the *ex post* with the *ex ante,* the observable result with the, originally purely mental, cause. In fact it is impossible to give an intelligible account of human action in any other way. The natural sciences may have had good reasons to discard the concept of "cause" and to confine themselves to observable "uniformities of sequence." There is no reason why the social sciences should follow them in this. Social causes have to be found in the creative acts of human minds. Economics explains that the reasons why certain prices are paid and quantities of goods produced, have to be sought in the choices made by consumers and decisions made by producers. Such causal genesis is a legitimate concern of the social sciences which has no counterpart in nature. It warrants the employment of genetic-causal schemes of interpretation which give rise to methodological problems *sui generis*.

A few words have now to be said about the relationship between knowledge and expectations. The impossibility of prediction in economics follows from the facts that economic change is linked to change in knowledge, and future knowledge cannot be gained before its time. Knowledge is generated by spontaneous acts of the mind. We may ask what bearing this has on the theory of expectations. How are expectations formed? How is prognosis related to diagnosis? In answering these questions we shall permit ourselves to restate briefly what we said on another occasion.[5]

All prognosis which is more than mere guesswork must be linked to the diagnosis of an existing situation. The business man who forms an expectation is doing precisely what a scientist does when he formulates a working hypothesis. Both, business expectation and scientific hypothesis serve the same purpose; both reflect an attempt at cognition and orientation in an imperfectly known world, both embody imperfect knowledge to be tested and improved by later experience. The difference between them consists in that, unlike many scientists, the business man cannot repeat experiments in conditions he can control. Tests have to be made in a world which not merely changes, but whose change is not governed by any known law.

While this does not deprive these tests of all value, it does mean that in business even more than in science a good deal will depend on interpretation of experience, i.e. on creative acts of the mind, and that the knowledge yielded will be imperfect.

On the other hand, each expectation does not stand by itself but is the cumulative result of a series of former expectations which have been revised in the light of later experience, and these past revisions are the main source of whatever present knowledge we have. Our present expectation, to be revised later on as experience accrues, is not only the basis of any plan of action we may contemplate but also a source of more perfect future knowledge. The formation of expectations is thus a continuous process, an element of the larger process of the transmission of knowledge, the process by which men acquire knowledge about each other's needs and resources.

It follows that any experience made conveys knowledge to us only insofar as it fits, or fails to fit, into a pre-existent frame of knowledge. But the frame of knowledge in terms of which we interpret a new experience is always "private and subjective." Knowledge always belongs to an individual mind. When we speak of the transmission of knowledge, we use this as a metaphorical expression for a process of interaction of minds. Knowledge spreads from mind to mind, it does not float from one individual to another as a piece of wood in a stream floats from one place to another. Its acquisition requires active participation in a social process. Following a different path, we have thus arrived at the same conclusion as Professor Shackle, viz., that expectations and the knowledge they reflect are always subjective. But this does not mean that the equilibrium of the isolated individual is necessarily the last word in dynamics.

Finally, we may view Professor Shackle's subjectivist dynamics in the perspective of the history of economic thought. In the history of our discipline objectivist and subjectivist tendencies have predominated at various periods, but the most remarkable progress of economics has been linked to the ascendancy of subjectivism.

The classical school, true to its 18th century origin, sought the ultimate determinants of economic life in certain "natural forces" like those reflected in the Malthusian law and the diminishing fertility of the soil, forces which were thought to shape

the distribution of incomes and to set limits to economic progress. An "objective" theory of value with hours of (unskilled)
labour as its measure crowned the classical edifice.

But about the middle of the last century subjectivism came into
its own. As it was gradually realised that human ingenuity can
overcome the obstacles presented by the classical forces, the
human mind and its manifestations, choice and decision, came to
occupy the centre of the economic stage. The "subjective revolution" of the 1870's presents only one aspect of this change, but it
epitomises it well. It came to be realized that the value of a good
does not reside in any measurable properties it might have, but
constitutes a relationship between an appraising mind and the
good.

The introduction of expectations into economics in this century, the realisation that what men will do in a given situation
depends largely on their interpretation of it and on the direction
of their imagination, was merely a further step along the same
route. The problem of expectations, implicit in the work of
Knight and Schumpeter, found explicit recognition by Keynes
and the pupils of Wicksell in Sweden. Professor Shackle's *Expectations in Economics* readily finds its place within this tradition.
Time in Economics, as we see it, is a more explicit statement of the
methodological presuppositions of this approach.

One problem remains open. Can expectations be introduced
into a general dynamic theory? The static equilibrium systems of
Walras and Pareto, the greatest achievement of neo-classical
economics, contain both, subjective and objective elements,
tastes and quantities of resources. This is possible because of the
timeless character of these systems. Once individuals have revealed their preferences, these become "data" like all others.

Individuals are free to choose, but having once chosen they
are not free to change their minds: there literally is "no time" for
that.

But expectations cannot be treated in this way if we want to
make them elements of a dynamic system. As soon as we permit
time to elapse we must permit knowledge to change, and knowledge cannot be regarded as a function of anything else. It is not

the subjective nature of expectations, any more than that of individual preferences, which makes them such unsuitable elements of dynamic theories, it is the fact that time cannot pass without modifying knowledge which appears to destroy the possibility of treating expectations as data of a dynamic equilibrium system.

This conclusion does not affect the possibility of a theory of the forward market on which individuals reveal their expectations by engaging in forward transactions in the same way as individuals reveal their preferences by purchases and sales on an ordinary market.

NOTES

1. G. L. S. Shackle, *Time in Economics* (Amsterdam: North Holland Publishing Co., 1958).

2. In *Economia Internazionale,* vol. VII, no. 4.

3. See L. M. Lachmann, "The Role of Expectations in Economics as a Social Science," *Economica* 10 (February 1943):15.

4. Of course, what is a useful concept always depends on what concrete problem we have to deal with. Whenever we have to describe a succession of events in chronological order, whether in society or nature, time as a continuum is an indispensable notion. We cannot but admire the Walrasian system, though we may recall the difficulties Walras had in trying to show how equilibrium is reached in actual market processes.

5. Cf. L. M. Lachmann, *Capital and Its Structure* (London: London School of Economics, 1956), pp. 23–34.

The Science of Human Action

This is Professor Mises's *magnum opus*. [1] It is a *magnum opus* in every sense of the word. Its majestic sweep embraces almost the whole field of economics and touches, at some point or other, on almost every social issue of our time. Not merely the formal-logical apparatus of economic theory, but the social structure of modern industrial society, its achievements, its weaknesses, and, most of all, its ideologies come under the relentless scrutiny of one who again and again confounds the smallminded within the precincts of our science and outside it. Perhaps his most outstanding merit is an intellectual courage which in these days of the cult of the "politically possible" has become all too rare. Throughout the 881 pages of the text the argument is presented with a pungency of style which rivals the clarity and vigour of his thought.

To render justice to a work of this nature on the few pages at our disposal is clearly impossible. All we can hope to do is to select a few topics for discussion.

When ten years ago Professor Knight reviewed the original German version[2] of the book in this journal[3] and found himself faced with the same dilemma, he selected one topic only for discussion, viz., the theory of capital. Quite possibly this is the best way of going about it. Undoubtedly the theory of capital occupies a prominent place in Professor Mises's doctrinal edifice. His theory of the trade cycle as well as his proof of the inadequacy of some recent "models" for a socialist market economy depend largely on his view of capital.

This article appeared in *Economica* 18 (November 1951): 412–27.

Yet we shall not follow the method Professor Knight adopted ten years ago. Unable though we are to take the reader on an extensive tour of the palace and to show him every part of the building, it seems to us wrong to confine our inspection to the basement. The wide vistas to be gained from some of the windows on the upper floors are too enchanting for that.

Human Action is, of course, far more than a treatise on the methodology of the social sciences. But its centre of gravity certainly lies in its first seven chapters which are devoted to the discussion of method in the social sciences. We shall therefore have to deal at some length with the issues raised in these chapters.

1.

In the study of human thought on any subject it is a fundamental principle that we cannot succeed in understanding what an author "really means" unless we understand the questions he is trying to answer. And an appraisal of Professor Mises's views on the methodology of the social sciences requires at least some knowledge of the history of the problems he is dealing with. In reading this book we must never forget that it is the work of Max Weber that is being carried on here.

Now, Max Weber's methodological writings had a dual purpose: to convince the historians who, at his time and in the German environment in which he grew up, were apt to claim a methodological monopoly for their "individualising" methods, that the social sciences offered just as much, if not more, scope for generalisation as the natural sciences; and that any historical "explanation" logically presupposes a generalised scheme of cause and effect. But at the same time he strove to uphold the methodological independence of the theoretical social sciences of the natural sciences by stressing the cardinal importance of *means* and *ends* as fundamental categories of human action.

This work has been carried on by others besides Professor Mises. There is Professor Hayek's famous essay on "Scientism and the Study of Society," well known to readers of this journal.[4]

There is the work of Dr. Schütz who has applied Husserl's phenomenology to the logical analysis of the structure of human action.[5] And there is, of course, Professor Robbins's *Essay on the Nature and Significance of Economic Science* (1932; 2nd ed. 1935), which firmly established the definition of our science in terms of scarce means and multiple ends.

It may be objected that this definition of the subject-matter of economics is too wide. At an election, for instance, each voter has one vote but more than one candidate to give it to; yet the problem is not usually regarded as an economic one.

Professor Mises's reply to such objections is that in our search for the causes of the market phenomena we observe, and the explanation of which is the primary task of economists, we have unwittingly strayed into the realm of *Praxeology*, the Science of Human Action. He therefore distinguishes between *Praxeology*, the Science of Human Action, and *Catallactics*, the science which deals with market phenomena (233). The theorems of the latter presuppose the categories of the former. In other words, what Professor Hayek has called "The Pure Logic of Choice" belongs to Praxeology rather than to Catallactics. In this way what we have come to regard as the main body of economics is seen to belong to two related but distinct fields. "Catallactics is the analysis of those actions which are conducted on the basis of monetary calculation. Market exchange and monetary calculation are inseparably linked together" (235).

Professor Mises claims *a priori* validity for the propositions of Praxeology. "Its scope is human action as such, irrespective of all environmental, accidental, and individual circumstances of the concrete acts. Its cognition is purely formal and general without reference to the material content and the particular features of the actual case . . . . Its statements and propositions are not derived from experience. They are, like those of logic and mathematics, *a priori*. They are not subject to verification or falsification on the ground of experience and facts. They are both logically and temporally antecedent to any comprehension of historical facts. They are a necessary requirement of any intellectual grasp of historical events" (32). At the same time

"Praxeology conveys exact and precise knowledge of real things" (39).

These statements raise two fundamental questions: How can Praxeology at one and the same time be *a priori* true, and "convey knowledge of real things"? Secondly, even if no *a priori* validity is claimed for the propositions of Catallactics, is it true that all the fundamental economic theorems that would clearly fall into the field of Praxeology are, like logic and mathematics, *a priori* valid?

As regards our first question, we must remember that the "real things" about which we learn from Praxeology are human actions. They can be studied in two ways: we can study them, as it were, "from outside," by observation and experience, like other phenomena of nature; or we can study them "from inside," that is to say, we interpret them as the products of *plans*, as manifestations of a directing and controlling mind. Looked at in this way all human action has a logical structure. There is therefore such a thing as a Logic of Action closely linked to the logic of our thought. We act by virtue of the fact that we think before. "The real thing which is the subject matter of praxeology, human action, stems from the same source as human reasoning. Action and reason are congeneric and homogeneous; they may even be called two different aspects of the same thing. That reason has the power to make clear through pure ratiocination the essential features of action is a consequence of the fact that action is an offshoot of reason" (39).

Our second question raises a fundamental issue in epistemology. It is not merely a question of whether "means and ends" have the same epistemological status as, for instance, "time and space." Behind it there lurks the even more fundamental question whether we can have any knowledge not ultimately derived from experience.

Fortunately this journal is not the proper place to raise such weighty issues in. *Economica* must not become a battleground for positivists and Neo-Kantians. It seems to us, however, that in this particular case it is possible to side with Professor Mises without taking sides on the wider issue. For we can, and in our opinion must, distinguish between different layers of experience. In

economics we are concerned with the action of the adult house-
holder and the business man. Even if we granted that our ability
to distinguish between means and ends is the result of some kind
of experience, it still remains true that this experience is not the
experience gathered from spending one's income or running a
business. Professor Mises is certainly right in holding that all
such action already *presupposes* the distinction between means
and ends.[6] We may therefore say that, whatever the source of
knowledge from which the distinction is ultimately derived,
means and ends are indeed "logically and temporally antecedent" to the household and business plans which economists
study. They may have their root in a layer of (juvenile?) experience, but it is a layer which precedes and underlies the layer with
which we are concerned.

2.

Having learnt that Professor Mises regards Praxeology as
methodologically similar to logic and mathematics, we might
expect him to welcome the use of mathematical methods in
economics. In fact, however, this is not so. On the contrary, the
section on "Logical Catallactics versus Mathematical Catallactics"
in the chapter on Prices, one of the most interesting and perhaps
the most characteristic of the book, turns out to be a devastating
criticism, not of mathematical economics as such, but at least of
the methods currently in use by mathematical economists. Two
classes of mathematical economists are the chief target of Professor Mises's onslaught.

There are, firstly, the econometricians trying to make
economics a "quantitative science." But "there is no such thing
as quantitative economics. All economic quantities we know
about are data of economic history. No reasonable man can
suppose that the relation between price and supply is in general,
or in respect of certain commodities, constant. We know, on the
contrary, that . . . the reactions of the same people to the same
external events vary, and that it is not possible to assign individuals to classes of men reacting in the same way" (348). Secondly,

there is the equilibrium school which refuses to study the Market Process, the central object of economics. "They merely mark out an imaginary situation in which the market process would cease to operate. The mathematical economists disregard the whole theoretical elucidation of the market process and evasively amuse themselves with an auxiliary notion employed in its context and devoid of any sense when used outside of this context" (352).

The reason for this confusion has to be sought in the inability of many economists to grasp the difference between the essential character of the natural sciences and that of the sciences dealing with human action. This difference is brought out in a characteristically Misesque passage:

"In physics we are faced with changes occurring in various sense phenomena. We discover a regularity in the sequence of these changes and these observations lead us to the construction of a science of physics. We know nothing about the ultimate forces actuating these changes. They are for the searching mind ultimately given and defy any further analysis. What we know from observation is the regular concatenation of various observable entities and attributes. It is this mutual interdependence of data that the physicist describes in differential equations.

"In praxeology the first fact we know is that men are purposively intent upon bringing about some changes. It is this fact that integrates the subject matter of praxeology and differentiates it from the subject matter of the natural sciences. We know the forces behind the changes, and this aprioristic knowledge leads us to a cognition of the praxeological processes. The physicist does not know what electricity 'is.' He knows only phenomena attributed to something called electricity. But the economist knows what actuates the market process. It is only thanks to this knowledge that he is in a position to distinguish market phenomena from other phenomena and to describe the market process" (352).

All this the mathematical economist ignores. In making equilibrium the central concept of his system "he merely describes an auxiliary makeshift employed by the logical economists as a limiting notion, the definition of a state of affairs in which there is no longer any action and the market process has come to a standstill. . . . A superficial analogy is spun out too long, that is all" (352).

In all this, to be sure, the word "causal-genetic" never occurs. Yet it is clear what Professor Mises is aiming at. The task of the economist is not merely, as in equilibrium theory, to examine the logical consistency of various modes of action, but to make human action intelligible, to let us understand the nature of the logical structures called 'plans,' to exhibit the successive modes of thought which give rise to successive modes of action. In other words, all true economics is not "functional" but "causal-genetic."[7]

"Logical economics is essentially a theory of processes and changes." And "the problems of process analysis, i.e., the only economic problems that matter, defy any mathematical approach. . . . The main deficiency of mathematical economics is not the fact that it ignores the temporal sequence, but that it ignores the market process. The mathematical method is at a loss to show how from a state of non-equilibrium those actions spring up which tend toward the establishment of equilibrium. . . . The differential equations of mechanics are supposed to describe precisely the motions concerned at any instant of the time travelled through. The economic equations have no reference whatever to conditions as they really are in each instant of the time interval between the state of non-equilibrium and that of equilibrium. . . . A very imperfect and superficial metaphor is not a substitute for the services rendered by logical economics" (353-4).

Two examples of the misinterpretation of economic phenomena resulting from the application of misleading mathematical metaphors are then given: Fisher's exchange equation, "the mathematical economist's futile and misleading attempt to deal with changes in the purchasing power of money"; and Schumpeter's rather unfortunate "dictum according to which consumers in evaluating consumers' goods *ipso facto* also evaluate the means of production which enter into the production of these goods."[8]

3.

We now have to face the central issue of Professor Mises's methodology. "Logical economics is essentially a theory of processes and changes." But is there, can there be, a "Pure Logic of Choice"? In the field of human action we "explain" phenomena as the outcome of the pursuit of plans. Each plan is a logical structure in which means and ends are coordinated by a directing and controlling mind. But the plans of different individuals may be, and as a rule are, inconsistent with each other. Now, it is an undeniable fact that far too many economists are preoccupied with examining the consistency of plans without ever bothering to tell us how in reality men overcome inconsistencies brought to light by failure, how they set out to revise their plans in the light of their experience, favourable or unfavourable.

In other words, there is a tendency in the economic theory currently in fashion to treat knowledge as a datum without explaining how knowledge is transformed as a result of the market process. This tendency is to be deplored. But if the transformation of knowledge is an essential element in the market process, then the latter cannot belong to the province of logical economics, for the acquisition of knowledge is *not* a logical process. How does our author overcome this difficulty?

He has an answer of a kind, and we believe it, on the whole, to be a satisfactory answer. Unfortunately it is nowhere explicitly stated, and the elements of the answer have to be pieced together from passages and ideas scattered throughout the text of 881 pages. The explicit answer, on the other hand, which Professor Mises provides for us cannot be regarded as adequate.

According to our author the logical principle which coordinates the plans of different individuals is the division of labour. "The exchange relation is the fundamental social relation. Interpersonal exchange of goods and services weaves the bond which unites men into society. The societal formula is: *do ut des*" (195).

At first sight this suggestion does not appear very helpful. For the division of labour to serve as the fundamental principle of human interaction it would be necessary for everybody concerned from the beginning to *know* everybody else's needs, resources, and abilities. In a world of processes and changes this is clearly impossible. It would be possible only in that static world Professor Mises disdains. He thus appears to be confronted with this dilemma: his principle for the coordination of social action is immediately applicable only in equilibrium, while a "theory of processes and changes" would first have to explain how men gain that knowledge which enables them to adjust their action to the needs of others, and to make use of their abilities and resources.

Professor Mises's real answer to the dilemma lies in his conception of entrepreneurship and the function of entrepreneurial profits, a conception which is really dynamic and remarkably similar to Schumpeter's. Profits, those temporary margins between today's cost of complementary factor services and tomorrow's product prices, are signposts of entrepreneurial success. In a symbolic form they convey knowledge, but the symbols have to be *interpreted*. In this ability men differ widely; its comparative rarity is the ultimate cause of human inequality. "If all entrepreneurs were to anticipate correctly the future state of the market, there would be neither profits nor losses. . . . An entrepreneur can make a profit only if he anticipates future conditions more correctly than other entrepreneurs" (291).

The market process, to be sure, conveys knowledge through profits realised. But it also promotes the rise of those better equipped than others to wrest economic meaning from the happenings of the market-place, the ups and downs of prices, the fluctuations in stocks, the doings of the politicians, and of those (they will always be few) who know how to learn from the mistakes of others. In other words, the market process is closely linked with what Pareto called "the circulation of élites," perhaps the most important of all social processes. "One should not forget that on the market a process of selection is in continual operation. There prevails an unceasing tendency to weed out the less efficient entrepreneurs, that is, those who fail in their endeavours to anticipate correctly (580). . . . This specific anticipative understanding of the conditions of the uncertain future defies any rules and systematisation (582). . . . The resultant of these endeavours is not only the price structure but no less the social structure, the assignment of definite tasks to the various individuals. The market makes people rich or poor, determines who shall run the big plants and who shall scrub the floors, fixes how many people shall work in the copper mines and how many in the symphony orchestras" (308).

The essence of the matter is that the market process promotes the spreading of knowledge through the promotion of those capable of interpreting market data and of thus transforming them into market knowledge, and the elimination of those who cannot read the signs of the market.

4.

We said already that the theory of capital occupies a prominent place in Professor Mises's doctrinal edifice. We must therefore look at it closely.

Broadly speaking, his theory of capital is more or less identical with that of Professor Hayek in the *Pure Theory of Capital.*[9] Böhm-Bawerk's doctrine is not uncritically accepted. His wage-fund interpretation of the capital stock is rejected; so is the "backward-looking" concept of the period of production. "The length of time expended in the past for the production of capital goods available to-day does not count at all. . . . The 'average period of production' is an empty concept" (486). Moreover, Böhm-Bawerk's "demonstration of the universal validity of time preference is inadequate because it is based on psychological considerations. However, psychology can never demonstrate the validity of a praxeological theorem" (485). While in expounding his theory of the higher productivity of roundabout methods of production he "did not entirely avoid the productivity approach which he himself had so brilliantly refuted" (486).

The essence of Professor Mises's argument can perhaps best be expressed by contrasting it with, e.g., Professor Knight's theory of investment. For the latter a man who saves faces merely the choice between a present segment of a service flow and a permanent income stream. For Professor Mises the man faces a choice between a number of present goods and a large number of future goods all maturing at different points of time. But he has a scale of preference ("time preference") which enables him to decide which combination of future goods he prefers to all others. Capital goods are thus future consumption goods *in statu nascendi,* and their valuation reflects the pattern of time preference between the various combinations of consumption goods of different degrees of futurity. The market rate of interest is the average rate of discount of future against present goods, the net result of these individual time preferences.

The question arises whether a form of economic organisation is possible in which there is a market for consumption goods, but no market for capital goods. Such a system has been advocated by the protagonists of the New Scientific Socialism. They would leave all investment decisions to a Central Planning Board, while output decisions about consumers' goods would be made by individual plant managers provided with "factor-price tables" and left with the general instruction to produce that output quantity for which market price equals marginal cost.

Professor Mises does not find it difficult to dispose of these schemes. He shows that they rest essentially on a misconception of the function of the entrepreneur in a market economy. "The cardinal fallacy implied in this and all kindred proposals is that they look at the economic problem from the perspective of the subaltern clerk whose intellectual horizon does not extend beyond subordinate tasks. They consider the structure of industrial production and the allocation of capital to the various branches and production aggregates as rigid, and do not take into account the necessity of altering this structure in order to adjust it to changes in conditions" (703). To be sure, the entrepreneur "invests," and he produces and sells output. But this is not all. He has another function which we all know but about which little is, as a rule, heard from economists: the "regrouping of capital assets" by buying and selling them, the incessant re-shuffling of the combinations of complementary capital goods with which he works and which in their complexity form the ever-changing basis of the capital structure.[10, 11]

5.

Almost forty years ago Professor Mises, through a brilliant interpretation of an idea of Wicksell, became the first exponent of what has come to be known as "The Austrian Theory of the Trade Cycle." In its fully developed form this theory contends that what happens during a boom is not merely that "incomes, output, and employment" rise and approach the "point of full employment," but that the capital structure becomes distorted. In some sectors of the economic system new capital goods are piled up, in others, owing to what Irving Fisher called "the money illusion," existing capital goods are not even being maintained. Under the relentless pressure of credit expansion sooner or later some resources become scarce, and others thus come to lack those *complementary* factors in the expectation of whose availability they had been produced. It is plain that the *heterogeneity of capital resources* of which during the boom some become scarce, some abundant, is of the essence of the matter.

For 15 years this theory has been under a cloud. During most of that time the stage was held by underconsumption theories. To many economists it began to appear unthinkable that economic crises could be caused by anything but "lack of effective demand." Keynesianism in all its forms ruled supreme.

But of late it has been possible to observe a gradual change of heart. Undoubtedly the high tide of Keynesianism is receding. In a mood of eclecticism an increasing number of economists appears to be ready to reconsider the evidence. In this new situation it is perhaps not too extravagant to hope for general, or nearly general, agreement that booms may collapse and depressions come to an end, for all sorts of reasons, that the economic systems of modern industrial societies are far too complex to offer much prospect of "stable progress," and that a theoretical one-model show must needs fail to give an adequate picture of the range of analytical tools required to cope with these baffling complexities.

This changing mood finds a clear expression in Dr. Hicks's recent book on the trade cycle.[12] Underconsumption crises are not impossible,[13] but they are unlikely to be frequent. The most important cause of cyclical downturns Dr. Hicks sees in the existence of the "ceiling," i.e., in the existence of physical obstacles to unlimited expansion of output. Of course, it is far from our mind to suggest that Professor Mises's theory is identical with Dr. Hicks's. Clearly it is not. But there are striking similarities, and the divergences are often more apparent than real. Of this we shall give three examples.

In the first place, Dr. Hicks relies heavily on the Acceleration Principle which Professor Mises scorns. But the essence of the boom is clearly, in both theories, and in open contrast to all underconsumptionist teaching, that entrepreneurs make investment plans the real resources for which do not exist. "The essence of the credit-expansion boom is not over-investment, but investment in wrong lines, i.e., malinvestment" (Mises, 556).

Secondly, Professor Mises, to whom capital resources are essentially heterogeneous, finds it easier to define the nature of malinvestment. "The whole entrepreneurial class is, as it were, in the position of a master-builder whose task is to erect a building out of a limited supply of building materials. If this man overestimates the quantity of the available supply, he drafts a plan for the execution of which the means at his disposal are not sufficient. He oversizes the groundwork and the foundations and only discovers later in the progress of the construction that he lacks the material needed for the completion of the structure. It is obvious that our master-builder's fault was not over-investment, but an inappropriate employment of the means at his disposal" (Mises, p. 557).

Dr. Hicks, on the other hand, throughout the greater part of his book treats capital as homogeneous, and thus, at the critical point, lacks the sharpest-edged tool for making malinvestment explicit. But it is interesting to note that, when in Chapter X he embarks on a "further inspection of the ceiling," his homogeneity assumption breaks down. He not merely contends that "resources needed for making investment goods are becoming scarcer than the resources needed for making consumption goods" (Hicks, 128). Four pages later we are actually told: "We could easily have made a further advance by splitting up these ceilings, and allowing a sectional ceiling for every product." The important point is "that the accumulating real pressure will usually precipitate a downturn before the general shortage has become so acute as to induce a general inflation." In other words, some resources will become scarce while others remain plentiful. This is precisely the situation the Austrian theory was designed to meet.

Thirdly, as regards the position on the morrow of the downturn, Dr. Hicks again relies on multiplier and accelerator, while Professor Mises, spurning such Keynesian devices, preaches the need for readjustment. But again the contrast is more apparent than real. For Dr. Hicks the downturn expresses the tendency of the system to return to the long-run equilibrium level (the danger being that this may be "passed by"). For Professor Mises "readjustment" means more or less the same thing. "The malinvestments of the boom have misplaced inconvertible factors of production in some lines at the expense of other lines in which they were more urgently needed. There is disproportion in the allocation of nonconvertible factors to the various branches of industry." Now "one must provide the capital goods lacking in those branches which were unduly neglected in the boom. Wage rates must drop; people must restrict their consumption temporarily until the capital wasted by malinvestment is restored. Those who dislike the hardships of the readjustment period must abstain in time from credit expansion" (575–6).

As regards the depression, the main difference between the two authors consists in that Professor Mises is less afraid than Dr. Hicks of the effects of secondary deflation (Mises, 565–6). This is perhaps a matter for judgment from case to case rather than for theoretical generalisation.

In conclusion we may note that on the whole the Austrian

theory has the broader scope, thanks largely to the fact that it is not tied to the homogeneity assumption. Dr. Hicks ignores existing capital goods and the problems of their versatility. We do not even learn whether his coefficients of production are fixed or variable. In the Austrian theory existing capital combinations can be reshuffled so as to release scarce resources. In fact, the constructive entrepreneurial task of the readjustment period consists largely in this, and not in indiscriminate investment. The core of the matter lies in this: the existence of unemployment and idle resources does not necessarily indicate "lack of effective demand"; it *may* indicate lack of complementary capital. When we reach his "ceiling" Dr. Hicks recognises this possibility; when we leave it its implications seem to fall into oblivion.

6.

A few words have to be said about Professor Mises's altitude to the wider issues of our time. Among the members of the governing class of present-day Western society he is not a popular figure. Politicians and bureaucrats dislike him; the intellectuals who produce the ideologies to sustain their rule abhor him. The Fabians worship other idols.

Equalitarianism is the favourite myth of our century. No thinking person can fail to notice that as societies become more civilised, inequalities are bound to increase. This is simply a corollary of the division of labour. As this reaches ever higher degrees, individual contributions to the social product become more and more specific and thus less substitutable. For is it not an accepted maxim of economics that the division of labour enables everybody to give of his best, and that, as it is carried to higher degrees of complexity, this, individual and highly specific, "best" tends to become very much better than anybody else's "best" in the same line? As inequality can thus be shown to be an inevitable concomitant of civilisation, arguments about its desirability or undesirability are seen to be largely irrelevant. Therefore "the inequality of incomes and wealth is an inherent feature of the market economy" (836). No prejudice, however, was ever shaken by argument, and our contemporary mythologists are no more given to critical reflection on major tenets than were their medieval ancestors.

But Professor Mises not merely refuses to accept the contemporary myth. He can see through it! "In endorsing the principle of equality as a political postulate nobody wants to share his own income with those who have less. When the American wage earner refers to equality, he means that the dividends of the stockholders should be given to him. He does not suggest a curtailment of this own income for the benefit of those 95 percent of the earth's population whose income is lower than his"(836).

Nor is much comfort offered to those who would create "equality of opportunity" through education, by "making educational opportunities more equal." The abilities by which men outdo each other in a complex society have little to do with education. Entrepreneurial ability is not to be acquired in lecture-rooms. Here Professor Mises makes an important point. "It is not generally realised that education can never be more than indoctrination with theories and ideas already developed. Education, whatever benefits it may confer, is transmission of traditional doctrines and valuations; it is by necessity conservative. It produces imitation and routine, not improvement and progress. Innovators and creative geniuses cannot be reared in schools. They are precisely the men who defy what the school has taught them" (311).[14]

The outlook for the praxeological sciences is not exactly bright. In our time they are bound to come into conflict with the dominant ideologies at almost every point. The high priests of "modern education" are unlikely to take kindly to any endeavour to substitute a scientific for a mythological view of the social function of education.

Yet, in the long run, society ignores the praxeological sciences at its peril. "The body of economic knowledge is an essential element in the structure of human civilisation; it is the foundation upon which modern industrialism and all the moral, intellectual, technological, and therapeutical achievements of the last centuries have been built. It rests with men whether they will make the proper use of the rich treasure with which this knowledge provides them or whether they will leave it unused. But if they fail to take the best advantage of it and disregard its teachings and warnings, they will not annul economics; they will stamp out society and the human race" (881).

It will be for History to judge.

NOTES

1. Ludwig von Mises, *Human Action: A Treatise on Economics* (New Haven: Yale University Press, 1949), p. 421.

2. Ludwig von Mises, *Nationalökonomie* (Geneva: Editions Union, 1940).

3. "Professor Mises and the Theory of Capital," *Economica* 8 (November 1941): 409–27.

4. In *Economica*, 9 (August 1942): 267–91; 10 (February 1943): 34–63; 11 (February 1944): 27–39.

5. See A. Stonier and K. Bode, "A New Approach to the Methodology of the Social Sciences," *Economica* 4 (November 1937): 406–24.

6. When he says: "There is no mode of action thinkable in which means and ends or costs and proceeds cannot be clearly distinguished and precisely separated" (40), we take him to mean: within the sphere of adult life, a particular household and business life. But what about games? Within each game the distinction can be drawn, but is this the "end" for which we play them?

7. The two concepts were originally used by Professor Mayer in "Der Erkenntniswert der funktionellen Preistheorien," in *Die Wirschaftstheorie der Gegenwart*, vol. 2 (Vienna, 1932).

8. *Capitalism, Socialism, and Democracy* (New York: Harper & Row, 1950), p. 175. See also Professor Hayek's criticism in *Individualism and Economic Order* (London: Routledge & Kegan Paul, 1949), p. 90n.

9. London: Macmillan, 1941.

10. "The operations of the managers, their buying and selling, are only a small segment of the totality of market operations. The market of the capitalist society also performs all those operations which allocate the capital goods to the various branches of industry. The entrepreneurs and capitalists establish corporations, and other firms, enlarge or reduce their size, dissolve them or merge them with other enterprises; they buy and sell the shares and bonds of already existing and of new corporations" (703-4).

11. Cf. L. M. Lachmann, "Complementarity and Substitution in the Theory of Capital," *Economica* 14 (May 1947): 108–19.

12. J. R. Hicks, *A Contribution to the Theory of the Trade Cycle* (Oxford: Oxford University Press, 1950).

13. For instance, the American situation in 1929 was, in our opinion, an underconsumption situation. In fact, most of the underconsumption theories of the last twenty years are simply "historical generalizations" of the memories of 1929–33.

14. As Professor Mises's detractors will probably dismiss this as "armchair philosophy," we may note what one of the most discerning students of modern business organization has to say on this subject: "On the whole it looks very much as if the 'integrated' business education tends to make a man unfit to be an entrepreneur by paralyzing his intellectual muscles, just as the training in mere technical skills of the business school of yesterday tended to unfit a man by destroying his vision. The more emphasis there is on 'administration,' 'organization,' 'policy,' 'analysis,' etc., the more there is emphasis on the known 'right' way of doing things and on routines rather than on the new—in short on the accepted, the safe, the bureaucratic way rather than on the way of the risk taker and the innovator" (Peter F. Drucker "The Graduate Business School," *Fortune* 42 [August 1950]: 94).

Model Constructions and the Market Economy

1.

INTRODUCTION

For almost two centuries concepts of the market economy have had a significant place in the development of economic theory. The market, not just as the product of economic history, but as a focus of meaningful action—as the product of, and also as a means of orientation for, economic agents in a society with division of labor—constituted one of the most important themes of classical political economy. It was certainly no accident that in the *Methodenstreit* the partisans of the historical school accused their opponents, often unjustly, of "Manchesterism." What they meant was that in classical theory the market and its institutions occupied such a predominant place, and this fact was to them an annoyance.

In recent decades, however, there has been a distinct change. Modern economic theory has become ever more abstract and occupied with the building of pseudo-Platonic models in imitation of the methods of the modern natural sciences. Within this framework, there is little room for a discussion of market processes or of the actions causing them. Even less attention is given to those mental acts from which these economic actions spring. Neoclassical formalism—as I shall designate the predominant trend in economic thinking that has gained such wide acceptance in recent decades—understandably does not find it a congenial task to explain economic phenomena in terms of underlying

This essay, "Marktwirtschaft und Modellkonstruktionen," *Ordo* 17(1966): 261–79, was translated from the German by Robert F. Ambacher of Millersville State College and Walter E. Grinder.

plans and actions.[1] One abstracts from all these and, following the example of the natural sciences, substitutes the functional determination of magnitudes, within a closed system characterized by simultaneous equations, for causal explanation.[2]

As a result of this development in economic theory, the vitality of our thinking about the market economy has been undermined. In this situation, the advocates of the market, faced with new problems, have to fashion their own analytical tools.

First of all, we must concentrate on the fundamental methodological problem facing us. The market is a focus of meaningful action. Market phenomena, quantities of goods and prices, result from the economic plans of market participants, such plans being based on the economic calculations of single individuals and enterprises. Economic plans, thus, are the components of meaningful action. To explain market phenomena therefore means to analyze these phenomena in terms of their meaningful components. If, however, as is done in modern economics, one views all economic phenomena, including market phenomena, as mere parts of a large complex of relationships, that is, the "economic system," one is limited to the "exact" determination of those quantitative relationships that can be determined at all. This manipulation is possible, of course, only within a closed system and then only when all relationships are fully coherent. This also explains the current preoccupation with conditions of equilibrium. The need to refer all economic phenomena to a central point, the "economic system," forces one to use such an approach.

Now the determination of economic quantities, as far as this is possible, is obviously a goal of any economic theory and thus of any market theory. But for a method of analysis that is also concerned with the interpretation of the meaning of action, this determination is only the first step. The real task is to explain how relations between quantities derive from mental acts.

The inadequacy of the models constructed by neoclassical formalism, which I shall deal with at length in the next section, stems, then, not from its high degree of abstraction as such, for all theory is abstract; nor from the fact that quantitative relations are determined, for all economic theory must achieve such determination; and most certainly not from the application of mathematics, for mathematics is a proved means of expressing quantitative relationships in all areas of knowledge. Rather, this inadequacy springs from the significance of the elements from which one must abstract: in macroeconomics one abstracts from the human actions and plans that underlie all economic phenomena, while in microeconomics these actions and plans appear all too often as an idealized distortion ("perfect competition").

Under these conditions the defenders of the market economy are confronted with new tasks. Three of these appear to me to be of particular importance.

First, it must be demonstrated that the stylized images of the market in the neoclassical models have little relevance to actual market processes. When, for example, linear programming theory shows that all rational economic activity implies a price system with prices equal to costs and that all production involving time implies a rate of interest, the similarity of this price system to that of the market economy seems evident. But this similarity only *seems* evident, and market theory can gain nothing from it. For in this linear price system we are dealing with equilibrium prices that result from a calculus and not from market processes. No account is taken of the central problems of market economics: what occurs in a state of disequilibrium, whether and under what condition equilibrium can be reached at all, how long such a condition would last if once reached, and so on.

No one denies the usefulness of linear programming for solving practical planning problems. But it has nothing to contribute to an understanding of market processes. The reason is that no individual actor in the market actually possesses that total knowledge of the data that linear theory assumes. Market processes and the calculation of optimal allocations are entirely different things. The close proximity of equilibrium and linear theory, which characterizes the neoclassical thought of our time, shows upon close investigation the weakness of the former rather than the fruitfulness of the latter.

Secondly, we must come to terms with the view that the market economy can function only in a stationary state, since only then could orientation to existing market prices warrant the success of economic action. In reality, we are told, the entrepreneur must act on his expectations, which of necessity are uncertain. It is hard to see what could coordinate these expectations. The price system certainly could not do it; and the forward markets of the real world are too little developed and too few in number to offer a solution.[3]

Without going into these important questions more fully, the following comment is in order:

First, such reliance on forward markets exaggerates the importance of well-coordinated expectations. Even in a world of perfect forward markets the future remains uncertain, and even the best coordinated expectations do not guard against disappointments. Second, the absence of forward markets does not by itself imply an unsatisfied demand for the services of specialized risk takers. In general, the market economy generates the institutions it needs. The lack of an institution may be attributable to the fact that it is not needed.

Finally, the decisive question is whether the market can offer methods for the quick and effective liquidation of malinvestments, even though it cannot prevent thwarted expectations and the failure of plans. For the market economy the revision of plans has no less significance than their original conception.

The third task of market-oriented theory is, in my opinion, the creation of a useful concept of competition. This is a subject that E. H. Chamberlin, J. M. Clark, and a number of others have tackled in the last thirty years. Even those who view the solutions offered with some skepticism should not belittle the accomplishments of these authors; for they have thoroughly investigated actual market processes, an undertaking of no small merit in our age of formalism.

Most important is recognizing that the market is not a state of affairs but a chain of events. It is therefore not possible to view competition as a market condition whose form can be deduced from assumptions about typical schemes of action *(market forms)*. These schemes of action themselves depend on market phenomena from which the actors in the market are continuously taking their orientation. I shall return to this matter in the third section.

2.

IN CRITICISM OF ECONOMIC MODELS

I shall now subject the neoclassical models to a critical examination, above all with regard to the problem of "economic growth." My reasons are that, on the one hand, theories of growth are really creations of the last twenty years, the neoclassical style of thought being particularly evident in this area, and, on the other hand, the unreal nature of the models often finds here its expression in striking ways.[4]

A characteristic common to most of these models is the search for, and the almost exclusive preoccupation with, so-called maximum growth paths. Since J. von Neumann's famous work,[5] the major task of growth theory has been to show how, under given conditions, the factors of production must be employed in order to attain enduring optimal growth. We are dealing here with a kind of "dynamic welfare economics." The solution of maximization problems, well known in microeconomics, is viewed here as the task of macroeconomics, although it is never revealed how each market participant gains the relevant partial knowledge he must have if total knowledge of all of market participants is to be equal to the total data possessed by the model builder. To conclude from the similarity of the formal characteristics of maximization problems that what is possible for an individual's personal economy is also possible for the economic system as a whole exactly characterizes the intellectual attitude of neoclassical formalism. At best, only the directors of a planned economy could possess such all-encompassing knowledge of the data—and even this is doubtful. All of this has nothing to do with the market economy.

Central to all activities of the market economy is the individual economic plan. It is one thing to show that all planned action is an attempt at problem solving. It is something quite different to examine "maximum growth paths," beginning with the assumption that all participants' problems have been successfully solved. Some plans will always fail. What happens in such cases *must* be of great interest to us. In reality there are no optimal solutions for all participants—except in the minds of welfare economists. Dynamic equilibria, maximum growth paths, and similar concepts are notions of economists with little interest in what matters in the market economy. The logic of choice leads us to the equilibrium of the household and of the firm, and perhaps of the single market, insofar as the market situation is intelligible to its participants. Beyond this point, the logic of choice becomes distorted and loses its meaning.

Every planner and actor must always be aware of a series of viewpoints and changing conditions that are often quantitatively determined and graded and that may be regarded as functions. But that gives us no right to see functions everywhere, or even to limit our investigation to their existence. Concepts that may have significance in the sphere of the individual economy and of the single market often lose it if a "macro" connotation is attributed to them without close investigation of the facts. Working with aggregates whose origins remain unexamined and whose mode of composition is assumed to persist without explanation allows the constructors of economic models to withdraw from the task of tracing market phenomena to the meanings people attribute to their economic actions.

Growth theory has thus become a branch of applied mathematics, in which one is satisfied with the deduction of optimal solutions from given "data," without having to be concerned with how many economic actors in the real world could possibly understand the meaning of these data. Methods borrowed from the natural sciences are applied without testing their applicability to the objects of the social sciences. The interpretation of complex relationships of meaning is replaced by a mechanical calculus. The market and its phenomena, however, are to be understood only as a focus of meaningful action.

However little the theory of the market economy, aspiring to interpret meaning, has to learn from economic models which lack such aspirations, it cannot afford to ignore it. The reason is simply that these maximum and optimum solutions—regardless of how unrealistic or how abstractly conceived—may be used as standards against which the real market economy can be measured and naturally found wanting. It is hardly an overstatement that most formalists seldom concern themselves with the phenomena of the real market economy except to prove, with great earnestness, that here the high ideal of "Pareto-optimality" has been missed. Unfortunately, we are not informed in what kind of society this could be achieved. The study of models is thus no idle occupation for an adherent to the market economy.

In particular my critique is directed against three features of these schemes: the unflinching use of equilibrium argument, the exclusively macroeconomic form of analysis, and the misunderstanding of the nature of technological progress.

In the individual economy the equilibrium concept obviously makes good sense, for here the actor tries to achieve such a state, even if it is never realized. This concept represents a real point of reference for mental acts. It also makes sense, in the single market, to speak of equilibrium between supply and demand. And where the actors respond very quickly, as, for example, in the stock market, such a condition is achieved every day. Only when we extend the concept to the entire complex of economic relationships do we encounter difficulty. Nevertheless, in a stationary world a general state of equilibrium is at least conceivable, and under certain circumstances it might even be achieved. But in a world of continuous unexpected change, this concept becomes highly questionable.

It is therefore remarkable that all modern growth theories are based on the same conceptual foundation, one that dates from Gustav Cassel's theory of a uniformly progressing economy, "steady state growth."[6] The creators of general equilibrium theory were aware that even in static analysis the conditions of equilibrium do not entail the achievement of a state commensurate with these conditions. They knew that the "road leading to equilibrium" conceals a number of problems.[7] They even attempted to circumvent these difficulties through the postulates of "recontract" theory. More than thirty years ago, in a famous essay, Lord Kaldor referred to these problems.[8] In recent economic models, however, they have been cast aside.[9] This is noteworthy since obviously such problems are bound to cause even greater difficulties in a dynamic economy than in static analysis. Whether even a temporary state of equilibrium will be achieved obviously depends on the velocity of reaction of the various elements in the system; their respective magnitudes, in turn, depend on the expectations of economic agents. Yet formalism avoids confronting these difficult problems by postulating the continued existence of a growth equilibrium, the very origin of which is not explained. The problems of human action in a world of unexpected change are concealed behind a smoke screen of formulae and functions.

Much has already been said about the competition between macroeconomics and microeconomics.[10] Here we shall come to grips with this problem in terms of market phenomena.

Obviously, a procedure that neglects to trace market phenomena to plans and fails to divide the complex relationships of these phenomena into their meaningful components is unsatisfactory. Furthermore, under what circumstances can the assumption be justified that changes in aggregates are independent of changes in their constituents? Assuming that the aggregates were composed of homogeneous elements, there would be no distinction between macroanalysis and microanalysis. Such an assumption, however, would obviously contradict reality. On the other hand, the assumption that aggregates follow "stochastic" laws rather than the causal laws of their elements would evidently signify the abdication of economic theory in its traditional sense. Finally, it might be contended that changes in the aggregates are accompanied by changes in the elements of precisely such a nature that regular and uniform growth of the aggregates results. In this case, the burden of proof rests on those who make such a claim.

The dilemma resulting from attempts to separate movements of aggregate quantities from the happenings in the individual markets may be illustrated by an example. The "production function" is a basic concept of modern macroeconomic theory.[11] Of these production functions the "Cobb-Douglas-function" is perhaps the best known. How is it possible for such a function to be valid and remain in a world of constant change? It could be so if all firms had the same production functions, but that can hardly be the case (our example of homogeneity.) In a world of heterogeneous individual production functions, constancy of the total function is possible only if the "steady growth" of the whole is accompanied by proportional progress in each sector. Economic growth is in reality, however, almost always accompanied by considerable fluctuation in the relative magnitudes of the individual sectors. This example shows where the improper abstraction of micro processes has led the model builders.

All thought is limited by the forms and modes it employs. Formalism, in opting for the functional mode making possible precise quantitative determinations within a closed system of variables, forgoes the possibility of making meaningful statements about human action. What we call "technical progress," however, encompasses a diverse complex of interrelationships consisting of many kinds of actions (such as of entrepreneurs and consumers). It is not surprising that formalism, which in its analysis of growth cannot but concern itself with technological progress, can master only those few aspects of the problem that can be compressed into the narrow ducts of its own mode of thought.[12]

Technological progress, viewed here *ex post,* is defined as an accomplished fact, as an increase in the productivity of the factors of production, uniform over time. The fact that *ex ante* it is by no means sure which technological changes will signify "progress" and which not, that this can only be established as the result of the interaction of numerous production and market processes, is simply disregarded. The fact that in a market economy many entrepreneurs continually experiment with new ideas, each in his own way and in another direction, and that final success or failure is determined only by the market lies beyond the model builder's imagination. At the same time, some of the difficulties encountered by them within their own mode of thought can be most instructive.

When technological progress occurs in "embodied form," that is, when machines built recently are more efficient than those built previously, the capital stock loses the homogeneity upon which the concept of the production function rests. Naturally one then attempts to introduce a new time function that will restore homogeneity. It is hard to see, however, why real productivity changes should conform to this function. The unqualified homogeneity of capital, once questioned, cannot be easily reinstated. Similarly, Kenneth Arrow's concept of "learning by doing" opens to us even broader and more intriguing vistas.[13]

To the formalist this means, first of all, that technological progress is a function not only of time, but also of the volume of production. No detailed argument is needed to show, however, that no ordinary production index could serve us here as an independent variable. In any case, these occurrences call for a more penetrating interpretation than that compatible with the functional mode of thought.

It is well known that experience in the use of tools and implements will often promote skills that permit their more effective use in the future. Technological progress is thus a concomitant of production as such. Clearly, we are dealing here with mental acts that turn experience into a new awareness, and then into new applications. Certainly, many errors are made in the process. Inequality of men once more becomes apparent in their unequal ability to learn by experience, a process that requires a certain amount of mental alertness. There can be no question of quantitative precision here.

Formalism, again, avoids coming to grips with these difficult problems, inaccessible to its methods. It postulates a functional relationship between aggregate quantities that would, even in the best of cases, prove nothing. The actual conditions of this interesting type of progress lie in the individual abilities of vari-

ous producers and their influence on others, and not in the
quantitative properties of aggregate wholes.

3.

SOME GUIDELINES FOR THE DEVELOPMENT OF A THEORY OF A MARKET ECONOMY

What then should be done to correct these deficiencies in
economic models and broaden the conceptual basis of the market economy? To this question I can, within the framework of
this essay, give no adequate answer. A few short hints to ideas
that might serve as guidelines for a reconstruction of market
economic theory, as it has now become necessary, will have to
suffice. While a complete outline of market economic theory
cannot be presented here, a few hints as to the style of our new
edifice and the place of some of its parts in the whole design are
in order. In doing so the major deficiencies of today's economic
models should be avoided as far as possible.

These models all suffer from the same defect: an exaggerated
significance is attributed to equilibrium concepts, and a consistency that does not exist is ascribed to the plans of individuals. To
the contrary, room must be left for the unavoidable inconsistency of plans. We must be able to speak not only of unsuccessful
plans and malinvestments, but also of the revision of such plans.
Essentially, each new plan rests on a revision of an earlier plan.

Functionalism in neoclassical formalism requires a closed system of variables, in which the magnitudes of a number of dependent variables are determined by functional relationships. It
is easy to see why such a mode of thought cannot do justice to the
market economy, which by its very nature is an "open system." In
the systems of Léon Walras and Vilfredo Pareto, to choose the
best known example, equilibrium prices and quantities of goods
are determined by the magnitudes of the data. In actual markets,
however, no one has such access to the complete constellation of
data as would enable them to arrive at the equilibrium quantities
and adjust his action to them. At best, one is familiar with the
data directly concerning him. For the rest, he depends on conjec-

tures, and for these, again, on inferences from available information. The market as a whole is fed by a broad stream of knowledge, which, although it flows constantly, provides each person with different information. The same information will be interpreted differently by an optimist and a pessimist. The same objective possibility will be used differently by an aggressive and by a restrained actor. In an uncertain world, in which economic agents are dependent on their expectations, a general coherence of plans is almost impossible. The objective existence of "data" that no one knows in their entirety is without significance.

The market economy is thus an "open" system, to which justice can hardly be done by the functionalist mode of thought. It requires, to the contrary, an "open" mode of thought that leaves room for the, at least temporarily, uncoordinated action of economic agents. Such a mode of thought of course does not permit "precisely" determined relations between quantities. It should help us to clarify, however, the manner in which human action is constantly oriented toward events; the interpretations of those events, which themselves change over time; the manner in which ideas are integrated and transformed over time into plans; and the manner in which all action flows from mental acts. In this sense, we may contrast the "genetic-causal" method with the functionalist one.[14] I should like to illustrate this point with two examples.

During the market process the participants orient themselves by each other's actions. Since dissimilar expectations cannot all be accurate, plans based on different expectations cannot all be successful. The market determines success and failure and forces unsuccessful actors to revise their plans. In this way the market process becomes a process of selection of the currently successful. This selection is the necessary result of the original inconsistency of the plans. In a game there cannot be only winners.

Success or failure of a plan is expressed in a capital gain or loss; for every plan requires a capital combination in which the stock of fixed capital is of significance. The successful entrepreneur not only obtains a higher income. His stock of fixed capital will also rise in value, since through the success of his plan it now becomes the source of a quasi-rent income stream. The opposite is true for an unsuccessful plan. The unsuccessful entrepreneur even runs the risk, if he is in debt, of losing control of his capital combination. Even if this does not occur, a capital loss ordinarily restricts the sphere of operation of the entrepreneur.

We may thus regard the stock of fixed capital, which, despite limited economic versatility, forms the backbone of every plan, as the vessel of the expectations for every plan. The market determines not only the distribution of income but also the distribution of wealth through changes in the value of capital goods.[15] It is therefore highly misleading to maintain that the distribution of income in the market depends on the existing distribution of wealth. For the distribution of wealth changes constantly as a result of changes in the value of capital goods that accompany the success or failure of every plan.

The above throws some light on the function of the stock market in the market economy.[16] Here, shares of different capital combinations, consisting essentially of fixed capital goods, are continually being evaluated. The stock exchange not only registers success and failure, but also expresses expectations about the prospects of plans already set in motion. The stock exchange may be viewed as the central forward market for future capital yields of indefinite horizon. Buyers and sellers on the exchange express their expectations about the chances of various plans, and thereby also evaluate the underlying capital combinations.

The function of the stock exchange is the same as that of any forward market, namely, to distill from many individual expectations a "market expectation," finding its expression in the stock price, to which each interested person may orient himself. The equilibrium price of the stock market is determined, not by an "objective" body of information, but by the respective expectations of buyers and sellers. That this price changes from day to day indicates the sensitivity of the price-forming mechanism with regard to expectations, and not the impaired capability of the stock market to function; for the function of the stock exchange, as of any market, is not to guess the future but to reconcile, as much as possible, present actions that extend into an uncertain future.

As a second example I should like to use competition to illustrate the genetic-causal method. It is hardly necessary to show why the "perfect competition" of the textbooks is a thoroughly defective concept and can contribute nothing to our understanding of actual competition.[17] Three points may be useful in the search for a better concept of competition.

In the first place, as indicated previously, competition should be viewed as a chain of events rather than as a state of affairs.[18] With competition as with the market as a whole, we are dealing with a process during the course of which the participants orient themselves to each other's actions. The most important point of orientation is here the size of the profits of competitors.

Second, we must discard the assumption, inherited from the classicists, that competitors all start from the "same position," whereas monopoly involves "privilege." On the contrary, the value of competition is precisely that buyers have a choice among unequal services. No one doubts that choice and decision are the most important attributes of the economic act. But what sense is there in a choice between equal services and identical goods? Here we see once again that the idea of "pure competition" springs from a mode of thought alien to meaning.

Third, two phases may be discerned in the process of competition, which constantly alternate. On the one hand, there is product differentiation, basically Schumpeter's "new combination," and, on the other hand, there is the leveling competition of imitators of a successful innovation. Both phases are necessary and complementary elements of the competition process. Without innovation and product differentiation there would be nothing to imitate, and competition could not exist. Without constant competitive pressure from imitators of successful innovations, innovations would remain a permanent source of monopolistic or oligopolistic income.

For economic progress and the functioning of the market economy, the first phase is as necessary as the second. How could aircraft, cars, phonographs, and so on of fifty years ago have been developed to their present forms without constant product differentiation? All progress, especially progress through quality improvements, calls for continual experimentation in different directions. The market passes its final judgment on the technological knowledge gained in this fashion.

Of the second stage of the process, or "competition in the narrower sense," little of a general nature may be said, other than that, here also, equilibrium concepts hinder rather than promote understanding.

Without price-cost differences no competition can exist in the sense of activity directed toward increasing one's share of the market. On the other hand, competition constantly diminishes these differences. For formalism this means that "ultimately" prices will everywhere be equal to costs. With regard to the actual market economy such a statement is meaningless; for reaching such a final stage simply means that the process of competition consisting of the two phases has come to a standstill. The continual emergence of new combinations with temporary profit possibilities in the first phase alone gives meaning to the leveling process of the second phase.

I have attempted to show why our thinking on the market economy has nothing to learn from contemporary economic theory, as long and insofar as it is dominated by formalism, and why its exponents will in the future have to go their own way. In the first section I briefly indicated those problems that seem especially important in the present situation. In the third section I attempted to outline a method that, in my opinion, promises to do justice to the actual tasks of market economy theory.

In evaluating the prospects of this undertaking, two points must be taken into account. On the one hand, formalism in its triumphal march through the contemporary world has met with resistance. On these islands of resistance we find schools of economic thought with roots in a tradition older than the one borrowed from the natural sciences, a tradition aimed at a meaningful understanding of human action. Although neoclassical formalism may justifiably invoke the analytic methods of its classical ancestors, nevertheless the subjective theory of value and the discovery of the significance of expectations have been achievements of the other tradition. This tradition survives even in this era of formalism. We should take it up again. Besides the work of Eucken and his disciples, there are above all the contributions of the praxeological school, of Mises, Hayek, and Röpke.[19] Furthermore, there is rich material in the field of economic history that can be utilized in the development of market economic theory. I refer here to the essays in *Capitalism and the Historians*[20] and the excellent work of Fritz Redlich.[21] Finally, it is a historical fact that, even in regard to economic growth, the market form of economic organization has been the most successful. It is a sign of the times that the recipes for rapid growth being peddled everywhere stem from the kitchen of formalism, even though economic history, whose phenomena to be sure have to be interpreted, offers abundant evidence of the true causes of economic progress.

NOTES

1. With a welcome lucidity, Paul A. Samuelson characterized the essence of the cognitive method of formalism: "Implicit in such analyses there are certain recognizable formal uniformities, which are indeed characteristic of all scientific method. It is proposed here to investigate these common features in the hope of demonstrating how it is possible to deduce general principles which can serve to unify large sectors of present day economic theory" (*Foundations of Economic Analysis* [Cambridge: Harvard University Press, 1947], p. 7).

2. "In every problem of economic theory certain variables (quantities, prices, etc.) are designated as unknowns, in whose determination we are interested. Their values emerge as a solution of a specific set of relationships imposed upon the unknowns by assumption or hypothesis. These functional relationships hold as of a given environment and milieu" (ibid., p. 7).

3. "To my knowledge no formal model of resource allocation through competitive markets has been developed which recognizes ignorance about all decision makers' future actions, preferences, or states of technological information as the main source of uncertainty confronting each individual decision maker, and which at the same time acknowledges the fact that forward markets on which anticipa-

tions and intentions could be tested and adjusted do not exist in sufficient variety and with a sufficient span of foresight to make presently developed theory regarding the efficiency of competitive markets applicable. If this judgment is correct, our economic knowledge has not yet been carried to the point where it sheds much light on the core problem of the economic organization of society: the problem of how to face and deal with uncertainty. In particular, the economic profession is not ready to speak with anything approaching scientific authority on the economic aspects of the issue of individual versus collective enterprise which divides mankind in our time. Meanwhile, the best safeguard against overestimation of the range of applicability of economic propositions is a careful spelling out of the premises on which they rest. Precision and rigor in the statement of premises and proofs can be expected to have a sobering effect on our beliefs about the reach of the propositions we have developed" (T. C. Koopmans, *Three Essays on the State of Economic Science* [New York: McGraw-Hill 1957], pp. 146–47).

4. A detailed survey of the state of growth theory at that time is offered by F. H. Hahn and R. C. O. Matthews, "The Theory of Growth: A Survey," *Economic Journal* 74 (December 1964): 779–902.

5. J. von Neumann, *Ergebnisse eines mathematischen Kolloquiums,* ed. Karl Menger (Vienna, 1935–36).

6. Gustav Cassel, *Theoretische Sozialökonomie* (Leipzig, 1918), chap. 1, para. 6.

7. In what we might call a semiofficial pronouncement from the headquarters of neoclassical formalism, that, too, is freely admitted today: "Granted that an economy possesses a general equilibrium constellation of prices and outputs, if that constellation is not already in effect are there mechanisms in the economy that will bring it into being? . . . Walras recognized this problem also, but was not able to give a satisfactory solution. In fact, the problem remains open to this day. We still do not have a satisfactory specification of the conditions under which the adjustment mechanism of an economy will guide it to its general equilibrium position" (Robert Dorfman, *The Price System* [Englewood Cliffs, N. J.: Prentice-Hall, 1964], pp. 107–8).

8. Lord Kaldor, "The Determinateness of Static Equilibrium," in *Essays on Value and Distribution* (Glencoe, Ill., Free Press, 1960), originally in *Review of Economic Studies* 1 (February 1934): 122–36.

9. A notable exception is the incisive study by G. B. Richardson, *Information and Investment* (London: Oxford University Press, 1960), esp. chaps. 1 and 2.

10. See, for example, Fritz Machlup, *Der Wettstreit zwischen Mikro- und Makro-theorien in der Nationalökonomie* (Tübingen: J. C. B. Mohr, 1960).

11. "It is commonly called 'neo-classical' but the appropriateness of the description must surely be questioned. There is no 'production function' in Jevons or Marshall, Walras or Pareto, Menger or Böhm-Bawerk. There is in Wicksell, but he is careful to confine it to his model of 'production without capital.' J. B. Clark can hardly be regarded as a major neoclassical economist. The originators of the 'production function' theory of distribution (in the static sense, where I still think that it should be taken fairly seriously) were Wicksteed, Edgeworth, and Pigou" (John Hicks, *Capital and Growth* [Oxford: Clarendon Press, 1965], p. 293n).

12. On this see especially, F. H. Hahn and R. C. O. Matthews, "Theory of Growth," pp. 825–52.

13. K. J. Arrow, "The Economic Implications of Learning by Doing," *Review of Economic Studies* 29 (June 1962): 155–73.

14. The term "genetic-causal method of inquiry" originated with Sombart *(Die drei National-ökonomien* [Munich and Leipzig, 1930], p. 121) and was then taken over by Hans Mayer ("Der Erkenntniswert der funktionellen Preistheorien," in *Die Wirtschaftstheorie der Gegenwart* [Vienna, 1932], 2:148–51).

15. See, for example, L. M. Lachmann, "The Market Economy and the Distribution of Wealth," in *On Freedom and Free Enterprise: Essays in Honor of Ludwig von Mises,* ed. Mary Sennholz (New York: D. Van Nostrand, 1956), pp. 175–87.

16. We trust our terminology will not cause a misunderstanding. *Functionalism* in modern sociology, whose terminology we use when we speak of the "function of the market" has, of course, nothing to do with the *functionalism* of formalistic economics.

17. F. A. Hayek: "The Meaning of Competition," in idem, *Individualism and Economic Order* (London: Routledge & Kegan Paul, 1949).

18. "Competition is by its nature a dynamic process whose essential characteristics are assumed away by the assumptions underlying static analysis" (ibid., p. 94).

19. The word *praxeology* was first used in Mises's *Nationalökonomie, Theorie des Handelns und Wirtschaftens* (Geneva, 1940) (translated as *Human Action* [New Haven: Yale University Press, 1949]). We would like to take this opportunity to refer to the works of two American students of Mises: I. M. Kirzner, *The Economic Point of View* (New York: D. Van Nostrand, 1960); and M. N. Rothbard, *Man, Economy, and State,* 2 vols. (New York: D. Van Nostrand, 1962).

20. *Capitalism and the Historians,* ed. F. A. Hayek (Chicago: University of Chicago Press, 1954).

21. Fritz Redlich, *Der Unternehmer* (Göttingen, 1964).

PART THREE
THE MARKET PROCESS

Some Notes on Economic Thought, 1933–1953

In commenting on the thought of an epoch immediately after its end, the commentator faces a task similar to that of the biographer of a contemporary. However intimate his acquaintance with his subject may have been, however copious the sources he can tap, sources which may no longer be available twenty or thirty years hence, he stands to lose by the lack of historical perspective. We all know that a biography written after fifty years will in many respects be different from one written soon after a man's death.

The problems of historical perspective are notoriously complex and intricate. No doubt, as time goes by author and readers gain a clearer view of their subject by being able to see it at a distance, but at the same time it becomes more and more difficult for them to appreciate the social climate, no longer their own, which prompted the actions of the men in whom they are interested.

There is of course no ready recipe for commenting on the recent past and not looking foolish in fifty years' time. But, unable as we are to forecast what future historians will have to say on our subject, we should probably not go far wrong if we—

first, endeavour to discount those events the influence of which is already visibly vanishing, i.e., clear our minds of what can already be seen to have been purely ephemeral; and
second, devote our effort primarily to discerning the major underlying trends of our epoch which will also shape the future, unless all of them are reversed or interrupted, which is unlikely.

Reprinted from *South African Journal of Economics* 22 (March 1954).

It goes without saying that reasons of space impose severe limitations on our endeavour. Of course there can be no question of our attempting anything even approaching a reasonably complete account of the ideas and discussions of the past twenty-one years. Nor is this all. All we can do here is to emphasize what appear to us to have been the "critical points" in the economic thought of our period. This means not merely that a good deal will have to be left out, but that the selection of these critical points for discussion in these pages will be highly subjective. The reader must bear in mind that, were somebody else to write this commentary, his selection of topics for discussion as well as his emphasis on the various topics selected, would necessarily differ from ours. In the present context this is inevitable, but it is in our view no serious sacrifice. All history is interpretation. The reader of what follows will be in a position to compare our interpretation of the thought of the period with his own, and thus to judge for himself.

As seen from the close proximity of 1954, three major events seem to characterise the economic thought of the past twenty-one years: the rise of the Keynesian economics, the evolution of various theories of mixed market forms, like monopolistic and imperfect competition, and the new developments in Welfare Economics associated with the names of Professor Hicks and Mr. Kaldor and their critics.[1]

Very little need be said here about the new Welfare Economics. In spite of its impressive name and the ingenuity shown by many of its protagonists, the subject matter is somewhat remote from reality. To be sure, this whole body of thought has been evolved ostensibly as a code to guide policy. But it is hard to see how in the world as it is it could ever be brought into operation. Its central concept, the "social welfare function," is not exactly a plaything for politicians. And all policy after all is made by politicians. In reality, as every newspaper reader knows, politicians pursue power, not welfare. In fact, one eminent welfare economist has candidly admitted that "our arrangements may perhaps be more properly described as constituting a discussion of a theory of rational behaviour rather than a complete theory of the state: for we are very little concerned with what a government does in fact do in any particular case, and in no case have we considered the ethical question of what a state *should* do."[2]

In the field of economic thought the rise of the Keynesian theory of employment and incomes was undoubtedly the most dramatic, as it was the most widely discussed event of the past twenty-one years. The products of both Keynesian and anti-Keynesian literature have by now reached mountain-size. To do justice to even a few of the problems raised is for us clearly impossible. To survey and assess the new doctrine, even were we to confine ourselves to the most hotly debated issues, would require a frame of discussion of at least the size of a book. Fortunately there is here no need for such an endeavour, as Professor Hutt will, elsewhere in this volume, deal with what is probably the most critical issue in the Keynesian doctrine, viz., the relationship between the scale of prices and the income level. But a few brief comments on the significance of the Keynesian economics *as a whole* will not be out of place.

If we look at it simply as a theoretical model, the Keynesian system is sound enough. It is consistent in the sense that, if we grant the premises, the conclusions will follow: the "level of incomes and employment" will be determined by the well-known determinants. The real issue is precisely whether the premises can be granted: to what extent they reflect reality. In Schumpeter's words, the realism of Keynes's "vision," not the logical consistency of his system is at issue.

It has sometimes been said that the Keynesian economics, so far from providing us with a "General Theory," reflects in its assumptions, explicit and implicit, the conditions of the Great Depression of 1929–1933 under the influence of which Keynes wrote his book. This is at best a half truth. It does less than justice to the great architect of the Allied economic war effort to whom we all owe so much, and to the man who devoted so much penetrating thought to the problems of the post-war world. Moreover, in "How to Pay for the War" (1940) Keynes showed with his usual brilliance how the "multiplier" technique can be used to describe inflationary processes. And in general we need not doubt that conditions of full and "over-full" employment, as we found them in the war and post-war years, lend themselves to description in Keynesian terms just as much as conditions of general unemployment do.

The truth appears to be that for the Keynesian model there lies the other limit of its validity. The Keynesian economics is an economics of extreme situations: it fits the circumstances of war and post-war inflation with the universal shortage of labour and material resources just as much as it did the world of the early 1930s with almost universal unemployment and "excess capacity." In other words, the Keynesian model fits reasonably well any world in which we find the various classes of factors of production in approximately similar conditions, and where they therefore can be treated *as though* they were homogeneous. In such a world the actual heterogeneity of factors may often be disregarded with impunity. It is here, but only here, that the famous "macro-economic" method works satisfactorily.

But by the same token our model can tell us little about what we may regard as the normal situation of a progressive economy. Where there is unemployment in some industries and labour shortage in others, where shortage of equipment in some rapidly expanding sectors coincides with excess capacity in others, the macro-economic notions are of little use. In such circumstances a "point of full employment" which we could hope to reach, but not to overshoot, by applying the familiar nostrums, does not exist. The assumption of universal homogeneity breaks down. Economists have to look round for other tools.

When we now turn to the theories of mixed market forms, of monopolistic and imperfect competition, to apply there, as we did in the Keynesian case, our twin tests of internal consistency and correspondence to reality, we see a very different picture. For one thing, the singleness of analytical purpose, the unity of structural design, which are such fascinating features of the Keynesian system, are here lacking. The theories of competition were not all cast in one mould. As a result we witness Professor

Chamberlin loudly disclaiming an intellectual affiliation which Mrs. Robinson protests does exist.[3]

On the other hand, most of the attacks made on the new theories on the grounds of lack of realism have been defeated with surprising ease. In staving off what, for a time, looked like the most dangerous of these attacks, the onslaught of the "full-cost pricing" enthusiasts,[4] the defenders have all shown considerable dexterity and usually a much better understanding of the actual circumstances in which business action has to be taken, in particular in the multi-product firm, than their opponents, for all their vaunted realism, could show.[5]

There are, nevertheless, some ominous cracks in the doctrinal edifice. Recently both Professor Chamberlin and Mrs. Robinson found it necessary to revisit the scenes of their earlier triumphs, a visit which, at least on Mrs. Robinson's part, seems to have led to considerable heart-searching, while Mr. Harrod has now submitted a revised version of the theory of imperfect competition.[6] No major structural alterations were found necessary, but there seems to be a common tendency to reassess the part of the marginal revenue curve which twenty years ago was widely regarded as the very linchpin of the new doctrines. While Professor Chamberlin dismisses it as "a piece of pure technique unrelated to the central problem,"[7] Mr. Harrod bases his rejection of the doctrine of excess capacity on a distinction between long-period and short-period marginal revenue of which, according to him, only the first determines price and output under imperfect competition.

But the most interesting problems in the theory of mixed market forms arise in connection with the question whether, to what extent, and, if at all, in what sequence the various market forms can be said to succeed each other in time. In this context the "inevitability of monopoly," or perhaps oligopoly, calls for particular attention. But these are questions to which it will be better to return after we have explored the wider issues of which they form part.

Thus far we have dealt with problems which loomed large in the discussions of the past two decades and occupied most of the literature. We must now turn to those wider issues which, though not recognised at the time, and even now perhaps barely visible, were in fact implied in, and underlay the questions which were currently discussed. But before we set out to plumb the depth of the stream of economic thought we have to deal with one issue which cannot be thus easily classified: a problem some aspects of which appeared on the surface and were widely discussed, but which had roots and ramifications that have not been laid bare. Throughout our two decades we notice a growing feeling of dissatisfaction with the traditional equilibrium methods of neo-classical economics, and a strong desire to make economic analysis "more dynamic."

Equilibrium analysis was felt to be unrealistic. In reality, we were told, equilibria are hardly ever found. In this form, to be sure, the criticism need not be taken too seriously. No theoretical model of course can ever provide a completely adequate picture of reality. The merits of a particular model have to be judged by comparison with those of another model, actual or potential, not by comparison with "reality" which is, and must always remain, beyond our theoretical grasp. The common sense case for the equilibrium method is that if we wish to survey a constellation of diverse forces, the easiest method of doing so is to perform the mental experiment of imagining that state of affairs which would be reached when all these forces have unfolded all their implications. This is certainly much simpler than to have to go through the laborious business of describing and classifying each force separately. The method can, however, be applied only if, first, the unfolding of the forces can take place without interference from outside and, second, the mode of interaction of our forces is known and can be predicted. The first condition, usually stated in the familiar *ceteris paribus* terms, is of course simply a fundamental postulate of all scientific method. But the second condition raises an issue peculiar to the social sciences. Our forces after all reflect human action prompted by knowledge. The second condition therefore means that the individuals acting will during the process of interacting which leads to equilibrium, not acquire new knowledge: otherwise their actions cannot be predicted. There are many cases (arbitrage is an obvious example) in which the process of interaction is so swift that the second condition will be approximately fulfilled, but there are others where it is not. The real objection to the equilibrium method is that it must ignore the process by which men acquire and digest new knowledge about each others' needs and resources. But during our period the problem was rarely seen in this light, except by Professor Hayek whose penetrating studies of these problems broke much new ground and opened up entirely new vistas.[8]

The wish to give the prominent ideas of the time a more dynamic colour than that with which they made their original appearance, was strong throughout the period under review.[9] In particular, Keynes's vision of the capitalistic economy bogged down in a morass of permanent unemployment clearly called for a theory of economic development to which the master himself had only contributed a few bare fragments. From Mr. Harrod's first "Essay in Dynamic Theory"[10] through his later contribution "Towards a Dynamic Economics" to Mrs. Robinson's "Generalisation of the General Theory"[11] there have been many attempts to "dynamise" the Keynesian doctrine. If none of these attempts has been very successful, this was, on the face of it, due to the fact that the model employed, that of an *expanding economy,* was somewhat too simple, just Cassel's "uniformly progressive economy" brought up to date to match the Keynesian background of the times, the "society making less than full use of its human and material resources." But we need only probe a little beneath the surface to see that the real reason for their discomfiture was the neglect of the problems of time and knowledge.

This is not to say that the rôle of time in economics was neglected during our period. It certainly was not,[12] but its implications were. Mrs. Robinson in a retrospective mood, has confessed: "In my opinion, the greatest weakness of the *Economics of Imperfect Competition* is one which it shares with the class of economic theory to which it belongs—the failure to deal with time."[13] As a generalisation about neoclassical economics this is hardly fair comment. Marshall after all had a good deal to say about time and its economic effects. But while time as a dimension of economic phenomena was by no means unknown to economists before 1933, its true economic significance was but tardily recognised.

Time brings change, and change brings the need for adjustment to new conditions. But a ready response to this need cannot be taken for granted. In a society based on division of labour men have to know each other's needs and resources in order to achieve their aims.

In a stationary economy, in a world in which to-day is as yesterday was and to-morrow will be like to-day, the question how men got the knowledge by which they live, offers no particular problem. We need ask it no more than we need ask, in general, how the stationary economy came to be stationary. Here it is not unreasonable to assume, as classical and neoclassical economists did, that all men have the knowledge requisite to go about their daily business.

But in a changing world the question cannot be eschewed. Here change implies that part of yesterday's knowledge is to-day no longer up to date. Men have to fight a running battle with the forces of change and ingorance, since every day that passes turns former knowledge into present ignorance. Here the economic problem begins to consist largely, if not exclusively, in "catching up" with the stream of change. He will be master who understands better, and more quickly, than the next man what recent change "means" in terms of needs and resources. Moreover, there now emerges the task of guessing accurately to-day what to-morrow's change will bring. It becomes clearly impossible to assume that new knowledge is acquired by everybody with the same speed with which conditions change, or even that, if there is a lag, it will be the same for all people. Change brings the need for adjustment to new conditions, but few people will at first understand what these new conditions are, or what they require, and the few who do profit at the expense of the others. (The typical reaction of the saving public to the secular inflation of our age provides ample illustrations for this.) Time thus entails changes in knowledge and its distribution, and thus also changes in the resources of the various individuals, a conclusion hardly congenial to equalitarians.[14]

This problem, which any serious attempt to bring time into economic theory has to face, has as a rule been hitherto ignored. The "dynamic models" of Messrs. Harrod and Hicks are prominent examples of this tendency, while the most ingenious attempt so far made to evade the problem openly, by assuming "perfect foresight," was soon seen to entail too many absurdities to find ready acceptance. Yet, during our period, again and again the problem came to the surface. This fact was reflected in the growing interest in *expectations*.

It would of course be quite wrong to think that expectations did not exist for economists before 1933. No economist who had to deal with concrete problems could ever permit himself to forget that in an uncertain world men base their actions not on what is, but on what they think will be. It remains true nevertheless that the introduction of expectations into economic theory was one of the major events of our period. We believe that future historians of economic thought will rank it as the outstanding event of our period.

We must first briefly outline the position as it existed in 1933. As early as 1912 Schumpeter[15] drew the distinction between the "entrepreneur," the man who has the mental power to imagine that to-morrow will be different from to-day and who is able to act accordingly, and the "static individual" who lacks this power and can only adapt himself to existing circumstances. Professor Knight, by a different route, reached virtually the same conclusion, viz., that in an uncertain world uncertainty-bearing becomes a function of specialists. In Sweden, by the late 1920s, the pupils of Wicksell had encountered the problem, and Professor Myrdal wrote the first book explicitly devoted to it.[16] Even in England Keynes, though probably unwittingly, had introduced expectations in 1930 when he discussed the influence of the "bullishness" and "bearishness" of the public.[17]

It remains true that only in the *General Theory* were expectations officially introduced into Anglo-Saxon economics. It is to be regretted that it was done in such a haphazard fashion. Thus the marginal efficiency of capital and liquidity preference are expectational magnitudes, but the all-important marginal propensity to consume is not, though it is hard to see why consumers' decisions should not be influenced by expectations of future prices. Moreover, in a world in which most durable, and semi-durable consumer goods, from television sets to clothes, can be bought on credit, consumers' expenditure is not limited to current income, and the consumer is in a position not really different from that of those who make investment decisions. It is difficult to avoid the impression that Keynes introduced expectations whenever it suited his argument, and left them out when it did not. Furthermore, in his Chapter 12 on "The State of Long-Term Expectation," the famous diatribe against the Stock Exchange, it becomes painfully evident that Keynes failed to grasp the nature of the problem posed by the existence of inconsistent expectations. Instead of studying the process by which men in a market exchange knowledge with each other and thus gradually reduce the degree of inconsistency by their actions, he roundly condemned the most sensitive institution for the exchange of knowledge the market economy has ever produced!

It cannot be said that the theory of expectations has made much progress since Keynes wrote. To be sure, we now have a set of impressive-looking tools of analysis. The Hicksian "elasticity of expectations,"[18] Dr. Lange's "practical range,"[19] and Professor Shackle's "potential surprise function"[20] all testify to the large amount of ingenuity that has been devoted to the subject during our period. If, for all the efforts made, the results have been rather meagre, the reason has to be sought in the mechanistic nature of the tools and the theories in which they are employed. None of these theories came to grapple with the central fact of a dynamic world: the human acts of interpretation by which men try to keep abreast of the changes in needs and resources. All these authors disregard the fact that man casts the material of his knowledge in the mould of expectations.

The dissatisfaction with the shortcomings of the equilibrium method mentioned earlier gave, during our period, rise to the first experiments with a new method of analysis which has come to be known as "Swedish Process Analysis." The common sense of this new method is, briefly, that while each individual, producer or consumer, at the moment at which he makes a plan, may reasonably be expected to co-ordinate his resources in such a way as to use them to his best advantage (so that "he is in equilibrium"), these various plans need not, and probably will not, be consistent with each other. Hence, from time to time, these plans will have to be revised in the light of the new knowledge prompted by their failure. In other words, Process Analysis takes account of the fact that in a changing world men only gradually and imperfectly acquire knowledge about each other's needs and resources.

The new method made its first appearance in the Anglo-Saxon world in 1937 in Professor Lundberg's *Studies in the Theory of Economic Expansion*. Its rationale was lucidly explained by Professor Lindahl in 1939.[21] It was used with dexterity by Professor Hicks in Parts III and IV of *Value and Capital*. Though it has not been without its critics,[22] it was perhaps one of the most hopeful departures of our period.[23] In the postwar years it proved most useful in the study of processes of inflation, open or suppressed.[24]

Dynamics has also invaded the theory of market forms during our period. With oligopoly this became inevitable as soon as it was realised that, for better or worse, oligopolists have to act on what they expect their rivals to do in the future. But here again, the real issue goes much deeper, and certainly passes the precincts of oligopoly. As long as competition was regarded as the principal market form, with monopoly as an exception, it was sufficient to ask what peculiar circumstances caused monopoly. But in the last two decades we have learned that most actual market forms are hybrids of monopoly and competition. The question arises now whether all these various market forms have to be regarded as alternative, though permanent types of market organisation, or as successive stages of a process. If the latter, we have to ask what is the typical sequence of this process, and also whether there is only one such type of process or whether there are several.

The problem finds its crudest expression in the neo-Marxists' assertion that "competitive Capitalism" is inevitably followed by "Monopoly Capitalism." But even outside the orbit of Marxism the problem is important enough to merit discussion. It is one of those issues which the discussions of the last two decades have raised without giving a conclusive answer to them.

Thus far the problem was as a rule discussed in the context of Increasing Returns. It has always been known that perfect competition is incompatible with increasing returns. This fact of course provided the original starting point for the *Economics of Imperfect Competition*. But do increasing returns necessarily lead in the end to monopoly or oligopoly? At the end of our period we find the problem by no means solved. Mr. Harrod thinks that "increasing returns are compatible with any kind of imperfect competition, but not with perfect competition."[25] Mrs. Robinson, on the other hand, has arrived at the conclusion that: "The chief cause of monopoly (in a broad sense) is obviously competition. Firms are constantly striving to expand, and some must be more successful than others."[26]

The inevitability of oligopoly is here inferred from the existence of increasing returns. To the extent to which the latter are due to "technical indivisibilities" the argument is plausible enough: the bigger firm has the advantage over the smaller firm. But, as Mr. Harrod has shown, increasing returns are also often a function of time. And time, as we saw, entails the diffusion of knowledge. It is hard to see why the knowledge acquired by one firm during the course of its expansion should for ever remain its exclusive possession, unless we assume that each firm's position at any moment is of such a unique character that no one else can learn from it anything to his profit, an assumption which would of course destroy most generalisations in our field and, in any case, make competition impossible.

It is, however, possible to feel that the whole discussion rests on a fundamental misconception of the nature of competition. Almost invariably it has been assumed that competition, perfect or otherwise, is one market form among others. In the discussion just mentioned the question at issue was merely whether it was a "stable" market form. In reality, however, as Professor Hayek put it, "competition is by its nature a dynamic process whose essential characteristics are assumed away by the assumptions underlying static analysis."[27]

In other words, competition is not a market form, but the very process by which one market form evolves into another. And this process is identical with the spreading of knowledge, not only from producers to consumers, but also from producers to their rivals. The "state of perfect competition" which in the last two decades has so often been made to serve as the standard model of the text books is, if at all, conceivable only as the end-product of this process of competition. For a situation in which all consumers are completely indifferent between the products of the various sellers must be a situation in which each consumer knows already all there is to be known about all goods on the market, and has nothing further to learn from it. On the other hand, all new knowledge, technical or otherwise, is at first necessarily the possession of a few on whom it will probably confer a temporary monopoly position. Gradually, as the new knowledge is tested in the workshop as well as in the market, more and more people come to know about it, and thus the spreading knowledge of it gradually undermines the erstwhile monopoly. In the course of progress we may expect that as one "wave of knowledge" reaches the periphery of the system, becomes "common knowledge," a new wave will emanate from somewhere else, and the process starts all over again. This, we need not doubt, is the real meaning of Schumpeter's "process of creative destruction."

A "state of perfect competition" in the text book sense would require therefore that this process has come to an end. In other words, it denotes a state of stagnation. In reality knowledge is always unequally distributed though at every moment forces are operating to widen its distribution. There is no reason to believe that these forces cease to operate under oligopoly. In order to understand what happens in a market it is not sufficient to count the number of sellers. What one has to establish is the existing degree of differentiation of knowledge, and whether and why it has recently increased or decreased.

As a final example of the misinterpretation of market forces likely to occur when elements of the competitive process are forced into the Procrustean bed of static analysis, we may choose the notion of *Product Differentiation* which has occupied a prominent place in the discussions of our period. Product differentiation is usually conceived as the result of deliberate attempts by entrepreneurs to protect themselves against the forces of competition. They are supposed to do this by spreading misleading information, by advertising and other means, among consumers who have no means of obtaining better knowledge. No doubt, if we look at a market at a given moment, we may often get this impression: but it is nevertheless likely to be a misleading impression. When set against the background of the process of economic progress, the assertion that product differentiation is practised by wily producers on an unsuspecting public appears absurd. Quality improvement is one of the hallmarks of economic progress. It is clearly impossible without product differentiation. Can anybody imagine how the aeroplanes, motorcars, typewriters, etc., of fifty years ago could have evolved into their present forms without product differentiation? The view of product differentiation here criticised thus appears to fall into the class of illegitimate generalisations.

We need not doubt that a producer will often attempt to hide a particular bit of information from the public, and for a time he may well succeed. But in this case he has to pay the penalty of not being able to utilise his own knowledge by testing it, and to improve it by utilising it. Sooner or later new waves of knowledge will sweep over him. The process of diffusion of knowledge is inherent in a society of specialists who exchange goods and services with each other. It is a concomitant of the division of labour. Even politicians cannot stop it altogether, though they may well slow it down.

NOTES

1. N. Kaldor, "Welfare Propositions of Economic and Interpersonal Comparisons of Utility," *Economic Journal* 49 (September 1939): 549–52; J. R. Hicks, "The Foundations of Welfare Economics," *Economic Journal* 49 (December 1939): 696–712. For criticism of the Hicks-Kaldor view see I. M. D. Little, *A Critique of Welfare Economics* (London: Clarendon Press, 1950), especially Chapters VI and VII.

2. W. J. Baumol, *Welfare Economics and the Theory of the State* (Cambridge: Harvard University Press, 1952), p. 140.

3. "I have never been able to grasp the nature of the distinction between imperfect and monopolistic competition to which Professor Chamberlin attaches so much importance. . . . It appears to me that where we dealt with the same question, in our respective books, and made the same assumptions we reached the same results (errors and omissions excepted). When we dealt with different questions we naturally made different assumptions" (Joan Robinson, "Imperfect Competition Revisited," *Economic Journal* 63 [September 1953]: 579n).

4. See P. W. S. Andrews, *Manufacturing Business*, 1949.

5. E. A. G. Robinson: "The Pricing of Manufactured Products," *Economic Journal* 60 (December 1950): 771–80; and "The Pricing of Manufactured Products and the Case against Imperfect Competition," *Economic Journal* (June 1951): 429–33; R. F. Harrod, *Economic Essays* (London, 1953), pp. 157–74; E. H. Chamberlin, " 'Full Cost' and Monopolistic Competition," *Economic Journal* (June 1952): 318–25.

6. E. H. Chamberlin, "Monopolistic Competition Revisited," *Economica* 18 (November 1951): 343–62; Joan Robinson, "Imperfect Competition Revisited," *Economic Journal* (September 1953): 579–93; R. F. Harrod, "The Theory of Imperfect Competition Revised," in *Economic Essays*, pp. 139–87.

7. *Economic Journal* 62 (June 1952): 321.

8. "Economics and Knowledge" and "The Use of Knowledge in Society" reprinted in *Individualism and Economic Order* (London: Routledge & Kegan Paul, 1949), pp. 33–56 and pp. 77–91.

9. For fairly obvious reasons this feeling found its strongest expression in business cycle theory. But as Professor Schumann deals with this field elsewhere in this volume we can neglect it here.

10. R. Harrod, "An Essay in Dynamic Theory," *Economic Journal* 49 (March 1939): 14–33.

11. Joan Robinson, *The Rate of Interest and Other Essays* (London: Macmillan & Co., 1952), pp. 69–142.

12. See e.g. P. N. Rosenstein-Rodan, "The Role of Time in Economic Theory," *Economica* 1 (February 1934) 77–97.

13. "Imperfect Competition Revisited," *Economic Journal* 63 (September 1953): 579–93.

14. On this whole problem see Ludwig von Mises, *Human Action: A Treatise on Economics* (New Haven: Yale University Press, 1949), especially pp. 308–11, and pp. 580–83. This important book has so far not met with the attention it deserves.

15. In the original German version of his *Theory of Economic Development* [English ed., Cambridge: Harvard Economic Studies Series, 1934].

16. Gunnar Myrdal, *Prisbildningsproblemet och föränderligheten* (Uppsala: Almquist & Wiksells, 1927).

17. *Treatise on Money*, vol. 1, Chapters 10 and 15.

18. J. R. Hicks, *Value and Capital* (Oxford: Clarendon Press, 1939), p. 205.

19. Oscar Lange, *Price Flexibility and Employment* (Bloomington, Ind.: Principia Press, 1944), p. 30.

20. G. L. S. Shackle, *Expectation in Economics* (Cambridge: Cambridge University Press, 1949), p. 4.

21. *Studies in the Theory of Money and Capital* (London: Allen & Unwin, 1939), Part I.

22. See for instance A. P. Lerner, *Essays in Economic Analysis,* pp. 215–241.

23. See also Karl Bode, "Plan Analysis and Process Analysis," *American Economic Review* 33 (June 1943): 348–54.

24. See Bent Hansen, *A Study in the Theory of Inflation* (London: Allen & Unwin, 1951).

25. *Economic Essays,* p. 186.

26. "Imperfect Competition Revisited," p. 592.

27. *Individualism and Economic Order,* p. 94.

Methodological
Individualism
and the Market Economy
1.

For over a century and a half, from David Hume to Gustav Cassel, the defenders of the market economy were able to draw intellectual strength no less than moral comfort from the existence of a body of economic thought which supported their cause and which appeared to show that interference with the free play of market forces would, at least in the long run, do more harm than good and prove ultimately self-defeating. During this period an attitude favourable to "interventionism" almost invariably went together with an attitude critical of the doctrines of classical economics. In the *Methodenstreit*, Schmoller appears to have felt that what his opponents were really defending was not so much a methodological point of view as the principle of the market economy—*"Das Manchestertum."*

In the course of this century all this has changed. Today economic theory, encapsulated in an artificial world of "perfect competition," coherent plans, and instantaneous adjustments to change, has come to rest so heavily on the notion of equilibrium, embodied in a system of simultaneous equations, that the significance of its conclusions to the real world is more than dubious. In a sense it is easy to explain what has happened. The notion of equilibrium which makes very good sense when confined to individual agents, like household and firm, is less easily applied to the description of human interaction. It still has its uses when

Reprinted from *Roads to Freedom: Essays in Honour of Friedrich A. von Hayek,* ed. Erich Streissler et al. (London: Routledge & Kegan Paul, 1969), pp. 89–104.

applied to a very simple type of market, such as Marshall's corn market. But "equilibrium of the industry" is a difficult concept to handle. Equilibrium of the "economic system" is a notion remote from reality, though Walras and Pareto showed its logical consistency. Equilibrium of an economic system in motion, "equilibrium growth," borders on absurdity. What has happened is that a notion which makes good sense in the description of human plans, within the universe of action controlled by one mind, has illegitimately been extended to a sphere where it has, and can have, no meaning. A formalistic methodology which uses concepts without a proper understanding of their true meaning and natural limits is apt to defeat its own ends and bound to lead us to absurd conclusions.

Professors Mises and Hayek have taken a prominent part in emphasizing the implications of this unfortunate state of affairs. They have both underlined the shortcomings of the notion of equilibrium when employed out of context. Mises in 1940[1] described this notion as "an auxiliary makeshift employed by the logical economists as a limiting notion, the definition of a state of affairs in which there is no longer any action and the market process has come to a standstill. . . . A superficial analogy is spun out too long, that is all."[2]

Hayek has twice dealt with the same problem. In Chapter II of *The Pure Theory of Capital* he pointed out why capital problems cannot be discussed within the framework of traditional stationary equilibrium theory.[3] And in "The Meaning of Competition" we were told that "competition is by its nature a dynamic process whose essential characteristics are assumed away by the assumptions underlying static analysis."[4]

Today the defenders of the market economy are finding themselves in a difficult position. The arsenal of economic thought, which served their fathers so well, no longer provides what they need. In fact it now often happens that what it has to supply proves more useful in the hands of their enemies than it does in their own. Their enemies will hardly fail to point out, for instance, that actual market competition, as distinct from "perfect competition," is bound to fall short of the high ideal of "Pareto Optimality," an equilibrium notion which occupies a prominent place in modern "welfare economics," another spurious offshoot of contemporary economic thought.

In these circumstances upholders of the market economy are confronted with two tasks which are as unenviable as they are inevitable. They must, in the first place, be ready to turn themselves into stern and unbending critics of the economic doctrines currently in fashion, ever ready to point out the aridity of their conclusions, the unreality of their assumptions, the artificial nature of their procedure. Secondly, and even more important, they must henceforth be able to forge their own weapons. What follows in this paper is offered as a modest contribution toward the achievement of these aims.

2.

The fundamental question, i.e. in what form we should conceive of the market economy, once we have rejected the general equilibrium of the economic system, has already been answered by Mises and Hayek: The market is a process of continuous change, not a state of rest. It is also clear that what keeps this process in continuous motion is the occurrence of unexpected change as well as the inconsistency of human plans. Both are necessary conditions, since without the recurrence of the first, in a stationary world, it is likely that plans would gradually become consistent as men come to learn more and more about their environment. The recurrence of unexpected change by itself, on the other hand, would not suffice to generate a continuous process, since the elements of the system might respond to each change by a finite process of adjustment to it. We would then have an "open system" on which external change impinges in the form of "random shocks" each of which the system, possibly with variable time lags, contrives to "absorb." But the existence of human action consciously designed to produce certain effects, prompted by expectations which may, and often do, fail, makes it impossible to look at the market process in this way. Conscious action oriented to a certain state of the market cannot possibly be conceived as a "random event." Nor is the inconsistency of the plans of different agents, without which there can be no competition, to be regarded in this manner without doing violence to the facts. For such plans have to be drawn up and carried out with great care if they are to have a chance of success. To speak here of "random shocks" would mean to profess ignorance where we have knowledge.

We now have to consider the significance of these facts for the methodology of the social sciences. It seems to us that they provide the justification for "methodological individualism" and the "compositive method."[5]

Let us retrace our steps. We have rejected the conception of the market economy as a closed system in a state of equilibrium, or at least with an inherent tendency towards it. We are unable to conceive of it as an open system on which random shocks impinge from "outside." Mere outside shocks without the inconsistency of plans would not necessarily generate a continuous process, certainly not the market process with which we are all familiar. This requires the inconsistency of plans prompted by divergent expectations, an inevitable concomitant of human action in an uncertain world. But in these plans the future as image affects the present as action in a way which makes nonsense of the notion of "random events." Hence, if we wish to explain the nature of the forces which propel the market process, we have to explain the nature of the relationship between action geared to the future and plans embodying a mental picture of the future.

The case for methodological individualism, for the method which seeks to explain human action in terms of plans conceived before action is actually taken, thus rests on a positive as well as a negative reason. The negative reason is, of course, that an event designed to take place in a certain situation, but not otherwise, cannot be regarded as a random event. The positive reason, on the other hand, is that in the study of human action we are able to achieve something which must for ever remain beyond the purview of the natural sciences, viz. to make events *intelligible* by explaining them in terms of the plans which guide action.

The scope of this principle of explanation is, of course, much wider than the area of significant action in a market economy. Needless to say, the fact that plans often fail and hardly ever are completely successful, provides no argument at all against our postulate. In fact it is only by comparing the outcome of action with the plan which guided it that we are able to judge success, another achievement which is beyond the reach of the natural sciences. The alternative principle of explanation is, of course, that of "response to stimulus." It is perhaps unnecessary to stress that the kind of entrepreneurial action mainly responsible for keeping the market process in motion, i.e. innovation and the formation and dissolution of specific capital combinations, does not lend itself to this type of explanation. Spontaneous mental action is not a "response" to anything pre-existent. Neither is it a random event. One might think otherwise of the process in the course of which, in a market economy, large numbers of producers are "learning by doing," and gradually find out more and more efficient, and cheaper, methods of producing goods, or ways of improving the quality of their products. Here, a formalist would speak of "adding a time dimension to the production function." But in reality this process is no more a response to stimulus than is spontaneous action in the form of innovation. The process is part and parcel of the general process of competition in the course of which even those who were unsuccessful in improving their own methods of production can benefit by adopting those of their more successful rivals. In any case, the continuous nature of the process reflects continuous acts of human will and effort, and emulation of the successful is here just as important as in the process by which innovations are diffused.

The method which explains human action in terms of plans, constituted by mental acts and linking an imagined future to an active present, has two aspects of which one is forward-looking while the other is backward-looking.

What Hayek has called the "Compositive Method"[6] denotes the forward-looking aspect. Here we start with the plans of the individuals, those mental schemes in which purposes, means and obstacles are welded together into a whole and, as it were, projected on a screen. We then ask whether the plans made by different individuals are consistent with one another. If so, the conditions of success do exist, a "general equilibrium" is possible, though in reality, of course, for a large number of reasons it may never actually be reached. If not, inconsistency of plans is bound to generate further changes. In this case we have to argue from the divergence of plans to their disappointment and hence to their revision. But while we can say that disappointed expectations will lead to a revision of plans, we never can tell what new expectations the acting individual will substitute for those which were frustrated by the course of events. It may be impossible to use a durable capital good for the purpose for which it was designed. That may happen for a large number of reasons. It will then have to be turned to "second best" purpose. But what this will be depends on the new expectations of its owner at the moment of the turning decision, and about that we can say nothing.

But we can also employ the method in the reverse order. Instead of asking what are the implications of a number of plans simultaneously carried out, we can reverse the procedure and ask what constellation of plans has given rise to an existing situation. This is the real meaning of the method of *Verstehen*, which is also, of course, the historical method. There appears to be no reason why the theoretical social sciences, when they pursue their enquiries into the typical causes of typical social phenomena, should not make use of it.

Methodological individualism, then, in its backward-looking form, means simply that we shall not be satisfied with any type of explanation of social phenomena which does not lead us ultimately to a human plan. This entails that explanations couched in terms of so-called "behaviour variables" are not satisfactory explanations of human conduct. We have it on Hayek's own authority that the main task of the theory of capital is to explain why existing capital goods are used in the way they are. But we may also enquire how the existing capital structure came into existence, i.e. in the pursuit of which plans the existing capital resources came to assume their present form. In fact, it is hardly possible to explain present use without answering these questions. But this means that we analyse an observed phenomenon in terms of the plans in the pursuit of which it came into existence. This is the obverse of the compositive method.

Such analysis of observed phenomena in terms of pre-existent plans has nothing to do with psychology. We are here concerned with purposes, not with motives, with plans, not with the psychic processes which give rise to them, with acts of our conscious minds, not with what lies behind them. As soon as our thoughts have assumed the firm outline of a plan and we have taken the decision to carry it out over a definite period of future time, we have reached a point outside the realm of psychology, a point which we can use either as the starting point or as the final goal of our enquiry. In the former case we make use of it as the starting point of the application of the compositive method, in the latter as the final point to which we carry the method of *Verstehen*. In neither case are we trespassing on the domain of psychology.

3.

We must now make an attempt to look at our principle of explanation (hereafter referred to as *Subjectivism*)[7] in the perspective of the history of economic thought.

Hayek has given it as his view that "it is probably no exaggeration to say that every important advance in economic theory during the last hundred years was a further step in the consistent application of subjectivism."[8] Naturally one thinks of marginal utility and expectations. But in exactly the same way as in writing the history of a realm an historian would not be entitled to confine himself to reciting the triumphs of its kings, soldiers, and statesmen, but must also deal with the vicissitudes they faced and the failures they suffered, the historian of thought has to record the defeats as well as the triumphs of subjectivism.

It seems to us that, from the point of view of methodology, the history of economic thought of the last 100 years has to be seen as a continuous struggle between subjectivism and its opponent (hereafter referred to as *Formalism*). In this long drawn-out battle success has by no means always been on the side of the subjectivists. They confronted a formidable foe with whose general character we are already familiar. The same late classical formalism which, as we saw, has brought about the alienation of modern economic theory from the market economy, is also responsible for the vicissitudes of subjectivism. Acts of the mind do not fit easily into the formal apparatus of a body of thought the main purpose of which is to produce a closed system within which it is possible to assign numerical values to a large number of magnitudes. But plans are products of mental activity which is oriented no less to an imagined future than to an experienced present. No wonder there were difficulties.

The story of the "subjective revolution" of the 1870s offers an instructive example of the vicissitudes which befell subjectivism. Its main thrust was directed against the classical theory of labour value. To the Ricardians value was a kind of economic "substance," a property common to all economic goods. The subjectivists were able to show that value is not a property inherent in goods, but constitutes a relationship between an appraising mind and the object appraised, a manifestation of mental activity. But most of the fruits of their victory were subsequently lost when neoclassical economics contrived to "absorb" subjective utility within the framework of its formal apparatus. "Tastes" were embodied in its system as a class of "data," a status which they came to share with resources and technical knowledge. Naturally the successful counter-revolution of neoclassical formalism raised problems of its own. Tastes can, and often will, change in an unpredictable fashion. Whenever this happens, the other elements of the system, i.e. the dependent variables, must adjust themselves accordingly. To be able to speak at all of "the system having an inherent tendency towards equilibrium," we should therefore have to assume that the velocity with which the other elements adjust themselves to changes in tastes is always so high that no new change will occur before a full adjustment to the previous change has taken place. It is difficult to imagine such circumstances.

From our point of view it is most important to realize that formalism, by assuming all tastes to be "given," whether in the form of utility functions or of indifference curves, is in fact evading the whole problem of how plans are made, a problem which is of crucial significance to subjectivism. The indifference curves which are imputed to consumers are in reality comprehensive lists of alternative plans to be put into operation if and when opportunity offers. In other words, what is really assumed here is that individuals never need make actual plans, because from the start they are equipped with such a large number of alternative plans that all contingencies are covered! The question how these lists of alternative plans ever came into existence is then ruled out of order as falling outside the sphere of economic questions! The whole purpose of the subjectivist revolt, which was to show that prices and quantities are the indirect results of the decision-making acts of millions of individuals who are renewing or revising their plans every day, is thus thwarted. Consumers' preferences, separated from the mental acts which daily shape and modify them, are turned into independent variables of a system in which there is no scope for planning and plan revision. Spontaneous action has been transformed into a response to stimulus. The formalists are able to claim that they have incorporated into their system the contribution of subjectivism, albeit in an emasculated form.[9] Robertson's famous *bon mot* on Keynes's theory of interest fully applies to the formalist theory of consumers' action: "The organ which secretes it has been amputated, and yet it somehow still exists—a grin without a cat."[10]

When we turn to expectations, our second instance of subjectivist success during the last 100 years, we see a very different picture.

In the first place, the problem of expectations did not make its appearance on the stage of economic thought in one thrust, as did marginal utility between 1871 and 1874, but rather by gradual infiltration. As a result it is virtually impossible to date its appearance. If we were to set the date e.g. in 1930 ("bullishness" and "bearishness" in Keynes's *Treatise*), we should be ignoring the fact that the problem was clearly foreshadowed in the work of Schumpeter and Knight, as well as in the early writings of Lindahl and Myrdal in the 1920s. But on the other hand, before 1930, at least in Anglo-Saxon economics, the problem was hardly recognized at all. It remains true that it began to make its impact in the 1930s.

From our point of view, the crucial significance of the emergence of expectations as a problem rests in the fact that, by contrast to what happened to utility, they have thus far proved refractory to all attempts to incorporate them into the formal apparatus of the late classical economics of our time. The reason is not far to seek. Expectations refer to processes of change. (In the stationary world of Walras-Paretian equilibrium they are in any case of no significance.) It is hard to see how they can be treated as elements of a system. They are not constants, since they are bound to change, while tastes can at least be conceived of as constants. Expectations, that is, always refer to a future point of time which we approach more closely as time passes. But neither can they be treated as variables. We cannot regard them as dependent variables since we cannot specify any mechanism of response. Different men's expectations will react differently to the occurrence of the same event. And if we regard them as independent variables, very little will be left of the rest of the system. Changes in expectations would then come to overshadow all other causes of change.[11] J. Schumpeter[12] and E. Lundberg[13] saw this very clearly already in the 1930s and reacted with characteristic vigour.

This does not mean that, if we compress our period of decision-making to a point of time, to "market day equilibrium," expectations could not be used and regarded as data. In this case they clearly can, but any conception of equilibrium over time, of "moving equilibrium," is incompatible with changing expectations. It is therefore hardly surprising that most of the authors of those macro-economic growth models which have gained prominence in recent years, such as Sir Roy Harrod and Joan Robinson, have on the whole preferred to keep the problem of expectations at arm's length. Only G. L. S. Shackle has been a vigorous and indefatigable exponent and student of its implications.

It is of some interest to cast a cursory glance at Keynes's contribution in the perspective of the continuous struggle between subjectivism and formalism. Fundamentally, Keynes was a subjectivist, aware of the contrast between the variability of expectations and the determinateness required of any formal system, such as his own short-term equilibrium model.[14] He mocked at long-period equilibrium ("In the long run we are all dead"), but then had to use what Marshallian tools lay most readily at hand for the purpose of giving unity to his thought. So he cast it in the mould of a short-period equilibrium system. Moreover, the *General Theory* was largely written as a polemic against what Keynes regarded as the neo-classical orthodoxy of his day. Since his argument relied so heavily on expectations, the polemical effect would certainly have been marred had the contrast between the rather indistinct character of the expectations he used to support his argument and the ostensible rigour of his model been too clearly revealed. In these circumstances he found himself compelled somewhat to "underplay" the significance of expectations. He introduced them where he needed them for his immediate purpose, as e.g., in the theory of investment and in liquidity preference theory, but left them out where he did not, as in multiplier theory.

But, when seen in the historical perspective which concerns us here, Keynes certainly was on the side of the subjectivists. As Professor Shackle has said so well:

The whole spirit of Keynes' book insists on the unfathomable subtlety, complexity and mutability of the influences which bear upon the decision to invest. To build a self-contained dynamic model would have been, for him, to contradict the very essence of what he was trying to say, namely, that it is uncertainty, the feeling of a helpless inability to know with assurance how a given course of action will turn out, that inhibits enterprise and the giving of full employment.[15]

No wonder that his successors found themselves somewhat embarrassed when they attempted to distil macro-economic growth models from his work.

Within the confines of this paper we are unable to do more than record a few episodes of the great struggle mentioned. But one such episode of recent years, which constitutes quite a remarkable success of subjectivism, should not go unrecorded.

In 1965 Sir John Hicks, who for many years had been one of the foremost exponents of formal analysis and one of its most skilful practitioners, appears to have changed sides. In an attempt to define the limits of the static method, which is of course *the* method of formalism, he showed that this method is incompatible with the existence of any planned action. "In statics there is no planning; mere repetition of what has been done before does not need to be planned. It is accordingly possible, in static theory, to treat the single period as a closed system, the working of which can be examined without reference to anything that goes on outside it (in the temporal sense). But this is not possible in dynamics."[16]

The implications of this passage are far-reaching and intimately concern the matters pursued in this paper. Sir John has not only made clear why it is that expectations, which must transcend the single period, cannot be fitted into any model which employs the static method. He has at the same time shown within what narrow limits the instruments of formalism can be at all usefully employed. And in doing so he has opened up a vast new area for economic research, an area which is of paramount importance to us. For the world "outside the single period," the world in which men have to act with a sense of the future and a memory of the past, the world of action and not merely of reaction, this world is none other than the realm of the market economy.

4.

At the end of our first section we promised to make a contribution to the arsenal of the market economy. The reader may well be wondering how far the methodological reflections presented in our second and third sections can be said to have furthered this cause. But what we in fact have done is to lay the ground for an attempt to cast what we hope will be new light on two notable features of the market economy which are all too often misunderstood—and not only by its critics.

The first of these is the Stock Exchange, perhaps the most characteristic of all the institutions of the market economy. In fact it is hardly an exaggeration to say that without a Stock Exchange there can be no market economy. What really distinguishes the latter from a socialist economy is not the size of the "private sector" of the economy, but the ability of the individual freely to buy and sell shares in the material resources of production. Their inability to exercise their ingenuity in this respect is perhaps the most important disability suffered by the citizens of socialist societies, however large their incomes might be, however wide the range of choice of consumption goods that may be available to them.

In the traditional view the chief function of the Stock Exchange is to serve as a channel through which savings flow before they become transformed into additions to the capital stock. Keynes taught us to regard the apportioning of the flow of savings to various investments as a function subsidiary to the constant turnover of an existing stock of securities prompted by divergent expectations. Thus, seeing the importance of expectations in asset markets, and disliking the implications of what he saw, he launched his famous diatribe on the Stock Exchange as a "casino."

The Stock Exchange consists of a series of markets for assets, i.e., future yield streams. In each market supply and demand are brought into equality every market day. Demand and supply reflect the divergent expectations of buyers and sellers concerning future yields. Transactions take place between those whose expectations diverge from the current market price. Since as much must be bought as is sold, we may say that the equilibrium price in an asset market reflects the "balance of expectations." As without divergence of expectations there can be no market at all, we can say that this divergence provides the substrate upon which the market price rests.

Since all assets traded on a Stock Exchange are substitutes, albeit imperfect substitutes, for one another, these markets form a "system." And as equilibrium is attained simultaneously in each market which forms part of it, our system is free of those problems which in the Walrasian system are apt to arise when equilibrium is reached in some markets before it is attained in others.

In this way the market economy accomplishes daily a consistent, because simultaneous, valuation of all its major productive assets. The practical importance of this fact is that it makes possible, whether in the form of "take-over bids" or otherwise, the transfer of the control of material resources from pessimists to optimists, i.e. to those who believe they can make better use of them than others can. Critics of the market economy who scoff at the continuous and often violent day-to-day fluctuations of share prices, have failed to notice that an equilibrium price which rests on a balance of expectations is bound to be flexible since it must change every time the substrate of this balance changes. For precisely the same reason for which equilibrium in an asset market is reached so smoothly and speedily, it cannot last longer than one day. For expectations rest on imperfect knowledge, and not even a day can pass without a change in the mode of diffusion of knowledge.

The methodological significance of these facts, which is of interest to us here, even transcends their practical importance for the market economy, great as this is. For we are now able to see that the market process in asset markets has a more restricted function than is the case in commodity markets. In the latter, as we said above, the market process is kept in continuous motion by the occurrence of unexpected change as well as the incoherence of human plans. But in asset markets, in which equilibrium is established every day, human plans are made coherent every day. Here the lapse of time between market days serves only to diffuse new knowledge and facilitate the re-orientation of expectations. It does not have to serve to display the inconsistency of, for instance, production plans, which is what must happen between "market days" in commodity markets if such are to exist. Equilibrium in asset markets, as in the Marshallian corn market, makes sense because it is confined to the exchange of existing stocks. Where these conditions do not exist, as in a flow market, and *a fortiori* in the relations between such markets, it makes no sense, and all there exists in fact is the continuous market process.

The formalists, in extending the equilibrium concept from asset markets, where it makes sense, to the Walrasian system of commodity markets, where it does not, have not only rendered a poor service to economic thought. They have rendered an even poorer service to the market economy by blurring one of its distinctive features. But in doing so, they have unwittingly provided the friends of the market economy with an instructive lesson that they must henceforth forge their own weapons.

A second feature of the market economy, with which we shall deal even more briefly here, is the fact that quantities produced and prices paid apparently depend on the distribution of wealth. We are, for instance, often told that "the Invisible Hand will only maximize total social utility *provided the state intervenes so as to make the initial distribution of dollar votes ethically proper.*"[17] We shall refrain from comment on the ethical propriety of such statements. But it is perhaps clear that the nature of the market process, which is a continuous process that cannot be interrupted, has here been misconceived. There is, of course, no such thing as an "initial distribution" before the market process starts. The distribution of wealth in terms of asset values at any point of time is the cumulative result of the market process of the past. In the asset markets, the sources of income streams are revalued every day in accordance with the prevailing balance of expectations, giving capital gains to some, inflicting capital losses upon others. What reason is there to believe that interference with this market process is any less detrimental than interference with the production and exchange of goods and services? Those who believe that such a reason does exist (and most of our contemporary "welfare economists" do!) must assume that asset holders, like Ricardian landlords, somehow stand outside all market processes and "get rich in their sleep." Nothing we have said about differences in the *modus operandi* of the market process, in asset and commodity markets respectively, can impair the validity of the simple truth that all these processes form part of an integrated whole.[18]

NOTES

1. In the original German edition of *Human Action*.
2. L. von Mises, *Human Action* (New Haven: Yale University Press, 1949), p. 352.
3. F. A. Hayek, *The Pure Theory of Capital* (London: Routledge & Kegan Paul, 1941), p. 14.
4. *Individualism and Economic Order* (London: Routledge & Kegan Paul, 1949), p. 94.
5. F. A. Hayek, *The Counter-Revolution of Science* (Glencoe, Ill.: Free Press of Glencoe, 1955), pp. 38–39.
6. *The Counter-Revolution of Science*, loc. cit., pp. 39, 212.
7. *The Counter-Revolution of Science*, loc. cit., p. 38.
8. Ibid., p. 31.
9. The Austrians alone stubbornly resisted this trend and retained a wholesome distrust of indifference curves in particular and the whole Lausanne approach in general. Unfortunately, they never were able to show, with the cogency their case required, the incompatibility between the idea of planned action, the very core of Austrian economic thought, and an analytical model which knows no action, but only reaction.
   See Hans Mayer, *Der Erkenntniswert der funktionellen Preistheorien* (Vienna, 1932).
   See also Ludwig M. Lachmann, "Die geistesgeschichtliche Bedeutung der österreichischen Schule in der Volkswirtschaftslehre," *Zeitschrift für Nationalökonomie* 26 (January 1966): 158–62.
10. D. H. Robertson, *Essays in Monetary Theory* (London and New York, 1948), p. 25.
11. This is, of course, what happened to Keynes's liquidity preference theory.
12. *Business Cycles*, 2 vols. (New York and London, 1939), 1:140.
13. *Studies in the Theory of Economic Expansion* (London: Allen & Unwin, 1937), p. 175.
14. "There is an arresting contrast between the method and the meaning of Keynes' book. The method is the analysis of equilibrium, the endeavour to account for men's actions as a rational, calculated and logically justifiable response to circumstances which in all relevant essentials they thoroughly know. The meaning is that such rationality is in the nature of things impossible and baseless, because men confront an unknown and unknowable future." G. L. S. Shackle, *A Scheme of*

Economic Theory (Cambridge: Cambridge University Press, 1965), p. 44.

15. Ibid., p. 98.

16. John Hicks, *Capital and Growth* (Oxford: Oxford University Press, 1965), p. 32.

17. Paul A. Samuelson, *Collected Scientific Papers,* 3 vols. (Cambridge, Mass.: M.I.T. Press, 1966), 2:1410. (Italics in the original.)

18. "There is no distributional process apart from the production and exchange processes of the market; hence the very concept of 'distribution' becomes meaningless on the free market. Since 'distribution' is simply the result of the free exchange process, and since this process benefits all participants on the market and increases social utility, it follows directly that the 'distributional' results of the free market also increase social utility." Murray N. Rothbard, "Toward a Reconstruction of Utility and Welfare Economics," in *On Freedom and Free Enterprise,* ed. Mary Sennholz (New York: D. Van Nostrand, 1956), p. 251.

Economics as a
Social Science[1]

In attempting to outline the main characteristics of
Economics, I shall maintain a triple thesis:
(1) that Economics is a Science,
(2) that it is a Social Science,
(3) that it is an Analytical Social Science.

By saying that Economics is a Science I mean that economists
endeavour to establish *systematic generalisations about observable
phenomena.*

The real nature of truth, the ultimate grounds of human
existence, the universal criteria of the Good and the Beautiful,
are the province of the philosopher, not of the scientist. For this
very reason the economist, as an economist, must refrain from
making value-judgements. He is concerned with the World as it
is, not with the World as it ought to be. About what ought to be
men will always disagree. Arguments of this kind cannot be
settled by an appeal to reason and experience. For each value-
judgement presupposes another value-judgement of a higher
order, and thus cannot be sustained without an appeal to the
ultimate grounds of human existence. Every discussion of a
value problem inevitably leads to a metaphysical problem, the
kind of problem the scientist has to eschew.

The object of Economic Science is Human Action, a class of
observable phenomena. But before we can begin to study its
characteristics we have to meet a possible objection. Can there be
a science which is not "deterministic"? If not, how can a science of
human action be reconciled with our consciousness of a Free

Reprinted from *South African Journal of Economics* 18 (September 1950).

Will? I believe this objection can be met, but the problem is undoubtedly a serious one. In answering it we must, for the reasons just given, keep clear of the philosophical depths of the Free Will problem. I shall merely assume that, where human affairs are concerned, Free Will is a useful hypothesis which has not hitherto been invalidated. It is, in fact, as hypothesis which is universally accepted, even by those who profess to disbelieve in it. For how otherwise could they take part in discussions without regarding themselves as mere human gramophones emitting strange but irrelevant noises, and how could they ever hope to "convince" anybody else?

Fortunately there is a way out of our dilemma. It lies in the distinction between means and ends. In choosing ends we are free. Choice indeed *is* a manifestation of Free Will. But there are some ends which are incompatible, "having one's cake and eating it" is a significant example in the economic field. Here, by making one choice, we eliminate the possibility of another. Moreover, the means at our disposal are almost always limited, and this sets further limits to our choice, whilst there are few, if any, economic problems in the Land of Cockaigne. But it is important to understand that where these means are of a kind to leave us no choice, no economic problem exists either. The nature of economic activity lies in that we have *some* choice, to the extent to which the means at our disposal have alternative uses. In this way the freedom of choice and the determinacy imposed on us by our limited resources can be reconciled. "Economics is the Science which studies human behaviour as a relationship between ends and scarce means which have alternative uses" according to Professor Robbins's well-known definition.[2]

It remains to clarify the difference between technical and economic problems. Technical problems can also be stated in terms of means and ends, but they only arise where we have one end and more than one means. How to produce gold is therefore a technical problem; whether to produce it at all, or to devote our resources to other ends, is essentially an economic one. It is the possibility of choice which makes it so.

The second part of my triple thesis contends that Economics is a Social Science as distinct from the natural sciences. I hasten to stress that the criterion of distinction does not lie in the nature of the objects studied. It would be wrong to think that "Man" constitutes a field of study intrinsically separate from "Nature."

Natural sciences of Man can and do exist: Anatomy and Physiology are obvious examples. But it is a materialistic fallacy to believe that the material nature of the objects studied determines the fields of the various sciences. The pursuit of knowledge consists in asking a series of questions, the answers to which we try to relate to each other. And it is the relationships between the problems thus raised, and sometimes solved, and not any relationship between material objects, which constitute the field of each science.[3]

The difference between natural and social sciences therefore lies in the nature of the questions they ask. I have defined the method of Economics in terms of means and ends. But means and ends have no measurable "material" existence. They are categories of the mind. The angle from which economists approach their problems assumes the form of a general classification into means and ends. To them all economic phenomena have, in the first place, to be interpreted as manifestations of the human mind, of decisions to seek certain ends with given means.

This means that among the observable phenomena which economists, like other scientists, attempt to relate to each other, *human decisions* play a most prominent part. In fact the business of the economist consists in very little else but asking what human choices have caused a given phenomenon, say a change in price, or output, or employment.

But behind these choices we must not go. Why female fashions change more rapidly than male fashions, why more people prefer the music of Irving Berlin to that of Stravinsky than the other way round, is no business of ours. The economic consequences (implications, if you like) of the choice once it is made, not the psychological causes, belong to the province of Economics.[4]

The difference between natural and social sciences may further be illustrated by the different part played in both by notions which originally were commonly used in both.

The concept of "Purpose," for example, has long been discarded by the older natural sciences like physics, and has now even been expunged from biology. Yet, it remains an indispensable tool of the social sciences. Where human action is concerned, a purely behaviouristic approach can answer none of our questions. It certainly cannot *explain,* i.e. *make intelligible,* a single human act, let alone a complex series of acts of production and exchange.

The same applies to the "continuity of environment." In the natural sciences this is an axiom. The "uniformity of Nature" has long been recognised as the logical basis of inductive inference. *Natura non facit saltum.* But in the social sciences where, of course, we also have to assume some continuity of environment, it is not an axiom. Its logical basis is here an assumption about purposes, and such an assumption may, in a concrete case, be falsified. Whether we turn on the wireless, post a letter, or wait for a train, in each case our conduct is guided by an implicit assumption that the purposes in the pursuit of which men yesterday operated the social environment in which we live, will continue to inspire them to-day. The probability we assign to such assumptions is evidently something entirely different from that with which we expect the moon to rise to-night. A general strike, for instance, would upset our assumptions in the former case, while Nature, broadly speaking, does not go on strike.

The idea of Causality falls into the same class of notions discarded by modern natural science, but which the social sciences must retain. The very "anthropomorphic connotations" which make the concept so suspect in the eyes of modern scientists eager to purge their terminology of anything not "observable," make it valuable to us. After all, we *are* concerned with the "anthropomorphic." For us it is not true that all we can observe are the uniformities of sequence between "events." Our object of study is the pattern of relationships between decisions made and the practical carrying out of these decisions, the co-ordination of means and ends. For us the category "means and ends" is logically prior to any observation we make, and the phenomena we observe are to us not just "events" in themselves meaningless.

For us our observations fall at once into two distinct classes, human decisions and all other social phenomena. And inasmuch as decisions have to be made before they can be carried out and have consequences, we are entitled to regard them as social causes.

That the making of decisions, the co-ordination of means and ends, takes the form of mental processes does not, of course, mean that it is not "observable." Without the assumption that we and our fellow-men, broadly speaking, "know what we are doing," there could not only be no social science, there could be no social life. The social scientist, we may conclude, not merely *describes* but *explains* social phenomena by reducing them to acts of the mind. We may therefore say that the "causes" of these phenomena are our choices, co-ordinated in the form of plans.

These plans may, of course, fail. Very few things ever go according to plan. In war, for example, nothing ever does, not even for the victorious side. It remains true none the less that the outcome of a war is the cumulative result of the conflicting plans of both belligerents. Could anybody describe the course of a war otherwise than in terms of the rival plans successively adopted, failures though they all were? We may therefore conclude that cause and effect as well as means and ends are fundamental categories of the social sciences.

Compared with the natural sciences the social sciences are in some respects inferior, in others superior. Their inferiority rests in their inability to *predict* and *control*. As human action is governed by choice, and choice is free, there can be no prediction of our actions. All attempts to smuggle in predictability by the large back-door labelled "the Law of large numbers" are bound to fail since human events lack the quality of "randomness" essential for this purpose. The essence of social life consists in that men get to know about each other and modify their conduct in accordance with such a knowledge. Human action, directed by knowledge gained in that *process of intercommunication* which is the very texture of society, can never be regarded as "random."

Nor can there be "control" in the full scientific sense of the word. A zoologist making a breeding experiment with guinea-pigs need have little fear that the guinea-pigs, knowing that they are being watched, will change their breeding habits. But a politician experimenting with taxation or import control measures will very soon find that the objects of his experiments are guided in their action by inspired guesses about how long he will stay in office.

I said that there can be no control in the full scientific sense of the word. I do not wish to be misunderstood. Nothing is farther from my mind than to deny the possibility of social control. The essential point is that social control requires the willing co-operation of those whose actions are to be controlled. And co-operation, like every other type of action, requires a continuous effort of the human will. Without it control cannot succeed.[5]

I do not wish to deny the possibility of what I would call "negative prediction," based on inconsistency. If an economist observes a government trying, at one and the same time, to reduce the cost of living and to create an export surplus, he *can* predict that one of these actions will be a failure. To uncover such inconsistencies and to warn the public that what the politicians propose to do cannot be done, is, in all countries, perhaps the most important public duty of economists in our time.

With such meagre and unimpressive contributions to human progress to their credit, wherein lies the superiority of the social sciences? In the fact that they can go beyond mere description and correlation, and render the social world *intelligible* by reducing the phenomena of human action to that irreducible final cause: human choice. The natural sciences, after all, adopted their present-day methods after centuries spent in a vain search for ultimate causes, not out of strength but out of despair. I can see no cogent reason why we, who are in a more fortunate position, should follow their lead. We shall never know why a rose smells as it does, but I can see no insurmountable obstacle to our knowing why a perfume, say Chanel No. 5, smells as it does. In the second case we can ask the creators what they had in mind; in the first we cannot. In the social sciences the quest for final causes is a meaningful enterprise, and in this lies their superiority.

The third part of my thesis is that economics is an analytical social science, as distinct from the descriptive social sciences, or History. In a moment I shall return to the very important relationship between Economics and History. Before doing so, however, I must stress that the only successful method of the analytical social sciences is the "compositive" method.

The *modus operandi* of all sciences consists in analysing complex phenomena into their elements. Where not causation but correlation is the type of relationship under examination, its degree may provide the standard of comparison. But where causation is our quest, the elements of our analysis must be the causes of the phenomenon observed. Only where we can account for all the necessary and sufficient conditions can we claim to have grasped all the elements of the problem.

The logical character of the relationship between a phenomenon and its elements raises, of course, a number of crucial issues with which I need not deal here. But at least the most fundamental aspect of this problem requires some comment. The question has been asked, with what right we apply the logic of our minds to the external phenomena of nature. There are, of course, a number of answers to this question, not all of them consistent in themselves, few consistent with each other. But where Human Action is concerned, fortunately the matter is much simpler. *For the Logic with which we think is also the Logic with which we act.* As Professor Mises has put it: "Human Action stems from the same source as human reasoning. Action and reason are congeneric and homogeneous; they may even be called two different aspects of the same thing. That reason has the power to make clear through pure ratiocination the essential features of action is a consequence of the fact that action is an offshoot of reason."[6]

The Logic of Action is essentially a Logic of Success. We start by imagining a desired state of affairs as aim of our action, and call its achievement "success." We then proceed to eliminate all those courses of action which, in the situation as we see it, would be inconsistent with this achievement. What remains is the course of action we take.

It is not hard to guess that I shall be accused of excessive methodological rationalism. "Where," I shall probably be asked, "is there any room left for the non-rational aspects of behaviour, for custom and habit, for the overwhelming force of passion, and the all-pervasive influence of human inertia?" The answer to this objection is that by making choice, whatever it is and however motivated, the starting point of our analysis we have already taken care of these objections. *Not the psychological causes of human decisions, but their logical consequences form the subject-matter of the analytical social sciences.*

The number of hours worked in a community is, as a rule, fixed by custom, but it certainly has an economic effect: it determines the magnitude of output. The remuneration of officials is everywhere determined outside the marketplace; it remains true none the less that it has an effect on the supply and demand of their services. The most ardent traditionalist who regards it as his main vocation in life to maintain an existing way of life and social order, must seek to make this order "work"; otherwise it will not survive.

I now turn to the relationship between the analytical social sciences and History. Perhaps a Professor of Economics and Economic History may crave the indulgence of his audience if, on an occasion like this, he spends a few minutes pondering the correct relationship between the two halves of his function. But something more serious is here involved. The relationship between the analytical social sciences and History encompasses, in the social field, the problems of "theory" and "fact," or, to be more precise, the whole set of problems which concern the relationship between the formal-logical apparatus of a science and its empirical material.

At once we are confronted with a dilemma. If Economic Science and Economic History both deal with the same empirical phenomena, is not one of them superfluous? Is there anything the one could tell us which the other could not? In trying to solve this dilemma it has been said that History deals with facts, Theory with inductive generalizations from these facts. If this were so, History could not be regarded as a science, for the mere accumulation of facts is, of course, not a scientific, but a prescientific activity. But it is readily seen that this view of the matter is quite wrong.

It is plainly impossible to write the simplest village chronicle, let alone a biography, or the history of wars and revolutions on a purely behaviouristic basis, without an attempt at causal explanation, that is to say, without referring to ends sought and means employed. This simply follows from the fact that all History deals with Human Action which cannot be rendered intelligible otherwise. It is also hardly an accident that the method I have described, the method of explaining social phenomena in terms of human decisions, possibly rival and conflicting decisions, was originally developed in the writing of History. Not in the sense that its logical character and implications were at all clearly realised, they were not, but for the simple reason that History cannot be written otherwise.

So we seem to be thrown back on our dilemma. If Theory and History both aim at causal explanation, is one of them superfluous? The answer has to be sought in the methodological principle I mentioned earlier in this address. It is not the nature of our empirical material, but the nature of the questions we ask of our material, that determines the boundaries between sciences. But do not the theorist and the historian both ask causal questions of their material? They do, but the questions of the one presuppose the answers to those of the other.

The work of the historian consists largely, though not exclusively, in applying the broad generalizations of theory to concrete facts. The relationship between the analytical social sciences and History is, broadly speaking, the same as that between pure and applied science. Whether the historian ascribes the vicissitudes of the British economy of the postwar period to "suppressed inflation" *(teruggedrongen inflasie)* or to Full Employment, in either case his historical judgement involves the valid existence of some general theory linking money and employment. Whether he sees the chief cause of the French Revolution in the stubborn blindness of a ruling class which failed to make concessions when there was still time to make them, or whether he sees it in the equally disastrous blindness of a rising professional class (to wit, the modern professional politi-cian of legal extraction), neither explanation would make sense without a theory about the relationship between social stratifica-tion and political power.

In the language of modern Logic, the function of the historian is to "fill in" the descriptive signs between the logical signs, to tell us what ends by what means men in a given situation pursued. In applying the general means-ends category to concrete historical facts new problems are encountered. The applied scientist knows many woes that are undreamt of in the philosophy of pure science. The general "scarce-means-multiple-ends" scheme, for example, works well enough where we have to deal with the action of one man, as in a biography, or an organized group, say, a company, a party, a nation. It works less well where the situation we study is the result of the complex interplay of a large number of social forces. Like every other scientist the historian dislikes having to handle too many variables. And the temptation to treat as constant what one knows not to be a constant is often very strong. In the worst cases this takes the form of seeking an explanation of phenomena observed by "personifying" the forces whose very *modus operandi* should be explained, and ascribing means and ends to such pseudo-characters, for example, if the evolution of the modern form of the joint-stock company is "explained" as an "indispensable tool of Capitalism." This, of course, is not History but mythology, somewhat reminiscent of the Olympian interventions in the struggles of the Homeric heroes whenever the author is at a loss to account for their actions. Explanations of events in the history of a group in terms of the Hegelian "group spirit," or the "cul-ture patterns" currently in anthropological fashion fall into the same class of pseudo-explanations.

Some economic historians explain almost everything that happened between 1815 and 1914 as either the result, or at least a concomitant, of the "process of industrialization." Here we postulate a given change, or rather, a given process of continu-ous change, as a quasi-external "cause," and assume that every-thing that happens constitutes a "response" of the social group concerned to the initial and continuous "stimulus." One can hardly grudge a working scientist an attempt to reduce the number of his independant variables to manageable proportions, but at the same time it is possible to feel that the cases in which the results of this method will be an unqualified success will be few. It is, for example, obvious that the process of industrialization in Britain, Germany, and the United States produced, besides a number of similar, also certain highly significant dissimilar results which it is also the task of the historian to explain. All this reminds us of a passage from Tocqueville:

M. de la Fayette has said somewhere in his memoirs that the exaggerated system of general causes provides wonderful comfort to mediocre politicians. I would add that it also does this admirably for mediocre historians. It always provides them with some really good reason which, in the most difficult part of their book, will promptly get them out of all trouble, and encourages the weakness or laziness of the mind, while all the time paying homage to its profundity.

I trust these remarks will not be construed as a criticism of historical method. They are not. The historical method, as outlined above, is the only method that enables us to understand complex social phenomena. My remarks were prompted by a desire to see some of the applications of this method improved, not to see it replaced by another method. I cannot help feeling that to the working historian notions like "Industrialization" or "Colonization" offer a frame of reference which is too wide and therefore can explain very little. I am pleading for a narrowing of the frame of reference used for the explanation of certain concrete events, not for a narrowing of the scope of historical method.

In fact, there are fields of study in which the historical method, if it were used more widely, might be used to great advantage. In recent years, in all countries, large quantities of statistical figures have been turned out by official and semiofficial bodies, by research institutions and *ad hoc* agencies. While it is always useful to know more facts, it is undeniable that from the point of view of gaining knowledge, the results have, on the whole, been rather meagre and often disappointing. The reason for this lies in the simple fact that statistical figures merely depict certain aspects of historical events, and these events, to become accessible to our minds, require an interpretation of the statistical picture. Without such an interpretation statistics have no meaning. By themselves they tell no story. From all the excellent statistical information about economic conditions in Europe which the Economic Commission for Europe has recently put at our disposal, we would yet fail to learn the most important single fact about Europe's economy in the post-war years: that in every country outside the British Isles and Scandinavia the attempts of the interventionists to impose and maintain a "controlled economy" have failed.

The so-called "Trade Cycle" offers another instance in which the historical method might be more widely employed. Almost from the time the ups and downs of modern economic life began to attract attention, economists have shown themselves eager "to explain it all," to grasp the essence of the phenomenon by various devices. Theorists tried to catch the elusive ghost by tying him up with long deductive chains derived from a few general assumptions. But as they could hardly ever agree on which assumptions to start from, their quest failed to succeed. "Empirical" economists, their positivistic faith undimmed by logical reasoning, sat poring over innumerable series of production, price, and employment figures, waiting patiently for a moment of inspiration that would show them what was cause and what effect.

To-day it is becoming more and more clear that these ups and downs do not conform to a single invariant pattern. There is no such thing as a Trade Cycle in the sense of a periodically recurrent movement of a given number of variables.[7] Unlike the celestial bodies the modern body-economic does not obey the laws of uniform rotation. Each economic crisis has to be studied as an historical event. But it is now also possible to see that the effort spent on the construction of so many theoretical models was by no means in vain. The inconsistency of the various models disappears once we realize that each historical crisis was due to a different configuration of circumstances. And to find its proper model of explanation for each crisis is essentially the task of the economic historian.

We may therefore conclude that the spheres of History and the analytical social sciences, so far from overlapping, are actually complementary. The historian endeavours to render his narrative intelligible by means of causal imputation. But if I study the causes of an event E, I can meaningfully attribute it to, say, factors A and B only if I have some *prior general knowledge* which makes me think that the class of events to which A and B belong may, in general, generate events of the class to which E belongs. If, on the other hand, two other factors, C and D, belong to a class of which there is no reason to believe that in any circumstances they could give rise to events of the class E, we shall refuse them causal status *a priori,* before even beginning the study of the facts. If we hear it suggested that a nation was ruined by the incompetence of its rulers, all we can do is turn to the facts. It is a plausible hypothesis, for in general it is possible for incompetence to have such results. But a hypothesis attributing the ruin of a nation to a lack of matrimonial virtues on the part of its rulers need not even be investigated.

The chief task of the analytical social scientist is to tell the historians what factors will *not* bear a causal imputation. The general analytical schemes of theory furthermore provide the historian with alternatives of explanation. But the actual choice of the alternative, the act of causal imputation itself, is very much the historian's own. It requires that specific understanding of a concrete situation, that ability to weigh each element of it in accordance with its proper significance, for which no general theory, however broadly conceived and elegantly formulated, can offer a substitute. On the other hand, all causal imputation has to depend on broad and general frames of reference describing connections between classes of events. It is the task of the analytical social sciences to provide, in the social sphere, such frames of reference and build a system out of them, for the historian and for all of us.

You may have noticed that in the later part of this address the concept of Economics became almost imperceptibly fused with that of analytical Social Science. This is as it ought to be. I trust I shall not be thought guilty of "economic Imperialism" if I claim that Economics has more nearly approached the ideal of a closed theoretical system in which all propositions are linked to each other and the number of fundamental hypotheses reduced to a bare minimum, than any other social science. This can hardly be an accident. No doubt such an achievement was easier for a science which deals with a sphere of life in which conduct *has to be rational,* on penalty of bankruptcy, and which can thus use the Logic of Action as the logical cement of its own edifice. But although possibly more difficult elsewhere, I do not think it is an achievement entirely beyond the power of other social sciences. After all, it is not merely in business life that failure carries extreme penalties. If Economics studies the implications of consumers' choice and business decisions, I can at least imagine a Political Sociology which applies the same method to voters' choice and political decisions. The fundamental principle that inconsistent action cannot succeed, that feasible plans must at least be free of inherent contradictions, applies wherever and whenever men strive for success.

At the beginning of this address I paid homage to my eminent predecessors. Let me, in this concluding passage, cast a glance into the future. My distinguished successor in this Chair, who fifty years hence may perhaps address a similar audience on "The Social Sciences in the Twentieth Century," will undoubtedly have much richer material to draw upon. But I venture to doubt whether he will find it necessary to modify in their essence, to add much to or to detract from, the few logical pinciples of Social Science I have set before you to-day.

NOTES

1. An Inaugural Lecture given at the University of the Witwatersrand on 19th April, 1950. The chair was taken by the Vice-Chancellor Dr. H. R. Raikes.

2. Lionel Robbins, *An Essay on the Nature and Significance of Economic Science* (London: Macmillan & Co., 1962), p. 16.

3. Max Weber, *Gesammelte Aufsätze zur Wissenschaftslehre* (Tübingen: J. C. B. Mohr, 1922), p. 166.

4. This delimitation is not arbitrary. It simply follows the natural frontier of our conscious thought, which is also that of Logic. Human Action controlled by the mind has a logical structure and can thus be "understood." Those subconscious processes, on the other hand, which precede the choice of purpose and the decision to act, lack this natural structure. They are to us "external phenomena," essentially structureless, just like any other event we happen to observe.

5. Forty years ago it was said of a highly civilized country in Europe that there the government was so universally loved and respected, that it was quite sufficient for them to say that they did not want a certain thing to be done, and everybody would start doing it!

6. L. v. Mises, *Human Action* (New Haven: Yale University Press, 1949), p. 39.

7. So much is now more or less generally agreed. Dr. J. R. Hicks, in his recent *Contribution to the Theory of the Trade Cycle* (Oxford: Clarendon Press, 1950), although he still speaks of "cycles," makes it clear that he does not mean uniform sequences of identical constellations.

"In the real world we shall not expect to find such uniformity; and in consequence we ought not to expect that actual cycles will repeat each other at all closely. Certainly the cycles of reality do not repeat each other; they have, at the most, a family likeness. Thus, in order to explain the facts, we do not want to assume uniformity in conditions; what we want is a theory which allows variation in conditions, but still leaves us with a cycle of the same basic character. . . . One of the things which give different cycles their different *histories* (our italics L.M.L.) may thus be found in a change in the investment coefficient. It looks very likely that variations in others of the fundamental conditions may explain other varieties of cyclical experience" (108–9).

Evidently this is a task for historians.

Ludwig von Mises and the Market Process

1.

In the thickening gloom of our age, an age of declining standards, rampant inflation, and egalitarian ideology, it is perhaps too much to hope that the realm of economic thought alone will remain unscathed and at least this province of the human mind escape invasion by our contemporary follies. In fact, what we find to-day is very much what one might have expected. We see a few thinkers engaged in a valiant but desperate struggle to defend and strengthen the great tradition they have inherited. The large majority of economists have to-day adopted an arid formalism as their style of thought, an approach which requires them to treat the manifestations of the human mind in household and market as purely formal entities, on par with material resources. Not surprisingly, the adherents of this style of thought have come to find the mathematical language a congenial medium in which to give expression to their thoughts.

They are fond of referring to themselves as "neoclassical" economists. This label is, however, rather misleading. The classical economists, in their great day, were concerned with human action of a certain type, the forms it takes in varying circumstances and the results it is likely to produce. They took the market economy of their time as object of their thought and asked why it was what it was. Gradually they built up a formal apparatus of thought in order to deal with these problems.

The "neoclassical" economists of our time have taken over, developed and considerably refined this apparatus of thought.

Reprinted from Friedrich A. Hayek, ed., *Toward Liberty: Essays in Honor of Ludwig von Mises*, 2 vols. (Menlo Park, Calif.: Institute for Humane Studies, 1971), 2:38–52.

But in doing so they have taken the shadow of the formal apparatus for the substance of the real subject matter. It will not surprise us to learn that when confronted with real problems, such as the permanent inflation of our time, neoclassical economics has nothing to say. "Late classical formalism" appears to us a much better designation of the style of thought currently in fashion in these quarters.

A prominent economist of this school has recently told us, "Until the econometricians have the answer for us, placing reliance upon neoclassical economic theory is a matter of faith." What a faith! Economics is by no means exclusively concerned with what happens, but also with what might have happened, with the alternatives of choice which presented themselves to the minds of the decision-makers. In fact, it is in terms of these alternatives alone that the decisions can be rendered intelligible, which is after all the main purpose of a social science. Statistics, as Mises has often explained, merely record what happened over a certain period of time. They cannot tell us what might have happened had circumstances been different.

Thirty years ago Mises warned us of the futility of late classical formalism. Characteristically he thrust his blade into his opponents' weakest spot. He showed the inadequacy of the main tool of the formalists, the notion of equilibrium. "They merely mark out an imaginary situation in which the market process would cease to operate. The mathematical economists disregard the whole theoretical elucidation of the market process and evasively amuse themselves with an auxiliary notion employed in its context and devoid of any sense when used outside of this context."[1] And he added, "A superficial analogy is spun out too long, that is all."

In voicing these strictures Mises gave pointed expression to that opposition to the work of the school of Lausanne in general, and its fundamental concept, the notion of equilibrium, in particular, which has for long been a characteristic feature of the whole Austrian school. From Menger's letters to Walras to the work of Hans Mayer and Leo Illy a succession of Austrian writers have expressed their distrust of the Lausanne approach and criticised the theory of general equilibrium. Schumpeter is the obvious exception, but in the sense relevant to our problem, as in several other senses, he may be said not really to have belonged to the "inner core" of the Austrian school. Mises, by contrast, established his claim to this title by his rejection of the equilibrium concept and thus showed himself to stand firmly in the true line of the Austrian succession. But he did not confine himself to criticism of the work of the school of Lausanne. He took an important step forward. He replaced the notion of equilibrium by the concept of the Market Process. We shall have more to say later on about this fundamental concept and its significance within the structure of Mises's thought. But there is another matter to which we must turn first.

In the 30 years which have now elapsed since Mises made his attack on the late classical formalism of our age and its notion of equilibrium a certain re-orientation of modern economic thought has taken place. Less is heard to-day of what Mises called the "evenly rotating economy" (*Kreislauf*) as the framework of the equilibrium concept. Instead the notion of "growth equilibrium" or "steady state growth" has come to acquire a place of prominence in contemporary thought. We shall therefore have to ask ourselves whether, and how far, this metamorphosis of the notion of equilibrium has affected the validity of Mises's criticism of 30 years ago.

In this essay we set ourselves two tasks: in the first place, to examine the question whether the new notion of equilibrium growth may be regarded as exempt from the criticism of the old variety of static equilibrium which Mises has presented. In the second place, Mises's hints about the Market Process as an alternative to equilibrium as a fundamental concept will have to be worked out more fully. We shall have to ask what are the conditions of the continuous existence of such a process. We shall also have to ask, what is, within the framework of the market process as a whole, the status of those equilibrating forces which tend to produce at least partial adjustments.

2.

In this section we propose to show that the new notion of "growth equilibrium" which has come into fashion in the last quarter of a century is even more inadequate than was the older version which Mises so trenchantly criticised. Though the new variety acquired fame and came into fashion as a feature of the Harrod-Domar model of economic growth, its origin has to be sought in Cassel's work in the second decade of this century. Cassel was critical of Wicksell's work, and in particular of the latter's attempts to analyse dynamic processes in terms of concepts, such as the "natural rate of interest," which can be given little meaning outside an unchanging world. He realised that economic processes in an industrial society subject to continuous change could not possibly be analysed with the help of such instruments of thought. But he remained enough of a Walrasian to want to retain the notion of general equilibrium and the static method. So he proposed the "uniformly progressive economy," the model of an economy in which output of all goods and services increases at a uniform rate all over the system while relative prices and the relative marginal products of the factors of production remain unaffected. Thus our economic system can remain in a state of general equilibrium all the time while output, population and the stock of capital grow steadily. We now have equilibrium persisting in a world of steady change. The static method remains applicable to a world which is not stationary. In a sense we might say that here we have another type of an "evenly rotating economy," only that the economic system as a whole achieves motion while it is rotating. Harrod and Domar, when they worked out their model, appear to have been quite unaware of Cassel's contribution.[2]

It is noteworthy that the protagonists of modern growth theories appear to believe that their models bear at least some resemblance to reality. Professor Solow asks, "What are the broad facts about the growth of advanced industrial economies that a well-told model must be capable of reproducing?" and, following Kaldor, then proceeds to state six "stylized facts." The first of them is according to him: "Real output per man (or per man-hour) grows at a more or less constant rate over fairly long periods of time. There are short-run fluctuations, of course, and even changes from one quarter-century to another. But at least there is no clear systematic tendency for the rate of increase of productivity in this sense to accelerate or to slow down. If, in addition, labour input . . . grows at a steady rate, so will aggregate output . . . ." The second is stated as "the stock of real capital, *crudely measured,* (our italics) grows at a more or less constant rate exceeding the rate of growth of labour input."[3]

That some fascinating games can be played with "macro-economic" aggregates, and the size of the capital stock in particular, is not a new discovery. When Cassel presented his model, at a time when macro-economics had not been thought of, he had to stress the need for a uniform rate of progress in all sectors. In our age this implication is conveniently forgotten together with the Cassellian original.

If the equilibrium of a stationary economy is an unsatisfactory tool of analysis for an industrial economy, growth equilibrium of the kind we described above is readily seen to be even less satisfactory. When real incomes per head increase, income recipients do not spend them in the same proportion as before. They will begin to buy some goods which previously had been entirely beyond their reach, buy more of some other goods, but less than in proportion to their higher incomes, and may actually reduce their consumption of some other goods they have come to regard as "inferior." The pattern of relative demand will certainly change. For the pattern of relative supplies to adjust itself *instantaneously* we at once have to assume that producers foresaw this change correctly as well as the time pattern of the change. We also have to assume that costs are constant over the relevant ranges of output in all industries affected and that wage rates do not change, otherwise relative prices will change. Such assumptions about constant costs and wages when relative output changes must be regarded as being already somewhat unrealistic. But the degree of lack of realism inherent in such assumptions pales into insignificance when compared with that of perfect foresight on the part of the producers without which we can have no instantaneous adjustments of supply to demand. In fact it is this assumption of perfect foresight that deprives the model of growth equilibrium of any resemblance to the market processes of the real world.

Yet, without such foresight the adjustment of supply to changes in demand will certainly be delayed, and during the delay there will be disequilibrium in the markets affected. If any transactions take place during the period of disequilibrium (and, in a continuous market, how could this fail to happen?) the conditions of our moving equilibrium will be changed for the very same reasons for which Edgeworth and Walras had to introduce "re-contract" to safeguard the determinate character of their final equilibrium position. To our knowledge, however, none of the many economists who have presented to us equilibrium growth models in recent years has attached the condition of re-contract for transactions during periods of disequilibrium. They have all, of course, assumed continuous and uninterrupted existence of equilibrium. It is this which, without instantaneous adjustments of supply to changes in demand, is impossible.

Similar problems arise in connection with the composition of the stock of capital. The maintenance of a constant capital-output ratio (whatever this vague notion may mean and imply) is, of course, not a sufficient condition of the maintenance of general equilibrium in a growing economic system. The actual composition of the capital stock in terms of the various capital resources must be appropriate to the composition of total output demanded. The capital stock must contain no single item which its owner would not wish to replace by a replica, if he suddenly lost it by accident, otherwise the stock cannot be in equilibrium. Such changes in demand for consumer goods as we discussed above must therefore be at once accompanied by a corresponding change in the composition of the capital stock, otherwise this stock cannot retain its equilibrium composition and we confront a new source of disequilibrium. Of course, so long as we regard all capital as homogeneous the problem does not arise. As soon as we face the fact that most durable capital goods, even if not actually specific to the uses for which they were originally designed, have at least a limited range of versatility, the continuous maintenance of the equilibrium composition of the capital stock in a world in which relative demand and technology are bound to change in quite unpredictable fashion, emerges as a serious problem.

It is instructive to look at the whole problem from the point of view of the convergence of expectations. A society in which economic progress occurs is part of an uncertain world. Nobody knows the future. In a stationary world it is possible to appeal to the constancy of the "data" and the continuous recurrence of events to justify the belief that all members of such a society will sooner or later become familiar with them and their expectations will converge on the recurrent pattern of events. In an uncertain world this is impossible. Experience shows that different people will entertain widely divergent expectations. This will be so not merely because some men are, by temperament, optimists and others pessimists. Differences in knowledge are here often of fundamental importance. The diffusion of new knowledge is not a uniform and not often a continuous process. Some sources of knowledge are only available to some, but not to others, while the ability to make use of new knowledge is most unequally distributed among men.

For all these reasons expectations in an uncertain world are bound to diverge. But divergent expectations cannot all be fulfilled. Some are bound to be disappointed. The plans based upon them will fail. Some plans will be even more successful than their makers had expected. In either case the planners will not be in equilibrium over time. At the end of the period they will wish they had pursued different plans, and this will apply to those whose plans failed as well as to those whose plans succeeded better than expected. They will thus have to revise their plans in the light of an unsatisfactory experience. But continuous equilibrium requires continuous success of plans. We have to conclude therefore that in an uncertain world in which expectations diverge and the plans based upon them cannot be consistent with one another the particular type of dynamic equilibrium known as "growth equilibrium" is impossible.

3.

Mises rejects the notion of equilibrium and proposes to replace it by that of the Market Process. In following him we confront a number of difficulties. Not the least of them stems from a fact of history which none of us can eschew. The ascendancy which the school of Lausanne has gained in this century has created a situation in which for most of us it has become difficult even to conceive of a world without equilibrium. It nowadays requires quite an effort to do so. So much of what we have learnt and thought seems to depend on it that without it we appear to be drifting helplessly on an uncharted sea without a possibility of taking our bearings. But the inadequacy of the Lausanne notion of general equilibrium has been established. We have to tackle the uncomfortable task of substituting for it something else, something at once more akin to reality and more congenial to praxeological thought.

Fortunately we have Mises's work to guide us in this task. In ridding our minds of the domination of the equilibrium notion the market process presents itself as a better alternative. Perhaps such a conception came more naturally to somebody who shaped his fundamental conceptions in the Vienna of the first decade of this century, the decade in which the reputation of the Austrian school was at its peak.[4] No doubt the young Mises, imbibing the "pure atmosphere" of the school of Vienna, not as yet contaminated by alien particles, found himself able to conceptualize, with little effort, the essence of the market economy in the form of the market process. For us, as we explained, an effort is here required. We should make a start by looking at different meanings of the notion of equilibrium.

First of all, we have to note that what has happened to the notion of equilibrium is that the economists of Lausanne and their successors to-day have stretched the meaning of equilibrium to such an extent that a notion, in its original meaning useful and indeed indispensable, has been applied far outside the borders of its natural habitat.

The Austrians were concerned, in the first place, with the individual in household and business. There is no doubt that here equilibrium has a clear meaning and real significance. Men really aim at bringing their various actions into consistency. Here a tendency towards equilibrium is not only a necessary concept of praxeology, but also a fact of experience. It is part of the logic inherent in human action. Interindividual equilibrium, such as that on a simple market, like Böhm-Bawerk's horse market, already raises problems but still makes sense. "Equilibrium of an industry" à la Marshall is already more precarious. "Equilibrium of the economic system as a whole," as Walras and Pareto conceived of it, is certainly open to Mises's strictures. "Growth Equilibrium," as we have tried to show, the equilibrium of a system in motion, is simply a mis-conception.

The vice of formalism is precisely this, that various phenomena which have no substance in common are pressed into the same conceptual form and then treated as identical. Because equilibrating forces operate successfully in the individual sphere of action, we must take it for granted, so the formalists tell us, that they will also do so outside it. From Walras to Samuelson we find the same manner of reasoning, the same arbitrary assumptions, the same unwarranted conclusions.

What, then, are we to do? If, with Mises, we adopt the Market Process as our fundamental *Ordnungsbegriff*, how much of equilibrium can we embody in it? We suggest that we envisage a world in which millions of individuals attempt to reach their individual equilibria, but in which a general equilibrium that would embrace all of these is never reached. The Market Process derives its *rationale* from, and has its place in, a world in which general equilibrium is impossible. But to deny the significance of general equilibrium is not to deny the existence of equilibrating forces. It is merely to demand that we must not lose sight of the forces of disequilibrium and make a comprehensive assessment of all the forces operating in the light of our general knowledge about the formation and dissemination of human knowledge.

If, with Mises, we reject the notion of general equilibrium, but, on the other hand, do not deny the operation of equilibrating forces in markets and between markets, we naturally have to account for those disequilibrating forces which prevent equilibrium from being reached. In other words, to explain the continuous nature of the market process is the same thing as to explain the superior strength of the forces of disequilibrium.

The market process is kept in permanent motion, and equilibrating forces are being checked, by the occurrence of unexpected change and the inconsistency of human plans. Both are necessary, but neither is a sufficient condition. Without the recurrence of the first, i.e. in a stationary world, it is indeed likely that plans would gradually become consistent as men came to learn more and more about their environment including one another's plans. Without the inconsistency of plans prompted by divergent expectations, on the other hand, it is at least possible that all individuals would respond to exogenous change in such a manner that general equilibrium can really be established. A good deal would here, of course, depend on the speed of such adjustments. Where this is high, each adjustment may have been completed before the next unexpected change occurs. What, however, will in reality frustrate the equilibrating forces is the divergence of expectations inevitable in an uncertain world, and its corollary, the inconsistency of plans. Such inconsistency is a permanent characteristic of a world in which unexpected change is expected to recur.

Within the general framework of the market process, prompted by the two permanent forces whose *modus operandi* we have just attempted to describe, equilibrating adjustments in individual markets, both price and quantity adjustments, will, of course, take place. The equilibrating forces will be found to do their work. But we can never be sure that the spill-over effects which an equilibrating adjustment in one market has on other markets will always be in an equilibrating direction. They may well go in the other direction. Equilibrium in one market may be upset when the repercussions of the equilibrating adjustments in other markets reach it. There is therefore no reason why the effects of such inter-market repercussions must always on balance be equilibrating. But our inability to assess the net result of this interplay of equilibrating forces in different markets does not amount to the discovery of another permanent force which keeps the market process in motion. It is a process within the market process.

We have never been able to understand why in the discussion on Keynes's so-called "under-employment equilibrium" some economists, opposed to Keynesian teaching, should have regarded it as either necessary or desirable to argue that in a market economy the market process, if only left unhampered, would "in the end" tend to bring about full employment. In the light of the considerations presented above such a conclusion appears unwarranted. If the outcome of the contest between equilibrating and disequilibrating forces is at best uncertain, why should it be less so in the case of the labour markets, affected as they are by a variety of factors, many of them noneconomic? If we have good reason not to believe in the generality of equilibrium, why should we want to assert that in the labour market alone equilibrium will always come about in the end? The cause of the market economy is not served by such assertions which a deeper understanding of the market process and the complex play of forces on which it rests will show to be fallacious. We have to learn to live with unemployment as with other types of disequilibrium.

4.

It may be useful to elucidate the ideas presented above on market process and equilibrium by restating them in terms of the diffusion of information, somewhat in the manner in which Leijonhufvud has recently interpreted some ideas of Keynes.

We pointed out above that a good deal always depends on the speed of the adjustments following disequilibrium. Where these are made rapidly, equilibrium may be reached before the next unexpected change occurs. Most economists agree that the market is an agent for the diffusion of information, but we may well doubt whether this can be at all regarded as a rapid process. Equilibrium theory, in order to affirm the existence of a strong tendency towards it, has to assume that correct information about equilibrium prices and quantities is readily distilled from market happenings and available to all participants. Otherwise there can be no immediate adjustment. With slow adjustments a good deal may happen in the meantime before equilibrium is reached.

In reality, of course, information will spread slowly because not all participants have the same ability to assess the informative significance of the events they observe. But even apart from this fact, which in any case prevents equal knowledge by all market participants, we have to take note of two further facts which in reality cannot but impede the diffusion of information.

Firstly, nobody can be certain whether an event he has observed constitutes a "real change" or a random fluctuation. He has to wait for confirmation and this takes time. Secondly, nobody knows for how long the information provided by a market event will remain relevant to his plans. In a changing world information which is relevant knowledge to-day may have become obsolete by to-morrow. These two facts, pulling the individual in opposite directions, account for the divergence of expectations.

We thus have to conclude that the diffusion of information does indeed form an indispensable part of the market process and by itself constitutes an equilibrating force. But it is in reality bound to be a rather slow process, likely to be hampered by the divergence of expectations and overtaken by unexpected events.

Mises, as a critic of equilibrium theory and exponent of the Austrian tradition, assumed the rôle of an innovator when he presented his conception of the Market Process as an alternative. It is, however, noteworthy how slowly and gradually the Austrian school evolved these fundamental concepts which serve to unify economic action in society.

In the Walrasian system the notion of equilibrium is employed as a formal device to unify economic action on the three levels of individual, market, and system. This unification is apparently accomplished at one stroke on all three levels. Hence the formal elegance and architectonic unity which have so fascinated many of our contemporaries. But, as we saw, poverty of content is here the price to be paid for elegance of form. While we learn something useful about what governs and unifies individual action, we merely learn a few half-truths about the forces operating in the system as a whole.

The Austrian school presents a very different picture. Here conceptualization and unification are often painfully slow. Even on the level of the individual it took half a century and was not achieved until Schönfeld's *Wirtschaftsrechnung* of 1924. In the development of Mises's thought as we said above, the idea of the market process was probably conceived 60 years ago, but it was not formulated until the 1930s.

But the slow progress has now brought its reward. We are now able to gain an insight into the complex nature of the forces operating, in particular between markets, which was never dreamt of in the halls of the palace on the shore of the Lake of Geneva.

Mises has provided his disciples with an instrument of thought which promises to be of superb power. In years to come it will be for them to prove their worth by handling it with care and adroitness.

NOTES

1. *Human Action* (New Haven: Yale University Press, 1949), p. 352.
2. *Theoretische Sozialökonomie* (Leipzig, 1918), I. Kapitel, para. 6.
3. R. M. Solow, *Growth Theory: An Exposition* (Oxford: Oxford University Press, 1970), p. 2.
4. "These years, during which Böhm-Bawerk, Wieser and Philippovich were teaching at Vienna, were the period of the school's greatest fame." F. A. von Hayek, "Economic Thought: The Austrian School," in *International Encyclopedia of the Social Sciences*, 4:461.

PART FOUR
PROBLEMS IN
MACROECONOMIC AND
CAPITAL THEORY

Complementarity and Substitution in the Theory of Capital

1.

Complementarity, introduced into economic dynamics by Professor Hicks in 1939,[1] has since given rise to a host of bewildering and intricate problems. Soon Dr. Lange, in defending the Hicksian view of complementarity against overt criticism by Professor Machlup,[2] had to warn us against confusing the effects of complementarity with those of a "sympathetic shift in demand."[3] But a few years later the same Dr. Lange relegated complementarity to a scornful footnote.[4] For this he was promptly taken to task by Mr. Harrod, who told us that "in the context of the enquiry, in which we are interested in changes of the prices not of highly specific factors, but of widely employed factors or categories of factors . . . the co-operant attribute predominates."[5] Mr. Harrod also expressed the view that "factors may be co-operant or alternative to one another. The latter attribute belongs to factors that are very specific. Thus if tool B becomes cheaper it may lead entrepreneurs to have no further use for tool A (which does roughly the same job)."[6] This view plainly contradicts Professor Hicks's statement that "there is a tendency for factors jointly employed in the same firm to be complementary."[7] There is thus good reason to believe that this is a field in which the wise walk warily.

We may start by recognising with Professor Hicks that goods subject to "sympathetic shifts in demand" will probably be also complementary goods, that "companiable commodities will very

Reprinted from *Economica* 14 (May 1947).

197

usually be complements."[8] Where the cause of a dynamic change lies on the demand side, the effects of complementarity and companiableness may therefore be almost impossible to disentangle. It follows that if it is our aim to study the effects of complementarity on dynamic change, it will be better to choose as our standard model a case in which the change originates on the supply side. This method we shall adopt in the latter part of this paper.

Next, we have to realise that the traditional treatment of factor complementarity in economic theory has been quite unduly narrow. The standard case discussed is here, of course, the labour-land-capital relationship in the distribution of incomes, Mr. Harrod's "widely employed categories of factors." But what precisely is our criterion of classification of these categories? And why cannot complementarity exist within each category? In this paper we shall endeavour to show that it is in the theory of capital that the concept of complementarity proves a most powerful lamp to throw light into some notoriously dark corners.

2.

To reduce that heterogeneous assortment of buses, blast furnaces, telephone kiosks and hotel-room carpets that we call Capital to an intelligible order, to exhibit the design of the pattern into which all of these have to fit, is the chief task of the theory of capital. This is usually done by representing capital as a "stock" or "fund" the component parts of which are units of money value. Our heterogeneous assortment is thus converted into a homogeneous aggregate by using Money value as a common denominator. As Professor Hayek has shown, this becomes impossible under conditions of dynamic change likely to cause relative value changes.

In a homogeneous aggregate each unit is a perfect substitute for every other unit, as drops of water are in a lake. Once we abandon the notion of capital as homogeneous, we should therefore be prepared to find less substitutability and more complementarity. There now emerges, at the opposite pole, a conception of capital as a *structure*, in which each capital good has a definite function and in which all such goods are complements. It goes without saying that these two concepts of capital, one as a homogeneous fund, each unit being a perfect substitute for every other unit, the other as a complex structure, in which each unit is a complement to every other unit, are to be regarded as *ideal types*, pure equilibrium concepts neither of which can be found in actual experience.

In reality we should expect individual capital instruments to be substitutes for some, and complements to some other instruments. Each locomotive, we may surmise, is complementary to a number of wagons, but at the same time a more or less perfect substitute for every other locomotive. If this is so, the next question we have to ask is whether, over the field of capital as a whole, complementarity or substitutability is the dominant relationship; or, more precisely, under what conditions we may expect one or the other to predominate. Mr. Harrod believes that among capital instruments substitutability prevails. But we should require further evidence. Enthusiasts of econometrics may well have a dreamy vision of new playgrounds to conquer and new toys to hug, for is this not precisely the kind of situation in which the harassed theorist has to "appeal to the facts"? But a little further reflection shows that here, as so often, "the facts" refuse to give a simple answer to our question.

The view that factor complementarity and substitutability are alternative modes of the relationship between factors *in the same situation* rests on a fallacy. There are too many instances of change, of which labour-saving invention is the most familiar, where complements are suddenly turned into substitutes; or, even more intriguingly, in which capital (our supposedly homogeneous stock!) is split into two parts one of which becomes a substitute for, while the other remains a complement to, labour. There are also cases where both relations appear to exist side by side. If a firm has four delivery vans, each delivering goods in a quarter of the town, are they complements or substitutes? According to Professor Hicks they are the former, as "factors jointly employed in the same firm"; according to Mr. Harrod they are bound to be the latter ("doing roughly the same job"). But are they not really both? Furthermore, while locomotives may be substitutes, and locomotives and wagons complements, from the point of view of the time table, the production plan for the railway system as a whole, all trains are complements. But if trains are complements, how can locomotives be substitutes?

These examples go to show that factor complementarity and substitutability are not exclusive alternatives. Factor complementarity and substitution are phenomena belonging to different provinces of the realm of action. Complementarity is a property of means employed for the same end, or a group of consistent ends. All the means jointly employed for the same end, or such ends, are necessarily complements. Factor complementarity presupposes a *plan* within the framework of which each factor has a function. It is therefore only with respect to a given plan that we can meaningfully speak of factor complementarity. Factors are complements insofar as they fit into a production plan and participate in a productive process.

Substitution, on the other hand, is a phenomenon of change the need for which arises whenever something has gone wrong with a prior plan. Substitutability indicates the ease with which a factor can be turned into an element of an existing plan.[9] A change in plan is possible without a change of end. The importance of substitutability lies in that it is usually possible to pursue the same end (output) with a different combination of factors. The importance of complementarity lies in that "technical rigidity" (invariability of the mode of complementarity) may often make it necessary to change the end rather than the means; an existing combination of factors is used to produce a different output.

The change in question must be possible but not predictable. If it were predictable there would be no need for substitution. We should take it into account in drawing up our plan. Here, as elsewhere in the theory of action, predictable change is indistinguishable from any other known element of the situation. The designer of a motor-car is as unlikely to forget the lamps as the mudguard.

A production plan involving a large number of factors and with a complex complementarity pattern is particularly vulnerable in case any of them breaks down. We safeguard ourselves against such occurrences by keeping a reserve stock of perfect substitutes for the operating factors (spare parts). We diminish its necessary size by devices calculated to increase substitutability, like the standardisation of equipment. Where the complementarity pattern of the plan is complex, a high degree of substitutability between operating factors and factors held in reserve may be required to keep it going. We have to provide for many minor changes in order to prevent a major one.

We now understand why the locomotives in our example gave us so much trouble. In saying that each locomotive is complementary to so and so many wagons we think of a given production plan (time table). In saying that each is a more or less perfect substitute for every other we are, as it were, turning our mind to an entirely different situation, one in which our original production plan with its allocation of locomotives to trains has been modified. In the first case we think of a given situation, in the second of a change in the situation.

This is not to say, of course, that every change will turn all complements into substitutes. Most factor complementarities, to be sure, can stand up to a number of changes, some of them, like the one mentioned, may outlast almost any change. Our point is merely that every major change is bound to upset some plans and disrupt some complementarities. On the other hand, it is impossible to speak of substitutable factors without defining the kind of change we wish to provide for. One cannot help feeling that the plant bred in the rarefied atmosphere of a static world with a given system of wants, does not stand up very well to the rough climate of a dynamic world which we cannot but study in terms of plans, but in which failure and revision of plans is an every-day occurrence.

It is now clear why factors jointly employed in the same firm tend to be complementary: they are all means to the same end, elements of the same plan. Unity of management here ensures consistency of action.

3.

We shall now extend the scope of our analysis from the individual enterprise and its production plan to the economic system as a whole. Shall we now find factor complementarity throughout the system? At first sight one might think that here, where factors are employed, not in one production plan but in many, there can be little or no complementarity. But further reflection shows that this need not be so. A firm, carrying out a plan extending over a period of time, is during that period in equilibrium, as equilibrium means essentially consistency of a number of acts by different individuals, or the same individual. We may now imagine an economic system in equilibrium in the sense that the acts of all individuals, producers and consumers, are consistent with each other, hence so are all production plans. The stationary state is the simplest type of such a system, but generally foreseen change will not affect the essence of the matter. In such an economic system in equilibrium, complementarity will exist between all factors in the system in precisely the same way as in each firm. For where the production plans of all firms fit into a coherent whole, they may, of course, be regarded as elements of one large plan constituted by this whole.

Let us now assume that an unforeseen change throws our system into disequilibrium. Substitution of factors ensues. It is important to realise that while factor substitution destroys one set of complementary relations, another will be created, though possibly of a different mode. If the factor substituted is a perfect substitute for the factor displaced, nothing further need be done. We fit the spare part into the machine, and it continues to run as before. But if the factor substituted is not a perfect substitute, there may have to be an adjustment of other factors. In the former case the new factor merely joins an existing combination, in the latter the *coefficients of production*,[10] the proportions in which the various factors are combined, will have to be altered. A change in the coefficients of production in one firm will, of course, have repercussions throughout the economic system and entail further acts of substitution in other firms. A sequence of changes will permeate the system, affecting prices, output and coefficients of production. But however many subsequent acts of substitution our first act may entail, as long as factors are used together in productive processes there will always be factor complementarity.

What we have said so far about complementarity and substitution applies to factors in general. Now, capital resources are more sensitive to unforeseen change than are either labour or permanent resources, and this marks them out for special treatment. Capital goods are products of the human mind, artefacts, produced in accordance with a plan. Capital gains and losses as effective tests of such plans will therefore affect decisions concerning capital production in a sense in which wage fluctuations, in general, do not affect the birth-rate.

Every capital instrument is designed for a purpose. Where it is highly specific, this purpose is identical with a certain kind of (anticipated) use. Where it is "versatile,"[11] it may cover a wide range of uses. But in any case it is planned for *some* kind of use, and failure to succeed in any of them as reflected in loss of earning power will result in revision of plan. At the moment at which a new machine is installed in a factory, one production plan impinges upon another. If the second plan, in which our machine is in use, fails, there will be repercussions on the first kind of plan: fewer such machines will be produced.

4.

We have seen that if capital is to be regarded as a homogeneous aggregate, all its constituent elements have to be perfect substitutes. But the complementarity of capital resources (plant, equipment, working capital) is a fact of experience. Hence, if we are to take account of it, we have to give up the "aggregative" conception of capital in favour of a structural conception. But if capital is to be regarded as a structure, what determines its shape? We have to allow for the heterogeneity of different capital resources which now have different functions. But what determines the character of these functions?

The shape of the capital structure is determined by the network of production plans. Each production plan utilises a given combination of factors. The proportions in which factors enter a combination, the coefficients of production, express the mode of factor complementarity in it. More particularly, the proportions in which the various capital resources enter it express the mode of capital complementarity in it, what we shall call the *capital coefficients*. The capital coefficients in each combination are thus the ultimate determinants of the capital structure, at least in equilibrium. In disequilibrium the degree of consistency between plans is a modifying factor.

Strictly speaking, of course, a capital structure in our sense can only exist in equilibrium, where all plans are consistent with each other, and the network of plans displays the firm outline of a clear and distinguishable pattern. But in dynamic reality this structure is in a state of continuous transformation. As production plans prove inconsistent and fail, the outline of our pattern becomes inevitably blurred. Plans have to be revised, new combinations formed, old combinations disintegrate, even those which persist have to undergo an often drastic modification of their factoral composition.[12] In reality the coefficients of production are ever changing. Every day the network of production plans is torn, every day it is mended anew. Under these circumstances we shall find some, at least temporarily, unutilised capital resources while others are scarce. In any case, in the world of our daily experience all unexpected change entails more or less extensive capital regrouping.[13]

The theory of capital has therefore every reason to occupy itself with the network of production plans. It is readily seen how failure of plans affects investment decisions and how, broadly speaking, complementarity serves as an amplifier of *internal* capital change. These phenomena of internal capital change the theory of capital neglects at its peril. Unfortunately, scant attention is paid to them in most of the economic thought of our time,[14] which, as regards capital change, seems almost exclusively preoccupied with problems of investment, i.e., problems of *external* capital change. Interrelations between internal and external changes are almost completely ignored.[15]

We now must pause for a moment and contemplate our results against the background of traditional capital theory. We have tried to show that a theory of capital based on a notion of homogeneity is bound to miss our problem entirely. It is to a structural conception of capital that we have to look for encouragement and inspiration. But in the sphere of human action Structure implies Function, and Function, where a number of factors is involved, implies co-ordination and complementarity.

Such a structural conception of capital is to be found in the system of Böhm-Bawerk. Contrary to what appears to be a widely held view, Böhm-Bawerk's chief contribution to the theory of capital was not the introduction of *time,* but of *complementarity over time.* Here, to be sure, the "stock of real capital" becomes a flow, but not a homogeneous flow. Its elements, the individual capital goods, are not, like drops of water, perfect substitutes, but each has its place in the flow. If it is true that Böhm-Bawerk's "stock of intermediate products" is essentially a wage fund in motion, we must remember that its different elements move at different speeds.

Hides, leather, and shoes in wholesale stocks, are not just physically similar goods at different points of time, but *products* at different stages of processing. And "processing" requires the existence of a production plan in which complementary factors come into operation in accordance with a time schedule. Time is relevant here as the dimension of processing, the medium of complementarity. Thus, what really matters is not time, but complementarity over time. On the other hand, under the stationary conditions characteristic of Böhm-Bawerk's system all capital instruments in existence at the same point of time are necessarily complements. Thus, whatever their position in time, all capital instruments are linked together by complementarity.[16]

We may say that within the realm of capital complementarity is an all-pervasive fact, at least as long as equilibrium is maintained.

If we regard capital as a complex structure the pattern of which is determined by the proportions in which the various capital resources co-operate in productive processes, it follows that all capital change, including new investment, is bound to modify the structure. Under these circumstances it is difficult to see how there could be "widening," or even "deepening" of capital. As Professor Hayek has shown, "widening," i.e., the multiplication of existing equipment, is, for the whole economic system, impossible in the absence of unused resources, while it is possible in some industries at the expense of other industries. "For the economic system as a whole the first of these alternatives is possible only if there is a labour reserve available. But in any particular industry the required additional labour may be attracted from another industry."[17]

Now, as we shall see in the next section, the existence of unemployed labour and unutilised resources is very important for the dynamics of capital, because they provide potential complements for the new productive combinations. But in their absence there can be no capital change which leaves coefficients of production unaffected. "Widening" of capital in some industries must be accompanied by disintegration of existing factor combinations elsewhere. The contrary impression is evidently due to the habit of confining our attention in matters of capital to what happens in a few expanding industries. The notion of capital "widening" is apparently an empirical generalisation of the well-known fact that the accumulation of capital as a rule takes the form of successive growth of new industries, and that at each moment a few expanding industries appear to bear the brunt of it. We may accept this empirical generalisation, but the impression that we may safely neglect what happens elsewhere, is nevertheless mistaken. Furthermore, even capital "deepening" is bound to modify not only the coefficients of production as far as labour and capital are concerned, but the capital coefficients. It is hard to imagine cases in which the proportion of capital assets to other factors increases while relative proportions of plant, machinery, tools, raw materials, etc., remain constant.

In other words, there can be no major change which leaves the existing structure and composition of capital intact. All such change tends to create situations in which there is too much of some capital assets and too little of others. In this fact lies the ultimate reason for that instability of the "capitalistic" economy which so many deplore and so few understand.

5.

We shall now test the efficiency of the analytical tools we have forged by applying them to a problem which in recent years has become a focus of economic controversy, viz., the effect of the accumulation of capital on profits and the inducement to invest. According to a powerful school of thought this effect is bound to be depressing. As more and more capital is accumulated, investment opportunities gradually become exhausted and the rate of profit declines. *"Other things being equal, the marginal efficiency of capital will be lower the greater the amount of capital goods already possessed."* (Author's italics.)[18] We shall endeavour to show that the accumulation of capital gives rise to processes which make it impossible for "other things" to remain equal. On the other hand, Professor Hayek has pointed out that there are cases in which investment actually raises the demand for capital.[19] An obvious example would be a copper mine in Central Africa in which we could not even begin to sink capital without having first built a railway from the coast.

It is clear that the issue hinges on complementarity and substitution. The "depressionists" evidently regard capital as a homogeneous aggregate; each unit of capital is a perfect substitute for every other unit, and accumulation means essentially an addition of further units to a pre-existing homogeneous stock. It is equally evident that Professor Hayek's view is based on complementarity. The "investment that raises the demand for capital" is investment in capital goods complementary to those to be constructed later.

The question now confronting us is, which of the two rival

influences, the stimulating influence of complementarity or the depressing effect of substitutability, will on balance prevail within the economic system. At first sight it might be thought that, as complementarity is all-pervasive while substitution will probably be confined to a few expanding industries in which new capital goods are installed, the former influence will prevail. But this would be a premature conclusion based on an unwarranted use of *ceteris paribus* assumptions. For the effect of new capital assets on the capital structure is not confined to those sectors in which they are installed and their immediate neighbourhood. By its effect on the coefficients of production, the breaking-up of existing combinations, and the formation of new ones, the accumulation of capital affects the whole economic system. But its *modus operandi* is gradual, depends in each case on the composition of the factor combinations affected, and is certainly very different from that usually assumed in capital theories based on the notion of homogeneity. We shall illustrate it by an example.

Let us assume that there is an increase of capital in the film[20] industry. More cameras, studio equipment, etc., are produced and installed. The greater number of films produced makes it necessary to have more cinemas[21] (complements). As film rentals fall cinema earnings rise. To the extent to which there is unemployed labour and unutilised resources new cinemas will be built. But this may be possible only within fairly narrow limits. The typical location of cinemas is in the central sector of urban areas where as a rule there are no empty spaces. Any considerable rise in cinema earnings, together probably with some decline in the demand for other forms of entertainment,[22] *will thus* cause existing capital equipment to be turned over to new uses. Theaters, ice rinks, dance halls, will be converted into cinemas. Existing factor combinations, house-cum-theatre, house-cum-ice rink, etc., will disintegrate. But while rents earned on such buildings will increase, considerable capital losses will be suffered on theatrical settings and costumes, freezing equipment, and musical instruments. In fact, unless these can be sold to somebody able to fit them into a new combination, they may altogether lose their capital character and become scrap. On the other hand, owners of "free" capital instruments complementary to them are now able to get them at "bargain prices" permitting large capital gains.

The accumulation of capital will therefore have what we may term a "chain reaction" effect. The initial change entails a sequence of subsequent changes as the final result of which the structure of capital becomes modified. The new capital instruments cause the disintegration of existing combinations, increase the earning power of elements complementary to them, and set free those for which they are substitutes. The latter will either lose their capital character or have to seek out other complements, new partners with whom to enter into new combinations. For this they depend on the existence of, at least temporarily, "free," i.e., unutilised capital goods, or on the breaking-up of other existing combinations. But the disintegration of the latter, by setting free some elements, would again create the same problem. The process will continue until all discarded factors have either found their way to the scrap-heap, or found "free" partners, or found owners willing to wait and hold them until a complement turns up.

This conclusion incidentally throws new light on the vexed problem of "excess capacity." We now realise that in a world of dynamic change unused resources have two functions. Firstly, they act as shock-absorbers when combinations disintegrate. Secondly, their existence provides an inducement to invest in those capital goods which are complementary to them.

We may therefore conclude that the production of new capital instruments will have different effects on the earnings of different existing capital resources. Those to which they are complements will earn more, those for which they are substitutes will earn less and often nothing at all. To ask what is the effect of the accumulation of capital on "the" rate of profit is to ask a meaningless question, since one of its main effects is to make rates of profit diverge. If in equilibrium it is possible to speak of "a" rate of profit, the accumulation of capital will destroy such equilibrium.

6.

We may now briefly survey the chief results of our enquiry.

Our first result, and the most general, is the inadequacy of static equilibrium methods in the theory of capital which clearly emerges as an eminently dynamic discipline. The concept of complementarity, which originated in a static three-commodity world, with a given system of wants, does not stand up well to its transplantation into the sphere of dynamics, and is not very well suited to the kind of plan analysis appropriate in this sphere.[23] At any rate, factor complementarity and product complementarity cannot be treated on the same level.

Secondly, it is useless to treat capital change as quantitative change in one factor under *ceteris paribus* conditions, when it is plain that at least some *cetera* will not remain *paria*. What is really needed is a new type of sequence analysis which enables us to follow up, sector by sector, the chain of changes set in motion by the impact of the original change. We may add that this applies at least as much to technical progress as to the accumulation of capital.

Thirdly, *internal capital change*, the regrouping of existing capital resources in response to unforeseen change, emerges as by far the most important topic of capital theory, although in present-day economic thought it is almost completely ignored. Undue preoccupation with mere *external* capital change, like investment, preferably in quantifiable money value terms, in the discussion of which internal repercussions are neglected, is seen to lead us nowhere. Furthermore, the question of the effect of the accumulation of capital on "the" rate of profit and the inducement to invest now appears as a meaningless question. Some profits will rise, some will fall. Unforeseen change always engenders capital gains and losses. It remains a question of some interest, to what extent the expectation of such gains and losses influences the inducement to invest. But in any case the installing of new capital instruments cannot meaningfully be regarded as "growth" of anything concrete or measurable. For it is bound to entail the, at least partial, destruction of some existing capital values.

Finally, if all this is important for the theory of capital, it is of equal, if not greater, importance to the theory of industrial fluctuations. Perhaps the concept of net investment pure and simple, as chief motor of economic change, has by now yielded us all that it is ever likely to yield. Between 1900 and 1915 economists like Cassel, Spiethoff, and Professor Robertson, basing their conclusions, not on alleged "psychological laws," but on a study of the actual events of the time, laid the foundations of a theory which takes account of intersectional maladjustment as a result of disproportionate growth of different groups of capital resources. The overinvestment theories currently in fashion are now seen to be fallacious. But what are we to substitute for them? This problem of factor substitution in economic theory will, if we may hazard a guess, occupy economists for many a day to come.

NOTES

1. In the realm of statics the theory of marginal productivity is, of course, a set of variations on this theme. In dynamics, on the other hand, most of Professor Hayek's work implies complementarity of different capital resources. What constituted the novelty was the explicit introduction of complementarity into dynamics.

2. "Professor Hicks' Statics," *Quarterly Journal of Economics* 54 (February 1940):277–97.

3. Oscar Lange, "Complementarity and Interrelations of Shifts in Demand," *Review of Economic Studies* 8 (October 1940): 58–63.

4. *Price Flexibility and Employment*, 1944, p. 9n.

5. R. F. Harrod, "Review of Oscar Lange's *Price Flexibility and Employment*," *Economic Journal* 56 (March 1946): 102–7.

6. Ibid.

7. *Value and Capital*, p. 98. Cf. also J. R. Hicks, *Théorie mathématique de la valeur* (Paris: Hermann & Lie, 1937), p. 49.

8. "The Interrelations of Shifts in Demand," *Review of Economic Studies* 12 (1944):73.

9. The factor in question may have to be taken out of another plan, or may be temporarily unemployed, or may be newly created for the purpose.

10. Walras's "coefficients de fabrication." Cf. his *Éléments d'économie politique pure,* éd. défin., 1926, pp. 211–12.

11. The term is due to Dr. G. L. Shackle. Cf. F. A. Hayek, *Pure Theory of Capital* (London: Routledge & Kegan Paul, 1941), p. 251n.

12. The revision of plans is the function of the entrepreneur, the carrying out of existing plans is the function of the manager.

13. Some economic and financial aspects of capital regrouping are discussed in "Finance Capitalism?" *Economica* 11 (May 1944):64–73.

14. Professor Hayek's work is, of course, the outstanding exception.

15. For example: "The prices of *existing* [author's italics] assets will always adjust themselves to changes in expectation concerning the prospective value of money. The significance of such changes in expectation lies in their effect on the readiness to produce *new* [author's italics] assets through their reaction on the marginal efficiency of capital." J. M. Keynes, *General Theory of Employment, Interest, and Money* (New York: Harcourt, Brace & World, 1936), p. 142.

In other words, changes in expectations have no significance for the regrouping of existing capital assets.

16. Böhm-Bawerk's "third ground," the higher productivity of roundabout processes, lends itself easily to interpretation in terms of complementarity over time.

17. *The Pure Theory of Capital,* p. 286.

18. J. R. Hicks, "Mr. Keynes' Theory of Employment," *Economic Journal* 46 (June 1936):249.

19. "Investment That Raises the Demand for Capital," *Review of Economic Statistics* 19 (November 1937): 174–77. (Now reprinted in F. A. Hayek, *Profits, Interest, and Investment* [London: G. Routledge & Sons, 1939], pp. 73–82.)

20. It is not necessary to assume that the film industry is the only expanding industry. But we have accepted the empirical generalization that at each moment current accumulation is likely to show itself prominently in a few expanding industries. What we wish to rule out, and would regard as highly unrealistic, is an increase of capital in all industries in the same proportions.

21. We assume that total demand increases *pari passu* with total supply. It is, of course, possible to deduce the depressing effect of accumulation merely from the postulate that total demand falls short of total supply, as "the marginal propensity to consume is always less than one." But there is no reason to believe that this is necessarily so. Cf. A. F. Burns, *Economic Research and the Keynesian Thinking of Our Times* (26th Annual Report of the Nat. Bureau of Economic Research, June, 1946, pp. 18–19).

22. That total demand increases *pari passu* with total supply does not entail that this will be so in every market.

23. In this respect, the discovery of the fact that "sympathetic shifts," i.e., dynamic demand changes, are liable to throw our whole system into indeterminacy, should have served us as a warning.

Mrs. Robinson on the Accumulation of Capital

1.

In the literature of this decade, not otherwise remarkable for the quality of its economic writing, Mrs. Robinson's latest book stands out as a landmark.[1] It is not merely the most elaborate contribution to post-Keynesian literature to date. It has, of course, all the qualities of rigour, lucidity and sophistication which we have come to expect from its author. But in certain respects it is quite unique.

The author, deliberately renouncing the instruments of marginal analysis, attempts to view the problems of economic progress from a classical perspective; her theme is the conditions of continuous expansion. Most of the analysis is conducted with the help of a model of a high degree of abstraction. But Mrs. Robinson has, as few other model-builders have, a flair for realism. She takes great care to tell the reader which are the important features of reality excluded from the model. From this endeavour to combine a measure of realism with a fairly high degree of abstraction there arise certain problems, as we shall see. But in the interest of more palatable economics than we have had of late, it is to be hoped that Mrs. Robinson's candour in stressing the limitations of her model will find many imitators.

The title of the book is, of course, borrowed from Rosa Luxemburg. Of its main problem the author says that it presented itself to her as "The Generalisation of the General Theory, that is, an extension of Keynes's short-period analysis to long-run development." In spite of these appearances, however, Mrs. Robinson is neither a Keynesian nor a Marxist, but a latter-day Ricardian.

Reprinted from *South African Journal of Economics* 26 (June 1958).

Keynes, of course, was mainly concerned with under-employment equilibrium, a short-run problem, whereas our author deals with the long run. Keynes, she says, "left a huge area of long-run problems covered with fragments of broken glass from the static theory and gave only vague hints as to how the shattered structure could be rebuilt." But Mrs. Robinson does not accept at least two major hints Keynes gave to his disciples for the long run. She explicitly rejects the "Psychological Law" of the declining marginal propensity to consume which, rather curiously, she terms the "Liberal underconsumption thesis," and which she ridicules as "the inevitable destiny of prosperous economies to drown themselves in cream." She also points out that a "lack of investment opportunities" is not a necessary result of rapid capital accumulation, but a possible result of a decline in the intensity of competition, while Keynes, of course, assumed perfect competition throughout. Mrs. Robinson's status as a Keynesian must, therefore, remain in doubt.

As a Ricardian, Mrs. Robinson embraces a cost-of-production theory of value, but not a pure labour theory. "Interest enters into the cost of capital goods both in respect of the period of gestation when equipment is being constructed and the pipe-line of work-in-progress filled up, and in respect of the period of the earning life of equipment," a sentence which would, of course, be anathema to Marxists.

A wish to return to the classical mode of thought implies, of course, a rejection of much of modern economics which is so largely concerned with human choice and decision. In Mrs. Robinson this rejection is quite deliberate. "Economic analysis, serving for two centuries to win an understanding of the Nature and Causes of the Wealth of Nations, has been fobbed off with another bride—a Theory of Value. . . . Faced with the choice of which to sacrifice first, economists for the last hundred years have sacrificed dynamic theory in order to discuss relative prices."

One may question the truth of this statement since modern economics is as much concerned with relative quantities as with relative prices. One may also wonder whether it is possible to discuss economic progress while ignoring not merely relative prices but also, for instance, intersectional shifts in output and resources. But such criticism would here be out of place. In the book Mrs. Robinson obviates it by assuming all output to be homogeneous. And although, as we shall see, this assumption gives rise to a host of difficulties, we must not question the level of abstraction as such on which an author chooses to conduct the argument.

In the next section an attempt will be made to present a brief and concise outline of the central argument of the book. The following two sections of this paper are devoted to critical reflections on what appear to be crucial issues arising from this argument. In the concluding section certain methodological aspects of the attempt to revive the classical style of analysis in the midst of the twentieth century will be examined.

There can, of course, be no question of doing justice to such a book within the space at our disposal. We shall have to ignore whole sections of it and some important strands of thought, and concentrate on what appear to us to be the crucial issues. The reader, we trust, will not allow himself to be misled by the preponderance of critical matter in this paper. In the first place, an argument such as this, fenced in as it is by such a formidable set of assumptions, can hardly be discussed adequately without criticism. But, secondly, it is precisely because the issues raised are so crucial for our science and, thirdly, because the book is in any case bound to become a focus of widespread discussion, that it requires to be subjected to close scrutiny. But on no account, we hope, will the reader allow himself to be deterred from reading the book itself. It is worth it.

2.

In the classical manner Mrs. Robinson's main concern is with the conditions of progress through capital accumulation, and in particular with its origin in and effects on the distribution of incomes between wages and profits. Her chief problem is whether, and in what circumstances, continuous progress under "the capitalistic rules of the game" is possible. These circumstances are enshrined in a model first set out in Chapter 7 and subsequently modified in many respects. "With the aid of this model we shall examine the problems of accumulation over the long run. . . . Our chief concern is with the relation between wages and profits, and the argument is conducted in terms of (1) the relations of the stock of capital to the available labour force, (2) the influence of competition, and (3) the technique of production."

At first our author assumes that all profits are saved and all wages consumed; there are, at this stage, no other incomes. The rate of accumulation is therefore identical with the rate of profit on capital and, if we assume a constant capital-output ratio, with the rate of expansion of output as a whole.

The assumptions embodied in the model engender a high degree of abstraction. All index number problems are eliminated by assuming complete homogeneity of labour and output. A "given technique of production" means fixed coefficients of production. The stock of capital goods "required to produce a given flow of output is rigidly determined by the technique in operation. Since commodities are produced in rigid proportions, the stock of equipment of all kinds must be in appropriate proportions." Technical progress thus means that the cost per unit of the composite commodity of which all output consists is reduced. The influence of variable expectations is eliminated by the assumption "that at every moment entrepreneurs expect the future rate of profit obtainable on investment to continue indefinitely at the level ruling at that moment; that they expect the rate of technical progress (which may be nil) to be steady; and that they fix amortisation allowances for long-lived plant accordingly. When something occurs which causes a change, we assume that expectations are immediately adjusted, and that no further change is expected." There are at first only entrepreneurs and workers in the economy, though rentiers and landlords enter later on. The economy is a closed system and there are no economies of scale.

Superimposed on this model there is another set of assumptions determining what Mrs. Robinson calls a *golden age,* a moving equilibrium of the economic system as a whole. It is thus described: "When technical progress is neutral, and proceeding steadily, without any change in the time pattern of production the competitive mechanism working freely, population growing (if at all) at a steady rate and accumulation going on fast enough to supply productive capacity for all available labour, the rate of profit tends to be constant and the level of real wages to rise with output per man. There are then no internal contradictions in the system." It is important to note that in this moving equilibrium not only does the rate of profit tend to be constant and uniform for all industries, but "total annual output and the stock of capital (valued in terms of commodities) then grow together at a constant proportionate rate compounded of the rate of increase of the labour force and the rate of increase of output per man." In other words, the capital-output ratio remains constant. Capital per worker increases, but output per worker also increases in such a fashion as to leave the capital-output ratio constant through time.

We are, of course, repeatedly warned that the conditions of a golden age are unlikely to be found in reality, but, says our author, "The persistence of capitalism till today is evidence that certain principles of coherence are imbedded in its confusion."

How is the rate of progress linked to the distribution of incomes? The answer is provided by the well-known Keynesian maxim that while workers spend what they earn entrepreneurs earn what they spend. "Thus each entrepreneur is better off the more investment his colleagues are carrying out. The more the entrepreneurs and rentiers (taken as a whole) spend on investment and consumption, the more they get as quasi-rent."

But there is an upper limit to the amount of investment possible at each moment which is set by what our author calls the *inflation barrier.* "Higher prices of consumption goods relative to money-wage rates involve a lower real consumption by workers. There is a limit to the level to which real-wage rates can fall without setting up a pressure to raise money-wage rates. But a rise in money-wage rates increases money expenditure, so that the vicious spiral of money wages chasing prices sets in. There is then a head-on conflict between the desire of entrepreneurs to invest and the refusal of the system to accept the level of real wages which the investment entails; something must give way. Either the system explodes in a hyper-inflation, or some check operates to curtail investment."

On the other hand there is no minimum level of profits as such. Profits are the result, not the cause of investment. But for the inflation barrier "accumulation is limited by the energy with which entrepreneurs carry it out" and nothing else.

Under the assumptions set forth the accumulation of capital by making capital less scarce and labour scarcer tends to raise real wages unless it is accompanied by such an increase in population that capital per worker cannot increase, or actually decreases. But the extent to which this happens depends upon the degree of competition. "The mechanism which ensures that actual output expands more or less in step with the rise in potential output due to technical progress is the competition which keeps prices in line with costs, and so raises the real-wage rate with productivity." When this does not happen, when entrepreneurs do not permit prices to fall as productivity rises, the economy is in danger of falling into stagnation, since entrepreneurs can succeed in keeping prices high only by keeping output low. Once prices have become inflexible "the main defence against the tendency to stagnation comes from pressure by trade unions to raise money-wage rates. When they succeed, the stickiness of prices tells in their favour, for entrepreneurs may prefer (within limits) to accept a cut in margins rather than to alter their price policy. Insofar as this occurs, real-wage rates rise. If by this means real wages can be made to rise as fast as output per man the root of the trouble is cut, and the economy can accumulate capital and increase total product at the rate appropriate to the pace at which technical improvements are being introduced just as though competition were still active."

But though such a "high wage economy" is better than stagnation it is far from being an ideal. "A kind of live-and-let-live system is then established, and provided that real wages are rising somewhat (over the long run) no one is concerned to inquire if they might be made to rise faster by a more rapid rate of accumulation."

What happens if output increases less than capital so that the capital-output ratio increases? The rate of profit will then tend to fall and entrepreneurs substitute capital for labour by choosing a more capital-intensive method of production. While, if capital accumulates faster than the population grows, the distribution of incomes shifts in favour of labour, this process will also be arrested when entrepreneurs choose a more capital-intensive technique. "They cross the mechanisation frontier" in Mrs. Robinson's terminology. "Our argument brings out the fact that it is accumulation as such which tends to raise wages, while mechanisation checks the fall in the rate of profit that would occur if accumulation continued in the absence of scope for mechanisation."

The argument is also significant in another way. It shows how far Mrs. Robinson has moved away from her Keynesian moorings. "A failure of accumulation to be maintained in actual economies is often attributed to a 'lack of investment opportunities' but, in a technical sense, there is never a lack of investment opportunities till bliss has been reached. There is always a use for more capital so long as it is possible to raise the degree of mechanisation. . . . The conception which underlies 'the failure of investment opportunities' is rather that the capitalist rules of the game create a resistance to a rise in the ratio of capital to labour when it entails a fall in the rate of profit."

The essence of Mrs. Robinson's thesis is that accumulation of capital raises real wages. Where it is accompanied by sufficient technical progress, capital-output ratio and rate of profit remain constant. Expansion then follows the path of a golden age. Where this is not so and output grows less than capital the rate of profit will tend to fall. Entrepreneurs then take evasive action by more intensive methods of production ("capital deepening") which check the rise in real wages. If they do not, if they reduce investment instead, they will thereby reduce their own earnings since they are the people who earn what they spend.

The model is later on modified in many ways which do not affect the validity of the main argument. Allowance is made for the fact that a part of profits is consumed. Hence, the rate of profit now exceeds the growth ratio of the economy by the proportion of their incomes capitalists devote to consumption. In Marxian terms, "The prices of consumption goods exceed their wages costs to a sufficient extent to permit of capitalists' consumption, as well as investment."

Other sections of the book are devoted to the short period, "a period within which changes in the stock of capital can be neglected but output can alter," to finance, land and various other topics. But the main outline of the analysis as described above is not affected by arguments presented in these sections.

3.

The notion of a stock of capital the growth of which accompanies the growth of output is crucial to Mrs. Robinson's analysis. It is also crucial that "over the long run the stock of capital corresponds more or less to the sum of all the net investments made" (p. 334). We shall call this the *integrability condition*. The author says that "it is broadly true" that this condition holds in reality. Evidently where this is so there can be no capital change other than investment and disinvestment. There can be no capital gains and losses, or at least, when they occur they are without economic significance. The model has no room for them. The question arises, however, whether the integrability condition is consistent with the conditions of technical progress, a question we shall take up in the following section.

But how can we measure capital? Our author emphasises that "the absence of tranquility makes it impossible to define precisely the meaning of a quantity of capital." How, then, can we make sense of the notion of a stock of capital in a changing world?[2] The answer is that this is just the purpose which the notion of a golden age is meant to serve: it enables us to combine "tranquillity" with change.

It is well known why in a world of unexpected change the quantity of capital is a meaningless notion, but in a golden age all change is expected change. In a stationary state the whole problem would not arise. Here all capital values can be ascertained without ambiguity since all capital goods are worth their cost; cost values and discounted earning values are identical. But our author is concerned with progress. The real significance of her golden age concept is that it denotes a moving equilibrium, a dynamic counterpart to the stationary state, the latest version to date of Cassel's "Uniformly Progressive Economy" of forty years ago, in which all those relationships the constancy of which enables us to determine the quantity of capital in a stationary state remain constant, yet are projected on to a dynamic world. In this moving equilibrium entrepreneurs always discount future earnings at the rate of profit which has obtained in the past, and there is only one such!

The reader is scarcely surprised to learn that in her endeavour to retain the benefit of stationary conditions when dealing with a world of change, our author soon runs into trouble. In the conditions of a golden age, to be sure, it is possible to measure the quantity of capital since "the value of the stock of capital is then determined by the rate of profit ruling in the given golden-age conditions." But how can we compare stocks of capital in economies at different stages of development, each of them in a golden age of its own, where the over-all homogeneity postulated for our model does not exist? "One set of difficulties flows from this difference in the composition of output in the different economies. Another set of difficulties flows from the fact . . . that a different wage rate in terms of output entails different relative values of commodities, capital goods and labour time, so that there is no simple unit of value in which to reckon."

In the chapter on "The Evaluation of Capital," perhaps the most penetrating discussion of this forbidding subject in the literature, our author, having at length expounded all these difficulties, rather surprisingly concludes that the problem of the measurement of capital is really a purely verbal one. "The problem of measuring capital is a problem about words. The capital is whatever it is, no matter what we call it. The reason for taking so much trouble about how we describe it is to save ourselves from being tricked by our own terminology into thinking that different things are alike because they are called by the same name. Since no way of measuring capital provides a simple quantity which reflects all the relevant differences between different stocks of capital goods we have to use several measures together."

Among the several measures of capital now introduced by our author, it becomes apparent that the key-concepts are *productive capacity* ("an outfit of capital goods that can be used by the appropriate quantity of labour to produce a flow of output specified in physical character and in its future time-pattern") and the *real-capital ratio* ("the ratio of capital reckoned in terms of labour time to the amount of labour currently employed when it is working at normal capacity"). The latter, we are told, "corresponds most closely to the conception of capital as a technical factor of production," and is really the measure of the degree of mechanization or capital intensity. We are warned, however, that this relapse into the labour theory of value does not mean that all labour time is homogeneous: the two kinds of labour time expressed in this ratio are not in *pari materia;* "one consists of past labour time, compounded at interest, embodied in a stock of capital goods, the other is a flow per unit of time of current labour." This, of course, is the heresy Rosa Luxemburg would never forgive.

The notion of productive capacity has no unambiguous meaning unless the output produced is homogeneous. This fact not merely precludes us from introducing into the model new products, a normal feature of economic progress. How are we to compare output in different economies with different rates of investment? Mrs. Robinson candidly admits that "this comparison has an exact meaning only for economies in a state of zero net investment. When, as is generally the case, accumulation is going on at different rates in economies using different techniques, the composition of output (which includes increments of capital goods) is different in each, and the comparison is subject to the same index-number ambiguity that we encountered above." It is, of course, common knowledge that international comparisons of production index figures make little sense.[3] To say that the growth of productive capacity is a measure of economic progress is therefore not to say very much, except in a world of homogeneous output.

What about the other key-concept, the real-capital ratio, our measure of the degree of mechanization? In a golden age it remains constant along with the capital-output ratio and the rate of profit since productivity increases uniformly throughout the system. But technical progress may affect the relative scarcity of labour and capital and thus the rate of profit. When this happens, and in general whenever entrepreneurs are impelled to change the degree of mechanization, the real-capital ratio changes in a situation in which the change in the rate of profit makes it impossible to compare the value of capital assets before and after the change. We have here a transition from one golden age to another, that is, from one equilibrium to another, a problem in comparative statics. But where is there a system of coordinates which, unaffected by the change, can serve to measure it?

To most economists this would be just another instance of the impossibility of comparing the quantity of capital in two different equilibrium positions. But our author is undaunted. She replaces the set of assumptions defining the golden age economy by another set of special assumptions "designed to make it possible to analyse the transition from one technique to another as though it took place without any disturbance to tranquillity. The argument, for this reason, is somewhat fanciful, but setting it out in this way enables us to see the workings of the mechanism, which are hard to follow in the hurly-burly of short-period disequilibrium in which it actually operates."

By then, however, the moment has come when even the most patient reader cannot but ask himself whether the game is worth the candle. Does an argument confined by such stringent abstractions throw any light at all on the industrial world as we know it? Why do we have to measure capital in circumstances in which we know that it cannot be done?

Mrs. Robinson, as a Ricardian, would probably reply that in labour time we have an "objective" measure of capital embodied in the real-capital ratio which we can compare before and after the change. There is, to be sure, the problem of adding up labour hours spent in different years and paid for at different wage rates. But if we have a constant "notional interest rate"[4] to compound our labour units, to compute the present value of hours worked in the past, the problem seems not insurmountable. It would appear that in this way a labour theory of value, albeit in a modified version, can be put to economic use.

But what have we really gained? What does an hour of work done in Britain in 1957 have in common with one done two hundred years ago except that they both last sixty minutes? The attempt to find in a changing world somewhere an unchanging entity to serve as a measure of change is bound to fail. Economic change affects the economic significance of hours of work along with everything else. Labour hours have no "intrinsic qualities" which do not change *and* have economic significance.

We cannot but suspect that this is another instance in which a method developed in the natural sciences is being used in economics without due care for the limits of its meaning. In physics (at least prior to Bohr and Heisenberg) the space-time continuum was used as the universal system of co-ordinates. All processes in nature were then reduced to changes in space and time which could be regarded as the "ultimate categories."

In the realm of human action, however, the mere lapse of time has no significance, except possibly as a framework of chronological order. As a dimension of human action a labour hour does not remain constant over the years since more or less may be done in it. When Mrs. Robinson writes, "Work takes time, but time does not do work," we have to add that the same work does not always take the same time. Labour hours are being bought and sold in markets and interact with other economic magnitudes in a sense which has no counterpart in classical physics. The heroic attempt to find a measure of capital invariant to time, whether as real-capital ratio or in any other form, thus far cannot be said to have succeeded. Mrs. Robinson has failed to do what cannot be done.

4.

It would be hardly fair to criticise our model for its level of abstraction, high though it is. The same might be said, after all, of such neoclassical notions as the stationary state, or of certain models of economic expansion which have of late won wide acclaim among economists. It is, on the contrary, Mrs. Robinson's striving for realism, the endeavour to let her model reflect circumstances and processes we know from the world around us, which so often arouses the reader's misgivings as to whether such circumstances and processes are at all compatible with the conditions of her model. It is when our author suddenly lowers the level of abstraction to enable her to "catch" an interesting feature she has observed, that the most embarrassing situations are likely to arise. Only too often the reader remembers well other occasions on which what must be regarded as at least equally important features of reality were left out, and had to be left out, because the model had no room for them.[5] This "selective" lowering of the level of abstraction becomes most awkward when our author has to deal with technical progress. A good deal of this section will therefore be concerned with the paradoxes which the introduction of this topic creates in Mrs. Robinson's model. But we shall first give a more general example.

Mrs. Robinson is much concerned with the *modus operandi* of what she calls capitalism. Again and again, we are told that "under the capitalist rules of the game" such and such will happen. The question whether these rules, and how many of them, are at all applicable to her model economy is, however, never asked. In reality the most important of these rules is surely that capital is invested where "net of risk" it promises to yield the highest return. But in an economy in which the stock of capital always has exactly the composition required to produce a given flow of composite output, the whole problem disappears. Malinvestment is abolished by definition. All investment yields the optimum return. The whole range of choices which in reality confront those who have to make investment decisions vanishes from sight. In what sense, then, can we still meaningfully speak of "the rules of the game" if we are actually confined to the choice between a very few moves? It would still be possible to play chess and obey "the rules of the game" even though each player is given, say, only a king, a queen and a bishop to play with. But most of these rules then become inoperative, for instance, all rules about the movements of knights and rooks. The reader of Mrs. Robinson's book is never warned that her rules of the game are a rather mutilated version of the real thing.

It is easy to see why the collision between realism and abstraction, latent in the whole of our author's technique of analysis, becomes most disturbing when she comes to grapple with technical progress. Homogeneity and progress are at bottom incompatible with each other. A progressive economy is an economy in which at each moment a number of experiments is being conducted with new products and new methods of producing old products. Even were all of these to succeed, their results would not be consistent with each other; at the very least relative opportunity costs would change. Mrs. Robinson later on admits as much. But even though some of these experiments will fail they are nevertheless indispensable elements of economic progress as they provide valuable knowledge, a kind of "negative know-how," to others. But they will also leave what our author calls "fossils" in the capital structure and thus affect the composition of the capital stock.

Nevertheless, if the same new methods of production were adopted by everybody at once there might not be much of a problem. But for Mrs. Robinson progress means the diffusion through competition of innovations introduced by entrepreneurs; her conception is here essentially Schumpeterian. The innovators at first make large profits, but sooner or later the imitators catch up with them, prices fall, real wages rise, and in the end the uniform rate of profit is restored. We are back in a golden age equilibrium.

Two problems arise. How can a capital stock of "appropriate

proportions" continue to exist during a period of technical innovation? And will the new equilibrium which will be reached at the end of the process of diffusion, when the innovation has gained universal acceptance, be independent of the events taking place during the period of transition?

As regards the first problem, Mrs. Robinson conceives of the change from one technique of production to another as a gradual process during which old equipment is being replaced by new equipment as it wears out. As long as this is so, the second problem does not arise as the duration of the process of transition is entirely determined by the age and durability of the existing equipment. During the transition, it is true, the rate of profit cannot be uniform. But competition is at work all the time, and if we confine ourselves to a comparison of equilibrium positions, viz. to a problem of comparative statics, it seems that we can keep the second problem at arm's length.

But our author has to admit that other forces will influence the transition process. "The speed at which new methods are diffused throughout the economy depends partly upon the physical life of capital goods," but where this is long it largely depends on the intensity of competition. The mechanism of competition "tends to grow weaker as the economy progresses, for the more vigorous is competition between entrepreneurs the more rapidly do the strong swallow up the weak, so that the number of separate sellers in each market tends to fall as time goes by." In other words, not all firms survive the transition process. What happens to the resources of those who do not survive it?

We are told that they may be forced to scrap their equipment before it has been fully amortized, a possibility which is of course inconsistent with the integrability condition. Another possibility, well known in industrial history, is that the strong "swallow up" the weak by taking them over as going concerns. But the strong are unlikely to make such "take-over bids" to the weak unless they see a possibility of using the resources of the latter in ways in which they have not been used hitherto. One of the things which will happen on our path of transition is that existing resources will be turned to different (more appropriate?) uses.

Technical progress does not mean merely the introduction and diffusion of new and better machines, it also means the more efficient use of existing resources. Even though we may ignore this possibility in our formal model we cannot keep it out of our description of the secondary processes of adjustment to change. Whatever may be the innovation with which we start, how golden the next golden age is going to be depends also on the changes in use of existing resources which are made on the path of transition from one equilibrium to the next.

In order to make a smooth transition plausible, from one technique to the next better technique, our author also has to assume that innovations come forward sufficiently slowly for the economy to have adapted itself completely to the first before the next begins to make its impact. Where this is not so, where innovations follow each other so fast that the economy never has time fully to digest one before the next appears, there never will be equilibrium. At each moment of time we shall find ourselves in the midst of a process of transition. When, then, do we return to the golden age? What happens to our moving equilibrium with its uniform rate of profit?

Mrs. Robinson's attempt to insert progress into her moving equilibrium model thus succeeds only where the speed of diffusion is very high and the speed with which innovations follow each other, i.e. the speed of progress itself, fairly low. The important case where different entrepreneurs attempt to improve their methods by experimenting in different directions without in the end all accepting the same new method, is of course excluded from the model, as are all cases of product differentiation. In the end it would appear that more features of progress as we know it are left out of the model than are included in it.

For Mrs. Robinson, as we saw, the stock of capital equals the sum of all investments. To measure capital means to add up the annual investments over the years. The integrability of these investments is the *sine qua non* of such capital measurement. But progress means that men acquire new knowledge. It is therefore inevitable that the capital goods existing at any moment in time will not provide a homogeneous structure. Some of them would not have been constructed at all had today's knowledge been available at the time of their construction. They are the "fossils" of an earlier age we mentioned above.

Our author's method of dealing with these, of safeguarding the continued maintenance of a homogeneous capital structure, is based on the assumption that these fossils will all be eliminated in the normal course of replacement, or even be scrapped earlier as soon as they cease to yield a return over prime costs, if competition is sufficiently fierce. But the latter possibility actually destroys the integrability of capital since it means that something that once was capital has ceased to be capital without being replaced. On the other hand, there are durable capital goods, like buildings, the productive capacity of which may be increased without replacing them, simply because men learn to utilise them more efficiently, for instance, by installing lifts. These capital resources can be made to fit into different capital structures reflecting different states of knowledge.

The parallelism between the growth of capital and output which underlies the constant capital-output ratio, a fundamental condition of the golden age, is therefore inconsistent with many manifestations of progress. Where capital has to be scrapped without being replaced, capital is being decumulated without being disinvested, yet in measuring today's capital such decumulation would have to be deducted from the current investment. On the other hand, more output now flows from the remaining capital resources.

But increased productive capacity of existing resources is also incompatible with a constant capital-output ratio. We may regard it as a "capital-saving innovation." Such capital-saving innovations, however, may not actually save much capital if the capital "saved" exists in such a specific form that it cannot be turned to other uses. Progress in the form of better utilisation of existing resources, so far from being capital saving, may actually increase the demand for capital by opening up new investment opportunities for complementary capital resources, for instance, an innovation may make it possible for more work-in-progress to be processed by the same plant. In all such cases capital gains and losses will be made which Mrs. Robinson, as a Ricardian, is forced to ignore, but which in reality often determine direction and magnitude of change and investment.

Mrs. Robinson who, with her usual candour, admits that we introduce a "patch of haziness into the analysis" whenever "the relation between the rate of investment in physical terms and in terms of value is highly variable," has carefully excluded all these possibilities by one of the special assumptions introduced when she deals with variations in the real-capital ratio in a "quasi-golden age" where accumulation takes place without inventions. Here she explicitly assumes that "the length of life of individual capital goods is short so that an individual entrepreneur can readily change his stock of capital goods from one form to another, without loss of value." But the very same problem arises wherever innovation makes existing specific capital redundant.

The conclusion seems inescapable that we face a dilemma here. We must either exclude all premature redundancy by assuming all capital to be sufficiently short-lived, that is, by extending the special assumption mentioned to *all* phases of a golden age, in which case a change of technique could hardly take the form of a process in time. It would then become clear that the model, revealing its true nature, works smoothly only where change is followed by instantaneous adjustment. Or, if in our model we wish to allow for such features of the world around us as durable equipment and time taken by processes of adjustment, we shall also have to allow for others. We then can, for instance, no longer regard the existing stock of capital (whatever that may mean) as the result of simple accumulation, hence the notion of a constant capital-output ratio becomes untenable. We also have to realise that investment opportunity is not independent of the efficiency with which existing resources are being utilised, and that new capital goods compete with some, and co-operate with other old resources.

When we have reached this insight it is not perhaps too difficult to understand why hardly any form of progress is compatible with the notion of a stock of capital which, whatever happens, invariably retains its "appropriate" composition.

5.

The distinguishing characteristic of the school of economics which flourished from 1871 to 1936 is the axiom that the ultimate causes of the economic processes we observe in reality have to be sought in the individual human minds, in choice and decision; and that economic phenomena are what they are because of the purposes pursued, the plans made and revised by millions of people in households and workshops. In this view, the quantities of the various goods produced and the prices paid for them are all compromise results reflecting the push and pull of these millions of decisions, of which there is of course no reason at all to believe *a priori* that they will be consistent with each other. It is only the continuous market process which gradually brings them into consistency as knowledge spreads throughout the market. The essence of the thought of this school of economics is the method by which we reduce objective market phenomena, like prices and quantities of goods, to the subjective preferences and expectations which give rise to them.

Every attempt to abandon this scheme of explanation has to find the causes of economic phenomena not in the multifarious variety of human minds, but in "something else." The classical economists, true to their eighteenth-century intellectual origins, found it in "natural forces," like the Malthusian Law or the diminishing fertility of the soil. These natural forces were the true determinants of all human phenomena. All economic action came to be regarded as merely a response to them. Since, moreover, it was a major classical tenet that all men respond to economic stimuli in a virtually identical fashion, the human mind and its acts (interpretation of experience, the making and carrying out of plans) could be ignored. It is well known that, for all its methodological crudity, the classical mode of thought proved remarkably successful in its time and day: it provided a unifying principle of explanation for a large body of experience.

But those who wish to return to the classical style of thought today are facing a peculiar dilemma. Since the demise of Malthusianism (at least in the West) and the rise of modern scientific technology, there are not many "natural forces" left to serve as the independent variables in the economic system. The most notable recent attempt in this direction, Keynes's "Psychological Law" of the declining marginal propensity to consume which, as we know, Mrs. Robinson rejects, has not been much of a success.

But Mrs. Robinson is not really a naturalist, the eighteenth century is not hers, and the attempt to dress in a rococo costume when discussing industrial progress in the twentieth century remains unconvincing. Confronted with the dilemma she falls back upon another classical device. The actors in her model are not real individuals but "ideal types" of economic agents with a restricted but predictable range of action. Thus "workers" and "entrepreneurs" become the protagonists of the drama, later to be joined by "rentiers" and "landlords." We are back in a Ricardian world in which the functional distribution of incomes between workers, capitalists and landlords is the main determinant of progress. This means a great simplification of the issues with which economists have to contend; since workers and entrepreneurs can act only in their collective capacities, we neither can nor need bother about all those cases in which different sections of each group move in different and often incompatible directions. The whole area of choice and decision-making in which some entrepreneurs show their mettle by being better than others at grasping what it is that the market wants from them, disappears from sight. If we think that the style of thought which freed us from the classical cliché of profit-maximising Economic Man and enabled us to explore the whole area of choice and decision, whatever the aim pursued, was a step forward, it is hard to avoid the conclusion that the reappearance of similar clichés in 1956 is a backward step.

It is interesting to observe that Mrs. Robinson, for all her devotion to the classical method, is on occasion unable to persevere in it. When she comes to grapple with the reality of progress she cannot but remember that some entrepreneurs are more progressive than others and that competition is sometimes more intense than at other times.

Would it be a very long step, one wonders, to the realization that all progress does not start with investment in new machinery, but often with thousands of entrepreneurs experimenting with, and in the process reshuffling, their existing capital combinations; or that in addition to the innovators and their imitators there are also those who try to go one better than those whose achievements they emulate, so that a new technique of production becomes modified and diversified in the very process of diffusion? How bold, then, would the next step be, viz. the realisation that the notion of a stock of capital which invariably has the "appropriate" composition required by circumstances, is an obstacle rather than a help to our understanding of the nature of economic progress?

NOTES

1. Joan Robinson, *The Accumulation of Capital* (London: Macmillan & Co., 1956).
2. The whole Keynesian edifice rests on the possibility that capital can be measured; Keynesian investment is net investment, Keynesian income is net income.
3. On the numerous ambiguities surrounding the meaning of productive capacity, see now G. Warren Nutter, "On Measuring Economic Growth," *Journal of Political Economy* 65 (February 1957):51–63.
4. The effect of changes in the rate of interest has therefore to be treated as negligible, see p. 144 n2.
5. Against what we have said it is no defense to claim that every author must be free to choose his own level of abstraction. Quite so, but once he has chosen it he must adhere to it. It is quite legitimate to abstract from any class of facts, but it is illegitimate, once such a class has been admitted into the model, to make an arbitrary selection between the members of the class.

Sir John Hicks on Capital and Growth

(Review Article)

1.

For thirty years or so the appearance of a new book by Sir John Hicks has been an event eagerly looked forward to by the *cognoscenti*. The title *Capital and Growth*[1] combines two subjects of peculiar interest today. The theory of Capital, after several decades of neglect, in which only investment, but not changes in the stock itself, had interested economists, has of late come into its own again. But this renaissance of the theory of capital is also closely connected with the other subject: economic growth can hardly be described, and certainly not explained, without reference to the composition of the capital stock as a whole.

In recent years the literature on Growth has grown to such an enormous size that a survey, or at least a guide for the baffled readers of economic journals, has become an urgent need. Professor Hicks is not the only one who has endeavoured to supply it.[2] But there are certain reasons why his proved talents seem particularly suited to this task. For many years his success in setting economic ideas in historical perspective, and in blending his own analysis with the writing of the history of ideas, has impressed his readers. Never content merely to present his own thought, he has shown an ability (alas, only too rare among contemporary economists) to set it out in a perspective in which various, apparently disconnected, aspects of known ideas, suddenly acquire new meaning and become related to one another in unsuspected ways.

Reprinted from *South African Journal of Economics* 34 (June 1966).

It is noteworthy that our author must be the only prominent British economist who grew up in the 1920s, but was not brought up in the Marshallian household. A Paretian and Wicksellian, rather than a Marshallian,[3] he displayed a certain aloofness towards the "Keynesian Revolution,"[4] a fact which permitted him to see in Keynesian theory a variant of, rather than a contradiction to, the neo-classical tenets. Starting from a fundamentally neo-classical point of view, he has been able to absorb successive waves of thought, first Keynes, then Harrod-Domar, later on Linear Theory, and to master them all with remarkable success and alacrity.

In this way he has become a prominent mediator between different strands of thought, a broker of ideas whose influence has been far greater than is often realised today. In this role he has been much helped by another Hicksian characteristic, viz. a sturdy sense of realism, an aversion to those "heroic" assumptions which may simplify analysis but will not pass muster before a critical eye. To be sure, he builds his models, and does so with skill and evident relish, but he usually manages to keep them down to earth. In this book his insistence on the heterogeneity of capital is a good case in point.

2.

The book consists of four parts of which the first two are concerned with the theory of growth as such, while the third is devoted to "Optimum Growth," the Welfare Economics of the subject, and the fourth to the implications of growth theory for other parts of economic analysis. It ends with five Mathematical Appendices.

The first part, "Methods of Dynamic Economics," at a superficial glance looks like a historical background to the Hicksian Growth Equilibrium model set out in Part II, a brief summary of growth theory from Adam Smith to Sir Roy Harrod. But, as is so often the case with Hicksian prose, the first impression turns out to be deceptive. The eleven chapters of the first part, which comprise almost half of the text without appendices, are a veritable seed-bed of ideas. With almost incredible terseness the author sets forth his main points on dynamic theory, drawing frequently on the history of economic thought for illustrations, but also often interspersing the historical chapters with analytical matter which is then brought to bear on features of contemporary reality.

At the end of the first chapter, after paying tribute to Cassel as the much neglected originator of the idea of steady growth, the author warns us "Growth Theory . . . is no more than a particular method of Dynamic Economics. It is not claimed (it ought not to be claimed) that it is *the* method—that there do not remain many dynamic problems to which some other approach would be more relevant. It may indeed be questioned whether it is 'dynamic' enough." (14) On the other hand, "In statics, equilibrium is fundamental; in dynamics, as we shall find, we cannot do without it; but even in statics it is treacherous, and in dynamics, unless we are very careful, it will trip us up completely." (15)

Chapter II, "The Concept of Equilibrium," contains the important distinction between equilibrium at a point of time and equilibrium over a period of time. (24) The former is thus defined: "The system is in equilibrium in this sense, if 'individuals' are reaching a preferred position, with respect to their expectations, as they are at that point." The latter equilibrium presupposes the existence of the former equilibrium at every point of time within the period. "But for period equilibrium there is the additional condition that these expectations must be consistent with one another and with what actually happens within the period." But consistent expectations are not the only requirement of Growth Equilibrium.

There is another requirement the need for which we realise as soon as we abandon the assumption of the homogeneity of our capital stock. "An equilibrium path . . . is a path that will (and can) be followed if expectations are appropriate to it, and if the initial capital stock is appropriate to it; both conditions are necessary." (116)

In a sense, this sentence contains the basis of all subsequent Growth Equilibrium analysis in the book. Our author insists that, whatever may be legitimate in statics, in dynamic theory we must give up the notion of a homogeneous capital stock. "It is the big thing that was wrong with classical theory. If there is just one homogeneous 'capital,' there is nothing to do with our savings but to invest them in this 'capital'; there can be no problem of malinvestment—or of savings going to waste." (35) The problem of the appropriate composition of the capital stock is thus shown to be one of the fundamental problems of all dynamic theory, whether of the growth equilibrium variety or otherwise. But the reader who had hoped that the causes and consequences of malinvestment in a world of uncertainty and divergent expectations would now be explored, is sadly disappointed. Except for the last chapter, in which Professor Hicks shows that technical progress will cause capital losses on specific resources, this remains the only time that malinvestment is mentioned in the book!

Two other matters of great significance are dealt with in the first part of the book. As others have done before him, Professor Hicks finds it necessary to stress, in his chapter on Marshall's method, that our world differs from that which Marshall took for granted in that we live in a world of prices "administered" by manufacturers, "but in those days even manufactured goods usually passed along a chain of wholesalers and retailers, each of whom was likely to have some independent price-making opportunity." (55) Again, like others before him, our author attributes the cause of this change to the virtual disappearance of the wholesale merchant and his price-setting function after 1900.[5] Formerly "the initiative would come from the wholesaler or shopkeeper, who would offer higher prices in order to get the goods which, even at the higher price, he could re-sell at a profit. Similarly, when demand fell, it would be the wholesaler who would offer a lower price. The manufacturer would have to accept that price if he could get no better." (56) Hence, while Marshall's was a world of flexible prices, even though not of "perfect competition," ours is a "fixprice world" with prices set on a "cost plus" basis and wage rates as ultimate price determinants.

The analytical significance of this historical change lies, on the one hand, in the fact that the "Temporary Equilibrium Method" which Hicks himself, following Lindahl, used in *Value and Capital* in 1939, has lost much of its validity. "The fundamental weakness of the Temporary Equilibrium method is the assumption, which it is obliged to make, that the market is in equilibrium—actual demand equals desired demand, actual supply equals desired supply—even in the *very* short period." (76) Hence we have to look for another method of dynamic analysis. To find it we must move nearer to Keynes and his successors who are here given credit for having understood, earlier than others, that a fixprice world requires a fixprice method of analysis. Here the reader cannot help wondering why, if we are to choose our method by the criterion of realism, we should have any reason to prefer Growth Equilibrium to Sir John's erstwhile favourite of 1939. We shall return to this point at the end of our penultimate section.

In Chapters IX and X we find another significant change of a Hicksian tenet: Sir John explicitly revokes not merely the Acceleration principle, but any "Stock Adjustment principle" for which universal validity is claimed. The revocation is announced, it is true, in almost an undertone. "It is hardly a discovery to find that we are unable to "simulate" the behaviour of intelligent business management by any simple rules." (102) But he adds significantly: "If we find—as we do find—that mechanical principles of adjustment do not offer a good representation, we shall have gained something in the way of scepticism about the use of such principles in more ambitious undertakings. And this . . . will be quite useful to us later on." It is possible to feel, however, that in putting this scepticism to work on some of the more esoteric growth models Sir John is practising the same excessive modesty as when announcing his recantation *sotto voce*.

3.

In Part II our author presents his own growth model. It is of the familiar 2-sector variety and, since constant returns to scale are assumed, relative prices are determined by cost of production. The wage level is "given" and the rate of profit thus determined as a residual. The rate of growth depends on the savings rate and the supply of labour. What happens if, in the Harrodian manner, "natural" and "warranted" growth rates diverge? It is shown that the ability of the system to adjust itself to such changes via price changes depends on the existence of a difference between the capital-labour ratios in the two sectors. In the following three chapters the author shows that these results are not seriously affected if we allow for a multiplicity of *known* techniques and of capital goods. But we are warned that technical progress is incompatible with a given growth path. "I insist that any particular growth equilibrium path is an equilibrium *with respect to a given technology;* changes in technology . . . must imply a shift from one equilibrium growth path to another." (171)

Chapter XVI, "Traverse," is perhaps the most interesting in the book, as here the notion of Growth Equilibrium is put to its crucial test. We shall return to some of the fundamental problems raised in it in our next section. It opens on a cheerful note which soon proves deceptive. "Now at last we begin to emerge from Growth Equilibrium . . . . It has been fertile in the generation of class-room exercises; but so far as we can yet see, they are exercises, not real problems . . . . They are not even hypothetical real problems . . . . They are shadows of real problems, dressed up in such a way that by pure logic we can find solutions for them." (183) Nevertheless there follow several pages of formal analysis in which the conditions of a successful Traverse are examined. Suddenly we are told, "Our analysis of the Traverse, in the one-capital-case, is no more than a bogy . . . it is quite misleading. An actual economy—any actual economy—does not, indeed cannot, work just like that." (190)

It appears that price flexibility is a major condition of a successful Traverse. "An economy which insists upon making its transitions on a Fixprice basis is doing so with 'one hand tied behind its back'." (196) But then there arises the question how, in the transition from old to new equilibrium path, the *right* new price system is to be found. This "cannot be an easy matter," yet on it the success of the whole Traverse depends, since choice of technique and appropriate composition of the capital stock depend on relative prices. At the end of the chapter we find our author throwing up his hands in despair: "In an actual economic situation, all these problems arise at once, while (because of the advance in technology) the equilibrium at which the economy is aiming is continually shifting. No wonder that there is a problem of business management!" (197)

In Part III, "Optimum Growth," Sir John turns with an audible sigh of relief from Positive to Welfare Economics, from the market place to the Turnpike. "The central problem of dynamic Optimum theory is the planning problem. Given an initial endowment of capital, embodied in particular capital goods . . . what is the plan of production, in present and future, which will enable some given aim to be reached in the most efficient manner?" (203) But to maximize the rate of growth over a period may mean either of two things: we may either try to maximize the flow of consumable outputs during it, or maximize the size of the terminal capital stock. The Turnpike Theory, which is considered first, "is concerned with an optimization problem of the second type." In Chapter XVIII the famous Neumann model which seeks to establish the conditions of continuous optimum growth (without consumption!) is set out in lucid language. In the next our author turns to the Turnpike Theorem itself. The problem here is: What is the optimum path to be followed by an economy which starts with a capital stock which is not appropriate to the balanced growth Neumann path; in what circumstances would it be better to discard the surplus parts of the stock for the sake of obtaining a balanced composition? Professor Hicks shows that it is largely a matter of time. Only over long periods would the advantages of balanced growth necessarily outweigh the capital losses from discarding surplus capital.

In the next three chapters he turns to the alternative type of Optimum theory which is concerned with a stream of consumption outputs. The argument here follows the line familiar from the second part of *Value and Capital*. With a given rate of interest, constant over time, there is an "intertemporal production frontier" in the sense that there is a limit to the substitution of future for present outputs. This frontier determines the optimum shape of the consumption output stream. At the end of Part III the author criticises Mr. Kaldor's Technical Progress function on the grounds that, to a large extent, technical progress stems from non-economic causes, such as scientific discovery. He therefore rejects a model "which would bring too much of the phenomenon into the strait-jacket of its 'equilibrium.' " (276)

The last part contains what apparently are Hicksian afterthoughts on matters of contemporary interest. In Chapter XXIII money is introduced and liquidity preference comes up for review. An extension of the concept of stock equilibrium to assets in general enables us to "generalize the conception of demand for money, and assert its equilibrium in the form of saying that the whole system of debits and credits must be in equilibrium." (281) In Keynes's theory "the rate of interest on long-term bonds is taken to stand for the whole gamut of rates and yields, on securities of all kinds, that are established on the market. As soon as one begins to ask questions about the structure of these rates, it becomes apparent that the choice between money and bonds is only one of the many possible choices between forms of asset-holding into which similar considerations of liquidity enter." (283) From these considerations the following picture emerges: "There is a maximum to all rates of interest, set by the expected rate of return on real investment (I simplify by the assumption that there is just one rate of return); there is a minimum set by the rate of interest *paid by* the bank. . . . All other rates of interest (those paid by firms to savers, and those paid by firms to the bank) must lie, in equilibrium, between these limits. Where they will lie will be determined by a balance of liquidity considerations in the balance-sheets of lenders and borrowers respectively." (286) Within this gap there is a place for financial intermediaries. "The financial intermediary can prosper if it can make use of specialized knowledge about the prospects of particular kinds of real investment; so that it can make advances to firms . . . which the bank would not know were sound investments; and if it can acquire resources which enable it to make these financial investments at a less loss of liquidity than they would entail upon the private saver." But while such action will reduce the gap, it can never close it altogether, a fact which has certain obvious implications for monetary policy in a Radcliffian world.

In the last chapter, "The Production Function," Professor Hicks examines Mrs. Robinson's famous criticism of this elusive notion.[6] Here at last technical progress is introduced, though it occurs discontinuously. "There are inventions (let us say) in 1900, 1910, 1920; in 1909 and 1919 the economy has settled into a *stationary state*." (295)

Technical progress requires a transmutation of the capital stock. "Can one treat the supply of capital as fixed, when capital has been transmuted according to our particular rule? The answer is that one can." (297) In fact "so long as we are only concerned with the comparison of equilibrium positions, the production function (or *a* production function) gets through." (298) But our mentor adds significantly: "How much use it is, when it has to be put into this sophisticated form, may indeed be questioned." He then admits "that the rate of profit on new investment is raised, while the profit that is earned on past investment may be lowered." (301) In other words, technical progress entails capital losses on specific resources.

This is certainly a matter of great importance. It is to be regretted that it is only mentioned in the concluding pages of the book. After all, technical progress is not the only cause of capital losses and gains. Any disappointment of expectations concerning the use of specific resources has the same effect. Why, the reader cannot help asking himself, did not Sir John tell us that before? Would it not have been useful, at least on the Traverse, to know that the transmutation of the capital stock will be affected by such losses and gains? Should we not also have been told that, together with the classical notion of a homogeneous capital stock, we must abandon the corresponding notion of *the* uniform rate of profit?

4.

We return to the Traverse. Chapter XVI is, in a sense, the pivot of the book. It is here that we have to decide whether the notion of Growth Equilibrium is a tenable conception. The problem is posed early on in the chapter: "But let us now suppose that the Harrod difficulty has been got over: that a suitable change in the overall propensity to save, for whatever reason, has occurred—will that be the end of the trouble?" (185) Our author has told us as early as on page 17 that, if the equilibrium assumption is to be justified, we must be able to assert the existence of a tendency to equilibrium, and that it must be a strong tendency. Can we assert this for the Traverse from an old growth path to a new?

The problem of the Traverse consists essentially in the need for a time interval to elapse before the new equilibrium path is reached, because the transmutation of the capital stock, the change of its mode of composition from that appropriate to the old to that appropriate to the new conditions, takes time. But if any of our conditions of equilibrium, which include expectations and wealth distribution, changes during the interval, the final equilibrium will be modified. This is an old and familiar problem which Edgeworth and Walras saw clearly and, within their stationary framework, attempted to solve by means of "recontract." Sir John spurns these "artificial arrangements." (54) But how does he tackle the problem?

Recontract is out of the question and a suspension of all business dealings during the Traverse hardly feasible. The transmutation of the stock obviously requires firm commitments. We are thus driven to the conclusion that, so far from being able to assert a tendency to it, we do not even know what the new equilibrium will be like until we get there—if ever we do. Nor are we entitled to speak of a transmutation of the stock since we are unable to specify the *terminus ad quem* beforehand. To speak of an "adjustment to new conditions" is positively misleading when we do not know what they are.

How does our author avoid these conclusions? He tells us that, when prices have to change, "a corresponding *Fixprice* policy would presumably imply that prices are adapted at once (or sought to be adapted at once) to the new equilibrium." (196) Nothing is said here about what would happen with flexible prices, but here, too, the system would evidently have to adapt itself to the new set of equilibrium prices *at once,* if malinvestment and the adoption of disequilibrium techniques are to be avoided. But this could only happen by a miracle and hardly permits us to assert a strong tendency to equilibrium.

What lessons are we to draw from this disconcerting experience?

In the first place, we must realise that our discomfiture is due to a misguided attempt to use the equilibrium concept in fields far away from its natural habitat. With the household and the firm equilibrium makes very good sense as here it is something actually aimed at. Interindividual equilibrium already raises issues concerning mutual knowledge which have never been properly appreciated or fully discussed. But in the Marshallian type of commodity market with flexible prices it still has a clear meaning. To extend the concept to the economic system as a whole was a bold venture, but Walras and Pareto showed that, *in a stationary state,* it could still be done. But to extend it even further, to an economic system in motion, would appear to lie beyond the range of the feasible.

Secondly, therefore, we must consider the possibility of a retreat to a more congenial terrain. Two positions can now be seen to have become untenable.

On the one hand, once we acknowledge, with our author, the inadequacy of all mechanical rules about human reaction to change, we also have to acknowledge the autonomy of expectations at every point of time, because this autonomy is the true cause of that inadequacy. But with this all possibility of an equilibrium over time, based upon convergent expectations, vanishes. For real expectations always diverge. This simple fact appears to destroy the, even theoretical, possibility of a determinable time path of economic processes. All this, however, does not invalidate the possibility of equilibrium at a point of time, an equilibrium in which each price reflects a balance of contemporary expectations.

On the other hand, there can be no such thing as a dynamic macro-economic equilibrium. For outside the stationary state there is, in general, owing to the ubiquity of "lags," no market mechanism to bring the divergent expectations of all individuals within the same economic system into simultaneous consistency with each other. Nor is there any reason why the quantities of the various capital goods held in different sectors should necessarily be such as to earn their owners an actual, let alone expected, uniform rate of profit.

We are thus forced back to a micro-economic version of the Temporary Economic Equilibrium at which Professor Hicks and Lindahl tried their hands in 1939. We have to assume *a* market, an intemporal market which of course permits of forward transactions, on which individuals express their expectations, with a resulting equilibrium price reflecting a balance of such expectations.

This may seem a poor "optimum" for equilibrium analysis. But we may draw some comfort from at least two qualifications (there may be more) which we may permit ourselves to make to the rule about the necessary micro-economic character of our markets.

In the first place, there is, in a market economy, a Stock Exchange, a market for future yield streams, in which expectations are brought into consistency every day and a price reflecting the balance of such expectations is struck. And since the Stock Exchange is also, in every reasonably developed economy, the central market for existing capital goods, or titles to them, we can say that expectations pertaining to the whole economy are here coordinated without a necessary lag. In fact, if the classical notion of a uniform rate of profit, the corollary of the assumption of capital homogeneity, is to retain any significance at all in the real world, it is only on the Stock Exchange, where a uniform rate of yield is produced every day by the price changes of existing assets, that we can really speak of it.

Secondly, once we recognise, with our author, the

heterogeneity of all capital, we must also recognise that existing capital combinations have to be dissolved from time to time, as expectations change. Existing capital combinations will thus have to be "re-shuffled," at intervals which may, but need not, coincide with those between our "market days," by the discarding of some and the purchase of other existing capital goods, such as buildings, equipment, ships, etc. This secondhand market for certain kinds of capital goods provides another link between various sectors of the economy. But here of course there will be lags.

Lastly, we should remember that equilibrium analysis, and indeed all formal analysis couched in terms of functional relationships, is neither the beginning nor the end of economic theory. When confronted with a disequilibrium situation, we certainly have to assume that each individual seeks to attain a (flow and stock) equilibrium. But these individual equilibria may not be compatible with one another and therefore be unattainable. Economists will have to learn to live with, and give an intelligible account of, circumstances which have no determinate outcome.

5.

In the opening section of this review article we described Sir John Hicks as a great mediator of economic thought, a most successful broker of ideas. In reality of course there is no broker, however successful he may be, to whom it does not happen, from time to time, that a deal falls through. Similarly, we find at least one conflict inherent in modern economic thought which our mediator has been unable to appease. We shall hardly be surprised that it first comes to our notice in the historical chapters of the first part, and even less that it fully comes to the surface in Chapter XVI. The question at issue is that of the compatibility of subjective attitudes (tastes, expectations) with the requirements of modern formal analysis in the shape of models. The elements of our models, parameters and variables, must be, at least in principle, objective and measurable entities. But are subjective attitudes?

This problem has existed, in one form or another, at least since the "marginal revolution" of the 1870s in which human preferences were acknowledged to be the ultimate basis on which the economic edifice rests. To trace it in the work of the major neo-classical writers would be a fascinating task. All we can do here is to make a few comments on the way in which it affects the present work.

Quantifiability is not, as has often been thought, the root of the matter. The outcome of the long discussion on cardinal versus ordinal utility showed that tastes qualify for inclusion in our models provided they can be *ordered;* it is unnecessary for them to be quantifiable in any cardinal sense. There seems to be no reason why the same should not apply to expectations.

The root of the matter is the autonomy of the human mind: men can and will change their tastes and expectations for no objectively ascertainable reason. Pareto saw this problem, as he saw so many others, far more clearly than most of his contemporaries. He insisted that the individual, having once recorded his preferences for us, "having left us this photograph of his tastes," as he put it, must disappear from the analytical scene and worry us no further with the unpredictable acts of his mind.[7] Whether he realised equally clearly that, by making this postulate, he also limited the validity of his whole system to the conditions of a stationary state, in which alone today's photographs will still be valid tomorrow, it is hard to say. But we may safely assume that he would have been willing to pay that price.

But around 1930, just about the time when our author joined the staff of the London School of Economics, expectations arrived on the scene. And expectations, since in a stationary state they are in any case without significance, cannot be disposed of in the Paretian fashion. The assumption of their continuous convergence, made in all the familiar growth models, is simply an attempt to sterilize them, as Professor Hicks sees clearly.

While constant tastes over a period of time are at least conceivable, expectations cannot remain constant as soon as they diverge, since some of them must turn out to be wrong sooner or later, hence be revised, though we can say very little about the mode of their revision. While therefore expectations cannot be constants, we must not treat them as variables either. They are clearly not dependent variables as they do not "depend" on any observable events. But if we try to treat them as "exogenous" data, we soon find that they will "take over" and "swallow up" most of our other data. This is the real lesson of the story of the Traverse. Divergent expectations, prompting transactions at non-equilibrium prices, will themselves affect the composition of the capital stock as well as the interindividual distribution of resources.

We must therefore conclude that expectations, and other subjective elements, constitute an alien body within the organism of formal model analysis. The conflict remains unresolved. Marshall was uneasily aware of it. Pareto saw it, drew his sword and cut the Gordian knot, but, alas, knew nothing of expectations. Our mediator, for once, has been unable to mediate in a conflict of the existence of which he is clearly aware. This of course is hardly his fault. Sir John Hicks has failed to do what cannot be done. It remains a tribute to the qualities of this remarkable book that for one brief moment, in Chapter XVI, a reader could bring himself to imagine that he might do it.

NOTES

1. John Hicks, *Capital and Growth* (Oxford: Clarendon Press, 1965).
2. See, e.g., F. H. Hahn and R. C. O. Matthews, "The Theory of Economic Growth: A Survey," *Economic Journal* 74 (December 1964): 799–902.
3. "We were such 'good Europeans' in London that it was Cambridge that seemed 'foreign.'" Hicks, *The Theory of Wages*, 2d ed. (London: Macmillan & Co., 1963), p. 306.
4. It is true that in the autobiographical sketch added to the 2d edition of *Theory of Wages* (1963) he says that in 1936 "I was (I think I may say) an almost whole-hearted Keynesian." (310)
Perhaps we should not take the author of the famous "bootstraps" argument at his word. Perhaps, as often happens, the enthusiasm of 1936 soon turned into the skepticism of 1939.
5. Cf. L. M. Lachmann, *Capital and Its Structure* (London: London School of Economics and Political Science, 1956), p. 64.

6. Joan Robinson, "The Production Function and the Theory of Capital," *Review of Economic Studies* 21 (1953–4): 81–106.

7. "L'individu peut disparaître pourvu qu'il nous laisse cette photographie de ses goûts." V. Pareto, *Manuel d'Economie Politique*, 2d ed. (Paris, 1927), p. 170.

Sir John Hicks as a Neo-Austrian

(Review Article)

1.

In the opening passage of the Preface of his latest book[1] Sir John Hicks tells us about the place it holds in his work on capital theory. "This is the third book I have written about Capital: *Value and Capital* (1939); *Capital and Growth* (1965); *Capital and Time* (1973). They were not planned as a trilogy. I had no idea, when I finished the first, that I would write the second.... Nor do the later volumes supersede the earlier, save in a few quite limited respects.... It is just as if one were making pictures of a building; though it is the same building, it looks quite different from different angles. As I now realize, I have been walking round my subject, taking different views of it. Though that which is presented here is just another view, it turns out to be quite useful in fitting the others together."

This is certainly true. We notice, e.g., that Part II of the new book, its central part, has the same heading, "Traverse," as had chapter XVI of *Capital and Growth*. In fact, what we now find here, in chapters VII to XII, is a careful restatement and elaboration, much qualified but also more sharp edged, of the earlier argument.

The real significance of the new book, however, lies elsewhere. It is impossible to describe its character adequately by indicating its place within the Hicksian *oeuvre*. It also has a place, which may turn out to be an important place, in the context of the present crisis in economic thought.

Reprinted from *South African Journal of Economics* 41 (September 1973): 195-207.

251

Value and Capital (1939) belongs to the epoch of neoclassical ascendancy of which our author was such a protagonist and during the struggle for which he won fame. *Capital and Growth* (1965) belongs to a period of neoclassical "expansionism" when the concept of general equilibrium was to be extended from the stationary state to economic growth. Our author then weighed up and critically surveyed various methods that might be employed to this end.

Today neoclassical economics is very much on the defensive. It is under fire from many sides. When Mr. Sraffa in 1960 gave his famous book the subtitle *Prelude to a Critique of Economic Theory,* few of his readers can have had a clear conception of the direction the critique might take. The end of the 1950s found neoclassical economics still powerfully entrenched. If, in 1973, Professor Shackle adds to the title of his book *Epistemics and Economics* the subtitle *A critique of economic doctrines,*[2] the reader cannot but realize that what is challenged in the plural is no longer a single predominant doctrine. Moreover, the challenge is issued in circumstances in which our certainties are few and the future of economic theory is by no means assured.

In this situation Sir John Hicks is taking command of the neoclassical forces already in some disarray. With the cool and dispassionate air of the veteran soldier he decides which positions are to be given up, and which must be defended at all costs. His strategy is the defence of the central neoclassical notion of general equilibrium, and in particular its modern extension, "steady growth." He tries to show that, on assumptions most of us would regard as reasonable, there are strong forces impelling the system towards a new steady growth path whenever a former growth equilibrium has been disturbed by technological change, and that some plausible generalizations can be established about the forms such *"Traverse"* might take. Growth equilibrium makes sense because the equilibrating forces are likely to be strong enough to prevail. Our author calls his approach *"A Neo-Austrian Theory."* As in Böhm-Bawerk, the production and use of capital goods are given a time dimension. The main difference, according to him, lies in the fact that Böhm-Bawerk used a model in which a flow of inputs produces a "point output," while his is a "flow input-flow output" model.

In a note to Chapter I he rightly points out that "the concept of production as a process in time" is nothing peculiarly "Austrian." "It is just the same concept as underlies the work of the British classical economists, and it is indeed older still." A poignant example from Boccacio's *Decameron* is given. Certainly Böhm-Bawerk was a Ricardian capital theorist who asked questions about the causes and magnitude of interest Ricardo had been unable to answer. "What Böhm-Bawerk did was to take the classical concept of capital, and to marry it with the theory of individual choice which he got from Menger" (p. 13). This is only partly true since Menger did not like Böhm-Bawerk's interest theory at all.[3] The question arises whether this neo-Austrian theory is not altogether too "classical" to be characteristically "Austrian." To his question, by no means of interest only to historians of thought, we shall return in the concluding section.

At the end of the note mentioned the Cambridge "post-Keynesians," today perhaps the best known, but by no means the only, opponents of neoclassical orthodoxy, receive actual praise. "It is the post-Keynesians who would better be called neoclassics; for it is they who, to their honour, have wrought a Classical Revival." But for all this Hicksian courtesy their arguments fare no better. We are reminded that, e.g., the Wage Fund, to which our author ascribes great importance, was also a Ricardian idea (pp. 58–62).

With so many labels lying scattered all over the floor of our wine cellar no wonder it is hard to know which one to stick on to the vintage Sir John is offering us here.

2.

The method of analysis employed in the book is described as *sequential analysis*. We are concerned with what happens in a sequence of "weeks." "The one-week relations . . . determine the course of the model in week *T*, when everything that has happened before week *T* is taken as given. Having determined the course in week T, we can then proceed to week $T + I$, applying similar relations, but with the performance of week T now forming part of the past" (p. 63). The method bears some resemblance to, but is not identical with, the kind of sequence analysis Lindahl[4] and Professor Lundberg[5] propounded in the 1930s as an alternative to short-run equilibrium analysis. An important difference is that in the Hicksian model the labour and capital market are the only markets. "All 'original' inputs are taken to be homogeneous, and all final outputs homogeneous; so there is just one non-intertemporal price, the input-output price-ratio" (p. 37). As with Böhm-Bawerk, we are in a one-commodity world. This sequential analysis is used to trace the effects of a technological change on the production system through time. As distinct from the Walrasian model, the effects of change are here not instantaneous but lagged. From our knowledge of the sequence of stages of production we can determine how long it will take such effects to permeate our system. Since technical change is mainly "embodied," the coexistence of old and new processes and gradual replacement of the former by the latter provide the time dimension of change. In a "steady state" all processes are of the same kind. A productive process is defined "as a scheme by which a flow of inputs is converted into a flow of outputs" (p. 14). We have to think of it as essentially a sequence of stages of production (coal, iron, steel, machinery, cutlery), but have to remember that there is only one "output good." Therefore in a "steady state" only one process is in operation.

In Part I, *Model*, the analytical tools are displayed, some of them already known to us. In Chapter II we have a *Fundamental Theorem:* "It is always true that a fall in the rate of interest will raise the capital value curve of any process—will raise it throughout—while a rise in the rate of interest will lower it" (p. 19). In the next chapter we are told "the fact that a process is in use does not imply that it would now be profitable to start it. When it was started, it appeared to be profitable, but conditions have changed. Either because of new invention, or because of changes in prices, its profitability has gone; so the starting of new processes of that kind would no longer be payable. It may nevertheless be profitable to carry on the remainder of such a process" (p. 32). How, we wonder, do prices change in a one-commodity world?

Chapter IV, "Technique and Technology," contains a discussion of the "Re-switching" problem. Like everyone else, Sir John admits the possibility of re-switching, of a fall in the rate of interest leading to a substitution of labour for capital instead of the other way around, "but it looks like being on the edge of the things that could happen" (p. 44). He notes that the re-switching possibility impairs the "lengthening of the period of production" of "the older Austrians" as much as the neoclassical substitution of capital for labour. "Both are special cases, in which the differences between techniques are reduced to differences in a single parameter. Neither, in general, is admissible" (p. 45).

In the next chapter, V, two important analytical tools are presented. We are reminded "that steady state theory . . . divides into these two branches. There is (1) the *Fixwage* theory, as I shall call it, in which *w* (the *real* wage) is given but employment is variable, and (2) the *Full Employment* theory, where there is full employment of a labour supply the movement of which is given exogenously" (p. 48).

In the former, with an elastic supply of labour, the limit of activity is set by savings. We thus have Full Performance as a counterpart to Full Employment. "We can nevertheless accept that an economy may run at less than Full Performance; and if confidence is insufficient, that is what it will do" (p. 52). We are warned "that Full Performance has nothing to do with the monetary system . . . . Money is not the cause of fluctuations; it is a complication, but no more than that" (p. 55).

Secondly, in this chapter the assumption of "static expectations" is adopted "since it probably throws as much light on actual processes of development as we can expect to get from our general approach" (p. 56). To this important assumption we shall have to return later on.

Thirdly, we have the distinction between *major* and *minor switches*. "A major switch is one that can only be made at the start of a process; but a minor switch can be made to a process that has already been started" (p. 61). We have to remember here that, since labour is our only input, all such switches refer to the amount of labour per unit of output within a process. Our author makes it clear that his "minor switches" are more or less the kind of supply adjustments permissible within Marshall's short period. There appears to be no place here for the reshuffling of existing capital combinations in response to unexpected change.

The chapter ends with a defence of the Wage Fund theory likely to give little satisfaction either in Cambridge or at M.I.T. Professor Kaldor's well-known views on wages are said, "more or less surreptitiously," to imply a resuscitation of classical Wage Fund theory. "It should never have been supposed that the Wage Fund (however carefully qualified) was a *complete* theory of wages; it does no more, at the best, than explain how the wage is determined in the current 'week,' the past course of the economy being given. It is a very short-run theory; it needs to be completed by the consideration of longer-run effects. Our method of dealing with longer-run effects will be developed . . . we shall try to exhibit them *sequentially*" (p. 60).

Mill is criticised for having abandoned this classical doctrine. "The article, in which the recantation occurs, is not one of Mill's better economic writings; one suspects that by 1868 he was much less interested in economics than he had been as a younger man" (p. 59).

3.

The problem of Part II (Chapters VII–XII) is the Traverse. "It is the determination of the path of our model economy (the Full Performance or maintainable path) when the economy is not in a steady state. Such a path must have a definite time-reference; for, out of the steady state, one point of time is not like another. In particular, it must have a beginning" (p. 81). Somewhat apologetically our author tells us he "would like to assume that this initial state is itself a mixed state, itself the result of a transition which is still incomplete; but a state of that sort we do not yet understand" (ibid).

Thus we have to start in a steady state, "and should proceed to trace out a path which will be followed when the steady state is subjected to some kind of disturbance . . . . We begin with an economy which is in a steady state, under an 'old' technique; then, at time *O*, there is an 'invention,' the introduction of . . . a new technology" (ibid). The new technology is embodied in new processes. Gradually, as these become completed and old processes disappear, the system adjusts itself to the change. While this process is under way our system can, of course, not be in a steady state since its capital stock does not have the composition requisite to either the old or the new equilibrium. We confront a "sequence, involving changes in wages and interest, in production and employment, which we have to work out. . . . It cannot be taken for granted that the sequence generated in this matter, will tend to a new equilibrium. It may or it may not" (p. 82).

To be assured of the completion of the Traverse, of the attainment of a new equilibrium growth path, we have to make a number of special assumptions one of which is that the relative periods of construction and utilization of our capital goods are not affected by the new technology. This is called the Standard Case.

It is then seen that the Fixwage Path (Ch. VIII) presents the simplest case. Here there is only one switch from the old to the new technology which then remains "dominant throughout the Traverse." All the benefits of progress accrue as profits (by assumption not to be consumed) and result in more investment and growth. When the new technology has been completely absorbed, wages rise in one jerk, the growth rate declines and we continue our journey on the new steady state level. Even here, however, the replacement of labour by better machines may cause temporary unemployment soon to be absorbed by increased accumulation. We are of course reminded that this is the problem of Ricardo's Chapter 31 "On Machinery."

Sir John is able to draw a practical lesson, perhaps of some relevance to African countries today: "To industrialize, without the savings to support your industrialization, is to ask for trouble. That is a principle which practical economists have learned from experience. It deserves a place, a regular place, in academic economics also" (p. 99).

As soon as we allow for wage flexibility, however, the problem of expectations naturally raises its head. Here "the choice should in general depend on expected wages as well as on current wages" (p. 110). But our author brushes it firmly aside: "I shall in this book leave that complication out of account. I shall assume *static expectations.*"

The main difficulty with flexible wages on the Traverse is of course that every time the wage rate rises a different technique (within the range of the new technology) becomes the most profitable. There will be repeated substitution against labour, but the wage rise is only slowed down, not held up. "The function of substitution, in an expanding economy, is to slow up the rises in wages that come from technical improvement; but the effect of the retardation is to stretch out the rise, making it a longer rise, so that a larger rise than would otherwise have occurred, is ultimately achieved. That is the Principal Proposition I am advancing in this chapter" (p. 115).

In Chapter XI, "Shortening and Lengthening," the Austrian aspect of the problems of the Traverse at last comes into view. If processes are "lengthened" by more investment in the construction industries, the even flow of their products through the system requires, at each processing stage, the presence of additional savings, in the form of working capital, to buy them. "Even when the wage is variable, lengthening of the construction period causes jerks .... When the wage is stabilized, the disturbances to the productive process (as a whole) are intensified" (p. 132). The intertemporal complementarity of some of our processes may fail, their parts no longer fit together.

At the end of the chapter Sir John pays a tribute: "To have drawn attention to vertical displacements was a major contribution; it is due to Professor Hayek.

"Where (I may as well emphasize here) I do not go along with him (or with what he said in 1931) is in the view that the disturbances in question have a monetary origin" (p. 133). We may point out here (as seems indeed to be admitted in the parenthesis) that already in his Copenhagen lecture of December 1933 Hayek put the main emphasis on divergence of plans and expectations rather than on "monetary disturbances."[6]

4.

In Part III the author is at last descending into the arena of Controversy, armed not with his sword but with his camera. The connoisseur of Hicksian art expecting revealing glimpses of the, as yet, imperfectly known, crevices where all seemed solid rock, is not disappointed.

Chapter XIII deals with The Measurement of Capital—Value and Volume. It is redolent of a famous wrangle on the same topic between Mr. Sraffa and our author that took place on the island of Corfu in 1958.[7]

Objective value is market price, but in the Hicksian model "there are no markets in intermediate products" (p. 157). After all, the reader reflects, the one-commodity world assumption exacts a price! "We nevertheless associated with every process, at every stage of its 'life,' a capital value. These values could not be market values; they must thus be subjective values, steps in the process by which technique is chosen" (p. 157). But, "Whose are the expectations, of future net outputs, from which the forward-looking value is to be derived? . . . The expectations of different individuals are not harmonious, and the statements which they record in their balance-sheets of magnitudes which depend on these expectations are not harmonious" (p. 161). Hence they cannot be added up. Most economists have concluded that it is therefore impossible to measure capital. Sir John Hicks seems hesitant. He spares a kind thought for the statistician and advises him to measure capital "by volume," though admitting that "it also, in its more sophisticated form, requires a value measure *at a base date*" (p. 163). The reader notices that the divergence of human expectations plays here a vital part.

In Chapter XIV "The Accumulation of Capital" comes under

discussion. We learn that the owners of capital invested in old processes will suffer capital losses even if these processes do not have to be cut short, because future output has to be discounted at the new, higher rate of interest. The word "malinvestment" is never used. It is noteworthy that no other case of it is ever mentioned.

Our author realizes that on a Full Employment path, with capital values changing all the time, the assumption of static expectations becomes hard to maintain. "A sequence of capital values, in which each term is calculated on assumptions that are belied by later elements in the sequence, does not look like being worth the trouble of writing it down" (p. 172). The only alternative, however, is "correct expectations of the wages and interest which in the course of the Traverse will be realized." Sir John firmly rejects it: "In positive economics we must not endow our actors with perfect foresight; for to do so would abolish Time, which is our subject" (ibid). But static expectations, the reader may feel, imply no less the abolition of Time as the dimension in which knowledge becomes diffused. And what entitles us to endow our actors with convergent expectations when we know that in reality they are bound to diverge? To "Austrian" thinking the diversity of expectations is a feature of the world no less significant than the diversity of preferences. They really belong together.

The chapter ends with another significant warning: "In a progressive economy, with wages rising, the increment of capital at cost is almost certainly much lower than appears from social accounting statistics. A great deal of saving is needed to prevent the volume of capital from declining. It should cause no surprise if it were found that there were happily progressive economies, with rising real incomes, in which the volume of capital was declining; the rise in real incomes would then seem to be 'due' to technical progress, and to technical progress alone. But that would not mean that the saving was unnecessary; it would be necessary, to keep the 'real' wage fund rising, so that full employment could be maintained with the rising real wages" (p. 176).

In the last chapter The Production Function, described as "the nub of the Controversy," comes under review. "So static a concept does not fit at all readily into our present line of thought" (p. 177). On the other hand, "it may reasonably be claimed that the neo-Austrian approach is richer; it gives us a deeper understanding . . . not only because it offers some comprehension of the whole of a process of adaptation . . . . Still more important is the inability of the static method to relate the process of growth to saving and investment . . . for it works with Equipment, not with Capital; it is negligent of Capital in any accounting sense" (p. 182). The chapter ends with the statement, "A reminder that the Distribution of Income is not, in the short-run, a well-founded economic concept is perhaps not the least important point which has emerged from our enquiry" (p. 184). An appendix, "The Mathematics of Traverse" ends the book.

5.

It is futile to quarrel about labels. A thinker who carries on Böhm-Bawerk's work cannot be gainsaid the predicate "Austrian" if he claims it. The question, however, whether this "neo-Austrian theory" is not more "classical" than "Austrian," inspired by Ricardo and Walras rather than by Menger and Hayek is more than a mere matter of intellectual genealogy.[8] It concerns the consistency of the new work. It also is germane to some aspects of the Grand Controversy now raging. Can neoclassical equilibrium theory be successfully defended on the macroeconomic level alone? Can Sir John Hicks defeat the neo-Ricardian counter-revolution now gathering strength at Cambridge by showing himself the more subtle Ricardian?

We may look at these important questions in various perspectives and should not confine ourselves to one of them. Seven years ago, when reviewing *Capital and Growth* in this journal, I raised the issue of *subjectivism versus formal analysis*. The issue remains as germane to the new book as it was to the old.[9]

Economics has two tasks. The first is to make the world around us intelligible in terms of human action and the pursuit of plans.

The second is to trace the unintended consequences of such action. Ricardian economics emphasized the second task, the "subjective revolution" of the 1870s stressed the urgency of the first, and the Austrian school has always cherished this tradition. The pursuit of the second task, to be sure, need not, in principle, impede that of the first. Experience has shown, however, that formal analysis on a fairly high level of abstraction is indispensable to accomplishing our second task, in particular where the number of possibilities is large and, in order to reach any firm conclusions, we have to limit this number by restrictive assumptions which may hinder us in the pursuit of our first task. For it is just part of this latter to explain the dazzling diversity of our world, and restrictive assumptions do not serve this purpose.

Seen in another perspective, even in the analysis of macro-economic processes the micro-basis, the true springs of human action, must not be abstracted from. Yet, in the present book it is almost completely ignored. It is not to be thought that the author of *Value and Capital* has really come to believe that autonomous changes in demand and the diversity of expectations do not matter. But so eager is he to "get results," to show that feasible forms of the Traverse are at least possible (since otherwise the "steady state" remains a mere figment of the imagination) that he seems ready to make any assumptions sufficiently restrictive to ensure them. We all understand that the present weakness of the neoclassical position may call for desperate measures. It is hard to see what is "Austrian" about them.

To substantiate our misgivings, two Hicksian assumptions lend themselves as ready examples, the one-commodity world and static expectations.

The weaknesses of Böhm-Bawerk's original construction were many. No doubt Sir John's flow output is a great improvement. But the fatal weakness of the former surely lies in the fact that we cannot apply it to a multi-commodity world which requires a price system invariant to changes emanating from the capital structure. Böhm-Bawerk's "subsistence fund" must always have that composition which corresponds to the tastes of the workers, otherwise there will be capital losses. Our author, of course, is not unaware of these problems (pp. 143–46), but the absence of a price system in his model does not seem to bother him. Yet, in the current controversy this problem plays a significant part.

In any transition from disequilibrium to equilibrium a good deal depends on the events occurring "on the path." In 1939 our author at least mentioned the consequences of trading at "false" prices.[10] In 1965 he dismissed Edgeworth's "recontract" and Walras's "tâtonnement" as "artificial arrangements."[11] In the new model there can be no trading at "false prices" while we are in our Traverse for the simple reason that there are no markets at all! Is this "arrangement" any less artificial than Edgeworth's or Walras's were?

We cannot but feel similar misgivings about the heterogeneity of capital. "This has often been thought to be a difficulty, but I do not think it is" (p. 178). The intertemporal complementarity of intermediate products at the various stages of our processes implies heterogeneity of one kind. Can we really neglect the "synchronical" heterogeneity of buildings, equipment, tools and stocks of goods? The faithful reader of Hicksian prose cannot help remembering how the assumption of a homogeneous "capital substance" was once said to be "the big thing that was wrong with classical theory. If there is just one homogeneous 'capital' ... there can be no problem of malinvestment—or of saving going to waste." (*Capital and Growth*, p. 35). Will not the "minor switches" of the new model in reality often take the form of the reshuffling of existing capital combinations? Will not "old" capital goods released from such combinations compete with some of the new ones? There is also the possibility that the same capital combination, in response to shifts in demand from one final product to another, will switch from one output stream to another, producing capital gains and losses. While in reality all the more interesting cases of "minor switches" appear to arise in this context, in the Hicksian model all this vanishes from sight. This is a good example of one of the ways in which the exigencies of macro-economic formalism impede our understanding of the ways the market economy works.

In turning, once more, to static expectations we can now see that they provide another instructive example of the same kind. Our author is compelled to maintain this assumption because otherwise the number of possible consequences is virtually infinite. As long as our sole aim remains to predict the unintended consequences of action it is legitimate enough to narrow the range of possibilities by means of restrictive assumptions in order to achieve "results." But if another of our aims is to render the world intelligible, exactly the opposite course of enquiry is indicated: we must convey to our readers an impression of the complexity and diversity of circumstances and try, as far as we can, to describe the range of possibilities. A widening, not a narrowing, of the scope of our enquiry is then what is required.

It was not personal caprice that prompted Menger's dislike of Böhm-Bawerk's capital theory and Walras's general equilibrium system; it was a conviction that in both a false picture of uniformity disguised the diversity of the world.

It is a curious fact that in 1965, when in *Capital and Growth* he renounced the Acceleration Principle of which he had made use in earlier writings, Professor Hicks did so in words suggesting that he was ready to follow this "Austrian" line of thought: "It is hardly a discovery to find that we are unable to 'simulate' the behaviour of intelligent business management by any simple rule . . . . If we find—as we do find—that mechanical principles of adjustment do not offer a good representation, we shall have gained something in the way of scepticism about the use of such principles in more ambitious undertakings" (*Capital and Growth*, pp. 102–03).

The Acceleration Principle is of course merely a special instance of static expectations. It is ironical that, just in a "neo-Austrian theory," an even more general "mechanical principle of adjustment" should occupy such a prominent place.

We have to remember that this work is part of a continuing *tour d'horizon*. "It is just as if one were making pictures of a building; though it is the same building, it looks quite different from different angles." Perhaps next time a few pictures will be taken at such angles that some of the problems mentioned will come into full view.

The book is, in a sense, a tract for the times, a powerful contribution to a current discussion of fundamental issues. What we are being told is that no answers to the questions raised can be found within the orbit of the Ricardian or Marshallian "long period," while this is precisely where the Cambridge neo-Ricardians and their neoclassical opponents are trying to find them. "New Equipment, the increment of Equipment, is among the least suitable of all macro-economic magnitudes to be treated as an independent variable. That is really what is wrong with the Production Function" (p. 182), the mainstay of the neoclassical position. But since even long-period forces must operate within short periods, we can (sometimes) determine what will happen by tracing their action over a sequence of short periods.

When, forty years hence or so, the history of economic thought in the twentieth century comes to be written, historians will find, no doubt to their delight, that in the work of Sir John Hicks they hold in their hands a true mirror of the age. The interplay of ideas, the impact some had and the changes all underwent as a consequence, are to be found there, reflected as in a glass. We are no less in his debt for being his contemporaries.

NOTES

1. John Hicks, *Capital and Time: A Neo-Austrian Theory* (Oxford: Clarendon Press, 1973).

2. G. L. S. Shackle, *Epistemics and Economics: A Critique of Economic Doctrines* (Cambridge: Cambridge University Press, 1973).

3. "This is the more noteworthy because Menger, far from welcoming that theory as a development of suggestions of his, severely condemned it from the first. In his somewhat grandiloquent style he told me once: 'The time will come when people will realize that Böhm-Bawerk's theory is one of the greatest errors ever committed.' He deleted those hints in his second edition." J. A. Schumpeter, *History of Economic Analysis* (Oxford: Oxford University Press, 1954), p. 847, note 8.

4. E. Lindahl, *Studies in the Theory of Money and Capital* (London: Allen & Unwin, 1939).

5. E. Lundberg, *Studies in the Theory of Economic Expansion* (London: P. S. King, 1937).

6. F. A. von Hayek, *Profits, Interest, and Investment* (London: G. Routledge & Sons, 1939), pp. 135–56.

7. See F. A. Lutz and D. C. Hague, eds., *The Theory of Capital* (London: Macmillan & Co., 1961), pp. 305–6.

8. "Böhm's analysis was much too one-dimensional for Menger, in whose own vision everything immediately ramified in some five to ten dimensions. Menger would describe the accumulation of capital as an increase in the range of capital goods and an ever-increasing complexity of the web of complementarities, while Böhm unified capital by the concept of the period of production." Erich Streissler, "To What Extent Was the Austrian School Marginalist?" *History of Political Economy* 4 (Fall 1972):435.

9. "Sir John Hicks on Capital and Growth," *South African Journal of Economics* 34 (June 1966):121–23.

10. J. R. Hicks, *Value and Capital* (Oxford: Clarendon Press, 1939), p. 128.

11. J. R. Hicks, *Capital and Growth* (Oxford: Oxford University Press, 1965), p. 54.

A Reconsideration of the Austrian Theory of Industrial Fluctuations

1.

The Austrian Theory of Industrial Fluctuations has lately been under a cloud.[1] By 1940, its most faithful adherents have to admit to themselves that few of the high hopes it held out in the halcyon days of the early 1930s have been fulfilled. To some extent this is, of course, due to the erstwhile ascendancy of the doctrines of Mr. Keynes and his followers, and although this is but a negative reason, it is probably the one that would readily occur to three out of four present-day economists.

It is probable, however, that to the historian of the future this ascendancy will be less of a problem than it is to some contemporaries of ours. For, when the history of economic thought in the second quarter of the twentieth century comes to be written, it will have become clearer than it is now that Mr. Keynes's theory—so far from being "general"—derives its fascination for the present generation of economists mainly from the fact that it is a most vivid description of a peculiar historical situation, an impressive picture of our world. In this disordered world the institutional and political framework of economic progress has broken down and in the resulting international chaos the capitalistically most advanced countries find it impossible to fulfil their natural function of assisting the economic development of the more backward parts of the world. The economic theorist of sterling purity, who in constructing his models chooses to ignore all this, may then, of course, summarise this

---

Reprinted from *Economica* 7 (May 1940).

Capital, Expectations, and the Market Process

situation by speaking of a "lack of investment opportunities"!

Reasons more positive—and of less ephemeral value—for the temporary eclipse of the Austrian theory may have to be sought in the manner of its first presentation and the intellectual milieu of its protagonists. Its theoretical pedigree was Wicksellian, and Wicksell's major claim to fame was to have linked the Böhm-Bawerkian theory of capital to the Walrasian equilibrium system. Hence, recent attacks on the former could not but affect its apparent derivative in the field of industrial fluctuations, while the charge of assuming "Full Employment" from the outset appeared no less serious a gravamen to a generation to which the monthly unemployment figures had become an integral part of its acquaintance with economic life.

Of both these charges Professor Hayek has now effectively disposed.[2] And if it could be hoped that the major obstacles to a more general understanding of the theory were thus removed, we might well leave matters at that. The only justification we have to offer for reconsidering the theory in the light of certain of its dynamic aspects consists in that we are unable to entertain any such hopes. For it seems to us that in the discussion about the Austrian theory "The Structure of Production" and "Full Employment" have received an altogether exaggerated attention, and that those who rejected it did so mainly because of its apparently too static character. It is curious to observe how the very same people would then wholeheartedly subscribe to another doctrine which, although at heart far more static than the Austrian, succeeded in conveying a distinctly dynamic impression, with all its static characteristics carefully tucked away.

In spite of this we believe that the reluctance with which the Austrian theory has met so far is actually due less to its being too static than to the fact that the mind of our generation, impregnated with static equilibrium notions, is incapable of realising its real dynamic significance.

In what follows we shall try, first to re-state what to us appear to be the essentials of the Austrian Theory of Industrial Fluctuations, a theory about the effects of cyclical fluctuations on the inter-industrial relationships between prices, profits and real wages. At the end of this paper we shall briefly confront this theoretical construction of ours with whatever knowledge we may be able to glean from trade cycle history in order to test its relevance to different periods of cyclical fluctuations. We hope to show that the Austrian theory is essentially dynamic, and we believe that any appearance to the contrary in its first presentation was really due to the upbringing of its protagonists to whom Walrasian equilibrium conditions appeared as the natural jumping-off ground for all excursions into the real world. We believe it to be vital to a correct understanding of the Austrian theory to stress its dynamic features and, in particular, to point out that certain of its assumptions, which have caused in the past and are likely to continue to cause much misunderstanding and bewilderment, have to be interpreted as symbols of a world of change.

That the Austrian theory does not readily fit into a static equilibrium system is easily seen, albeit in a very general and simplified manner, if we bear in mind that while *reversibility* is the essence of the latter, the Austrian theory rests fundamentally upon the non-reversibility of the investment operation. Once "free Capital" has been converted into buildings and machinery, any failure of events to conform to expectations will upset everything.

We do not revert to our initial position, but are worse off than we would have been had we never departed from it. For all static equilibrium analysis, on the other hand, it is essential that every deviation from the equilibrium point will set in motion forces which will lead us back to this point.

If the foregoing is thought to afford some justification for a reconsideration of the case, there are two special reasons why the present moment appears particularly propitious for this endeavour. On the one hand, the recent publication of Professor Schumpeter's *Business Cycles*[3] will no doubt rekindle interest in the dynamics of the process of capitalistic evolution, and his concept of "Innovation," as we shall see, provides us with a most valuable tool of analysis. By its help, we shall try to explain the peculiar function of the capital-goods-industries in a world of change. On the other hand, in the new version of the Austrian theory real wages begin to fall at the moment that "Full Employment" is reached.[4]

This result, at first sight rather astonishing, is based on the assumption of an intercyclical increase in the productivity of Labour so that in successive cycles identical output quantities are produced by less and less Labour, and "Full Capacity" may mean considerably less than "Full Employment." Here again the theory requires dynamic interpretation.

It goes without saying that if in what follows we endeavour to set forth what to us appear to be the essentials of the Austrian theory, we are acting entirely on our own responsibility. As long as thought is free, there is no guarantee whatsoever that, because some men's ideas coincide at some moment, they will do so at the next. By the same token, "schools of thought" lead a precarious life. At best of a transitory nature, they grow and wither as the human spirit moves.

We earnestly believe that what we have to say will be unobjectionable to all who are counted among the Austrian school, but we may well be wrong. We shall try to present the doctrine in such a way as will safeguard it against most of the attacks to which so far it has been exposed, but here we may well fail. In the end the reader will have to judge for himself whether he is able to recognise in our sketch essential features of the world in which we are living.

2.

In this and the following sections we shall state our assumptions regarding the structure of the industrial system and the relations between the various factors of production. Thereafter we shall study the cyclical process, i.e., our system in motion, and at the end of the paper make a brief attempt at verification.

In every economic system in which the division of Labour has reached a certain stage it is possible to distinguish:
  (1) industries producing consumers' goods,
  (2) industries producing the equipment for the production of the former,
  (3) industries producing raw materials.

For the sake of brevity we shall speak of C-, E-, and R-industries. But in a progressive economy there will exist a further group of industries, the special function of which is the provision of the means for progress. And in an economy that is liable to change there will have to be industries providing the means for change.

Our first task consists in convincing the reader that Growth is but one aspect of Innovation and that therefore the industries providing the means for both will be identical. There is little we have to add to Professor Schumpeter's brilliant analysis of the problems of industrial change. It is, of course, the fashion to-day to describe all dynamic phenomena in terms of aggregate quantities (like investment, incomes, output) and to regard Growth as an upward movement of a system of variables interpreted as the response of the system to changes in external conditions, say population. As such an attitude is only too prevalent among contemporary economists it is necessary for us to insist that there is no such thing as "natural Growth" and that a casual glance at the economic history of countries like India and China is sufficient to make us understand that industrial Growth is the outcome of conscious and sustained human effort about which "dynamic equations" tell us less than nothing. Growth then is the cumulative effect of individual efforts directed towards the improvement of the productive apparatus of society.

To deny that the results of these efforts can be adequately described in dynamic equations is, however, not the same as to ignore the effects they may have on the structure and composition of the economic system by stimulating some industries while thwarting others. On the contrary, it would be true to say that the Austrian theory is a theory about the inter-industrial effects of certain dynamic processes.

In a progressive economy it is usually possible to discern industries which are particularly sensitive to entrepreneurial efforts towards change and innovation. We might call them "dynamic key industries" and shall refer to them as K-industries. If the reader is satisfied that Growth does not just consist in aggregate quantities sliding harmoniously upwards along an imaginary "trend," he will have made the first step towards understanding why the demand for the products of these industries is unlikely to be closely geared to that for consumers' goods.

Our next step consists in showing that "capital-intensification" or the "deepening of capital" is merely another form of Innovation. Once we have rid ourselves of the notion of capital as a homogeneous aggregate and bear in mind its essentially heterogeneous character as an agglomeration of houses, ships, machinery, etc., it is easy to see that "an increase of capital per unit of output" does not just mean the addition of another piece of machinery to an otherwise unchanged equipment park, but that as often as not it will entail a complete re-arrangement of the existing productive apparatus, including depreciation of specific factors, and possibly a change in the character of the final product. This is but another way of saying that the "deepening of capital" is a non-reversible process by which the conditions of production are definitely changed.

For our purpose what matters is that the industries which in a progressive economy provide the means for capital-intensification are identical with those providing the means for changes in production in general (i.e., under modern conditions the "heavy" industries producing iron and steel). In economic history, as a matter of fact, it is often virtually impossible to distinguish between the one and the other: the evolution of the railways can be described either as the production of an entirely new service or else as capital-intensification of the pre-existing transport system. The same applies to electrification.

3.

Furthermore, we shall assume that labour in each of the industries described above is homogeneous—which does not, however, exclude differences between average and marginal product where homogeneous labour co-operates with equipment of different quality—but that it is not mobile between industries. In other words, labour in each industry is a non-competing group.

Furthermore, we are assuming a fairly rapid intercyclical increase in the productivity of labour as a result of technical progress. Thus we shall expect to see in successive cycles physically identical output quantities produced either by a steadily diminishing labour force or in shorter working weeks or by a combination of both.[5]

Let us now analyse our system in terms of complementarity and competitiveness. Broadly speaking, consumers' goods industries (C), equipment goods industries (E), and raw material producers (R) are complementary in the sense that, on the whole, a change in demand for C will entail a corresponding change in demand for the other two. As to our dynamic key-industries (K), they certainly compete for raw materials with C and E. But what determines the demand for K-products? Is K-output complementary to or competitive with the output of C and E? It is impossible to answer this question straight away, yet it is on this answer, as we shall see, that the issue between the Austrians and their opponents ultimately turns.

There is no prima facie reason for a belief that demand for the products of our K-industries must be closely linked to that for consumption goods. It is true that these industries are partly engaged in building up new C-industries, but just because the latter are new, their demand schedules are unknown and it is in no way possible to deduce such schedules for particular industries from any general demand function. Demand for K-products depends thus largely on expectations regarding a distant, unknown and uncertain future. We only know two factors which are most likely to have a decisive influence on it:

(1) The relationship between present costs and expected future yield. "The rate of interest relates a future income stream to a present capital outlay. With a given rate of interest, the investor's decision depends on the cost of this present outlay and the size of the expected future income stream, i.e., he has to compare a present outlay exclusively determined by the present level of costs and prices with an expected income stream which . . . is unlikely to be affected by this at all. It follows that, in the case of durable investment, the average yield of which is independent of present conditions, a rise in costs will check the inducement to invest and vice versa."[5]

In referring to this factor we shall speak of the *Lundberg effect*.[6]

(2) Real Wages. By the real wage paid in an industry we mean the ratio between money wage and price of the product of the industry. Real wages in different industries may hence be expected to be different. The higher the real wage in an industry the stronger is the urge to substitute labour-saving machinery and to increase the amount of capital per unit of output. Equally, where real wages are low, they will set up a tendency to diminish the amount of capital per unit of output and to turn over capital more quickly. In referring to this factor we shall speak of the *Ricardo effect*.[7]

From all this it follows that if our two factors were moving together, if real wages were to increase at the same time that investment costs rise relatively to future yields, this would tend to stabilise our system. For it would mean that while one source of demand for capital goods which is particularly sensitive to the cost-yield ratio became exhausted, another one—demand for labour-saving machinery—would help to maintain the level of investment activity. This is what, prima facie, we should expect to happen during the later stages of prosperity: While raw material prices soar and their forward quotations begin to display ominous "backwardations," will not the point of Full Employment be approached? Unfortunately, in our economic system this is unlikely to be the case owing to the intercyclical increase of the productivity of labour. There is no reason to believe that in an economy such as ours the introduction of labour-saving machinery has to wait for Full Employment to become profitable. Moreover, inspection of British and American statistics for the 1920s and 1930s suggests considerable increases in the productivity of Labour at considerably less than Full Employment.[8] In this case, unless there has been a corresponding increase in equipment, Full Capacity will be reached before Full Employment. Hence, real wages will begin to fall at exactly the moment that the boom gets under way, and the Ricardo effect will come into play. As the percentage of profit per unit of output rises, it will pay to turn over capital more quickly rather than to invest it for longer periods. Hence, the dynamic relation-

American railroad promoters, confronted with the same dilemma, were "in every major instance" only rescued by the timely arrival of European—mostly English—capital, what else can we infer but that the mobile resources of the American economy—raw materials and consumption goods—were insufficient to carry the burden of as large an investment activity as the railroad plans involved, and that a large rise in imports from Europe was needed in order to bridge the gap? Moreover, whatever price and commodity stock data we have for the period seem to indicate that, in every major instance of a breakdown, scarcity of resources (industrial raw materials) did actually exist.[14]

But we must admit that as an explanation of the crisis of 1929 and of the developments leading up to it our model does not fare so well. To all our knowledge there is no evidence to suggest that the economic evolution of the 1920's was stopped short by scarcity of resources. We shall not dwell upon the continued existence, in Britain and the United States, of unemployment throughout this period, for, as was shown above, where industrial productivity increases rapidly, unemployment is not inconsistent with a strain on resources (the combination of labour with equipment under conditions of non-optimum cost). More important as a symptom of the absence of any such strain is, of course, the stationary behaviour of consumption goods prices between 1924 and 1929. But what we should regard as most significant in this connection, since it stands in open contradiction to all our other experience, is the increase in raw material stocks after 1925.[15]

It is thus not easy to account for the crisis of 1929 by the help of the Austrian theory. We may infer that the economic conditions of the 1920s must have been very different from those on which our model is based. It is hardly possible for us, in this context, to go beyond the stage of tentative suggestion. All we can do is to hint at two facts which appear to us to be germane to the issue.

First, the evolution of the automobile has changed the economic function of the "heavy" metal industries. In the ages of railroad construction and electrification the cyclical position of these industries corresponded, more or less, to that of our K-industries. Demand for their products was not geared to that for consumers' goods, and a sufficient degree of competitiveness existed within the system. The evolution of the automobile, the demand for which is so large y dependent on consumers' incomes,[16] has changed this. Thanks to it, th iron and steel industries have to-day adopted the character of E-industries in the sense of our model.

Second, where much of the investment activity of the upswing is directed towards increasing the production and productivity of raw materials, there need be no scarcity of them. There can be little doubt that between 1920 and 1930 the production of most industrial raw materials underwent revolutionary innovations,[17] mostly of the capital intensification kind (e.g. tin dredging and the selective flotation process for copper and zinc) and that the rise in raw material stocks was largely consequent upon these changes in productive technique. An industrial society which increases the output of industrial raw materials and lays in a handsome stock of them *before* setting itself to the task of making available more and better consumption goods is acting as prudently as an agricultural community which will not release half of its labour force for the construction of a bridge before a stock of grain which is sufficient to maintain them during their absence from primary production has been piled up.

We are inclined to think that such a society would, indeed, be relatively immune against the type of crisis that has been sketched out in this paper. Yet, as we had to learn to our grief, not even such prudence will protect us from other calamities of a dynamic world. The extreme complexity of such a world in which almost any constellation of circumstances is capable, without notice, of giving rise to destructive forces, defies all facile generalisations. What chances of success under the circumstances all attempts at "social planning" that are based on such facile generalisations are likely to have is one of the melancholy reflections which, by 1940, the student of economics cannot eschew.

NOTES

1. The present paper contains results of an investigation into problems of secondary depressions which the author undertook as Leon Fellow of the University of London during 1939–40.

2. F. A. von Hayek, *Profits, Interest, and Investment* (London: G. Routledge & Sons, 1939).

3. J. A. Schumpeter, *Business Cycles,* 2 vols. (New York: McGraw-Hill, 1939).

4. F. A. von Hayek: *Profits, Interest, and Investment,* p. 11. The description of the point at which scarcities begin to make themselves felt as one of "Full Employment" seems to us most unfortunate. As will be seen presently, what is meant is Full Capacity (of first-line equipment) rather than Full Employment of Labor. Its theoretical significance consists in that it is the point at which cost curves begin to slope upward.

5. L. M. Lachmann, "Investment and Costs of Production," *American Economic Review* 28 (September 1938):475.

6. Erik Lundberg, *Studies in the Theory of Economic Expansion* (Stockholm Economic Series, 1937), p. 230. Dr. Lundberg, it is true, relates receipts to the rate of interest only. But, as the present author has shown (i.e., p. 475), it is easy to extend the theorem so as to cover costs other than interest.

7. F. A. von Hayek, *Profits, Interest, and Investment,* pp. 8–10.

8. For Great Britain: G. L. Schwartz and E. C. Rhodes, *Output, Employment, and Wages in the United Kingdom, 1924, 1930, 1935* (London and Cambridge Economic Service, Special Memorandum No. 47). See in particular the Introduction by Professor A. L. Bowley. For the United States: D. Weintraub: *Technological Trends and National Policy* (National Resources Committee, Washington, 1937).

9. The reader will notice that we distinguish between the cyclical and intercyclical aspects of capital intensification. To the former belong its effect on investment, employment, and incomes in K, to the latter its effect on employment in C. In Dr. Hawtrey's terminology, while the effects of capital being deepened are confined to the Cycle ("The Short Period") those of capital having been deepened extend over a longer period of time. It is only with the latter that we are here concerned.

10. L. M. Lachmann and F. Snapper, "Commodity Stocks in the Trade Cycle," *Economica* 5 (November 1938):445–6.

11. J. A. Schumpeter, *Business Cycles,* 2 vols. (New York: McGraw-Hill, 1939) 1:296n.

12. E. V. Morgan, "Railway Investment, Bank of England Policy, and Interest Rates, 1844–48," *Economic History* 4 (February 1940):331–34.

13. J. A. Schumpeter, op. cit., p. 335.

14. Lachmann and Snapper, "Commodity Stocks in the Trade Cycle," p. 436, table I.

15. Lachmann and Snapper, op. cit., p. 437, table II.

16. S. I. Horner, et al., *The Dynamics of Automobile Demand* (New York: General Motors Corporation, 1939).

17. Melvin T. Copeland, *A Raw Commodity Revolution.* Harvard Business Research Studies, No. 19.

PART FIVE
ON ECONOMIC POLICY

Causes and Consequences of the Inflation of Our Time

1.

The subject with which I am to deal is of an economic, but at the same time of a historical nature. While inflationary processes have been the concern of economists for almost as long as coherent economic thought can be said to have existed, any comparison between the outstanding features of "the inflation of our age" and those of other epochs, such as my subject clearly requires, involves the perspective of history. This dual nature of my task presents a problem of method and approach. This problem stems, not from any fundamental incompatibility between the economic and the historical approach, but from a certain tendency inherent in modern macro-economic analysis. In economic analysis, as in all generalizing thought, we build in our minds "models" of reality by deducing necessary consequences from hypotheses arbitrarily chosen. Of course we are all aware that the more "realistic" our assumptions are, the closer to reality we may hope our conclusions to be. But since it is always impossible to include the whole of reality in our set of assumptions, the selection of the components of this set cannot but be arbitrary. The historian studying the changes which a given society has undergone through time faces the same problem of selection since he, too, has to confine himself to a limited number of features. There is thus, in principle, insofar as the arbitrary selection of topics for inclusion in either the analytical model of the economist or the "observation model" of the historian is concerned, no incompatibility at all between the two approaches.

But the recent development of economic theory in the direction of a stronger emphasis on macro-economic problems

Reprinted from *South African Journal of Economics* 35 (December 1967).

analysed in terms of variables and the relationships between them, makes it in fact very unlikely that an economist constructing a model of inflation and a historian studying inflationary processes through time, will both select the same features as of primary importance, and will abstract from the same features as of only secondary significance. The modern economist, immersed as he is in examining systems of functional relationships between macro-variables, has to abstract from the human purposes, attitudes, and ideas which lie behind them, while the historian can hardly follow him in this practice as these very things form the essential subject-matter of all history.

We hear much nowadays of consumption functions, input-output tables, and capital-output ratios. Nobody bothers to explain why, in a world of rapid changes in attitudes, tastes, and techniques, such variables as these should be expected to subsist, nor why, if there is change, such change should follow a definite and predictable pattern. But it must surely be clear that where our task is the explanation of change in time, no argument in which human ideas and attitudes which might prompt such change are ignored or abstracted from, will be worth serious consideration. When we try to explain the specific character of the inflationary processes of our time it must be one of our foremost tasks to grant ideas and attitudes a prominent place in our scheme of explanation.

2.

When we look at any of our price indices, whether of wholesale or consumer prices, either before or after 1958, it is the relentless character of the annual price rises which leaves the most striking impression. Between 1939 and 1966 we find not a single year in which the price index is not higher than in the preceding and lower than in the next year.

Two contrasting aspects of this situation appear to us to call for notice. On the one hand, one cannot but be surprised at the extent to which this state of affairs has come today to be generally accepted as a perhaps undesirable, but inevitable feature of economic life in advanced Western society. We all know that we are living in a world in which prices can only rise but never fall. When we speak of "fighting inflation," what we really mean is that we hope to reduce the rate of price rise. Perhaps, in our bolder moments, we even imagine a period of stable prices which might last a number of years. But I have never met anybody, economist or layman, who actually thought that the continuous price rise of the last three decades might one day be reversed and that we may live to see a decade or so of falling prices. I imagine that if such a person were to turn up at this conference, he would at once create something of a sensation.

Economists, on the other hand, notoriously slow to grasp and absorb into their thinking historical change in thought and institutions that happens during their own life-time, have thus far been reluctant to probe the implications of the facts mentioned for theory and practice. Recent discussions of the so-called "reverse yield gap" are evidence of this reluctance the main reasons for which have to be sought in the history of economic thought. So much of our thinking on prices and monetary matters, classical, neo-classical, and Keynesian, is consciously or subconsciously based on the assumption of a world of prices flexible in both directions, upward and downward, that our reluctance to recast some of our conceptual tools in a mould more appropriate to a world of unidirectional price change is not perhaps altogether surprising. Nor is it inexcusable. When we remember that all modern economists are trained to think in equilibrium terms, in terms of a coherent "economic system" of which the "price system" forms part, we shall find it easy to understand why their minds boggle at what Sir John Hicks has called The Fixprice Method,[1] a description by which, as its author puts it, "It is not implied . . . that prices are never allowed to change—only that they do not necessarily change whenever there is demand-supply disequilibrium."[2]

After all, even Keynes, as late as in his *Treatise on Money* of 1930, assumed prices flexible in both directions. It is only natural that the facts of the new situation should permeate our thinking but gradually and that we are slow, perhaps slower than we should be, to come to grips with them.

On the other hand, it is not often realised what a new situation it really is that we confront. It gradually came into existence, so far as I can judge, in the course of the 1920s. Before that time prices often did fall, even as late as in the years immediately after the First World War. In that world, so different from ours, it was generally taken for granted that periods of rising prices will be followed by falling prices.

Perhaps the most striking example of this change is found in the fact that a hundred years ago, in what was already an industrial economy, it was taken for granted that the results of inflation have to be wiped out by deflation and falling prices: the liquidation of the "Greenback period" in America in the years after the Civil War took the form of a prolonged process of deflation. Between 1865 and 1879, with a mild rise in the stock of money which had been inflated between 1861 and 1865, a very rapid rise in the gross social product caused a "drastic and sustained price decline." As Schumpeter put it, in those 14 years, "the economic organism was allowed to grow into its monetary coat." As Professor Friedman and Mrs. Schwartz have described it, "The price level fell to half its initial level in the course of less than fifteen years and, at the same time, economic growth proceeded at a rapid rate. . . . Their coincidence casts serious doubts on the validity of the now widely held view that secular price deflation and rapid economic growth are incompatible."[3]

While prices were halved within 14 years, the net national product doubled between 1869 and 1879. Net national product per capita (at 1929 prices) rose from 188 to 295 dollars.[4] The rapid growth was not confined to manufacturing industries in which employment increased by one-third during the decade.

"The number of farms rose by over 50 per cent from 1870 to 1880 for the U.S. as a whole. The average value per acre apparently increased despite the sharp decline in the price of farm products—clear evidence of a rise in economic productivity. The output of coal, pig iron, and copper all more than doubled and that of lead multiplied sixfold."[5]

3.

Why do all these facts sound to us like tales from a lost world? This is an economic no less than a historical question.

Inflation means that the social product falls short of the total claims made upon it. The "real value" of each money claim is then reduced by the price rise. With given claims a sufficient rise in the social product may eliminate inflation. But in a growing economy inflation will become endemic if the rate of growth of claims continues to exceed the rate of growth of the social product. This is evidently the situation of Western society today. The fundamental cause of our inability to stop the inflation of our age is our inability to control the creation of claims to shares in the social product.

It may be thought that the problem might be at least mitigated, if not cured, by inducing at least some holders of claims to postpone them. No doubt increased savings will reduce inflationary pressure. But in a world in which prices do not fall, such persuasion as is required to make people save more is increasingly less likely to succeed as these holders realise that by postponing their claims they can only lose but never gain. They are far more likely to convert their claims into real resources which, if at some hazard, may be turned into sources of future real income streams, thus safeguarding them against certain loss. But this of course means that such claims are not postponed but, on the contrary, currently exercised.

Every attempt to assess the major causes of the inflation of our age will therefore have to start from the fact of the creation of excessive claims to the social product. Here we have to distinguish, more carefully than has been done in the past, between the sources of such claim creation and the monetary channels through which the claims are exercised. Economists appear to have taken it for granted that control of inflation means control of the monetary channels through which such claims flow. We shall have to take a wider view. But it may well be, as a matter of history, that at a time when the number of possible sources of such excessive claims was small, virtually confined to governments and large business concerns with easy access to the capital and money market, control of the monetary channels was in itself sufficient to check inflation.

History shows many examples of successful anti-inflationary credit policy. In our world the sources of claim creation are more diffuse while our monetary system is, at the same time, more complex and more difficult to control. We can no longer take it for granted that successful control of the monetary channels means success in the struggle against inflation.

Nevertheless it remains true that one major cause of the inflation of our age lies in the high degree of elasticity of our supply of money. With a metallic money the inflationary process we have witnessed during the last three decades would have been impossible. A system of credit money in which the creation of money requires little beyond agreement between lender (bank) and borrower, and in which a large and widely held stock of near-money assets will at once start flowing into any gap opened by a "credit squeeze," is evidently something very different from, and far more unwieldy than, anything the central bankers of *la belle époque* ever had to contend with.

A second major source of the inflation of our age we have to find in the manner in which prices of industrial goods are determined in our world. These are very largely "list" or catalogue prices. In the case of resale price maintenance the producer even determines the price which the consumer will have to pay. But with or without resale price maintenance, the producer in the large majority of cases determines the price at which he will sell the product to his customer who is a "price taker": he can only accept the price or refuse to buy. The producer is his own price setter. In setting his price, to be sure, the producer must take his bearings from the market and has to take account of the elasticity of demand confronting him. But, firstly, in our age of inflation most producers have learnt to distinguish between the short-run elasticity of demand immediately after a price increase and the long-run elasticity which will prevail once the economy has digested another bout of all-round inflation. Secondly, to take one's orientation from sales expectations is in principle something different from taking it from current market prices. The latter is not a mere figment of the imagination of economic theorists building models of "perfect competition." In the nineteenth century world such a mode of orientation really existed.

Price setting by industrial producers is a relatively new phenomenon, and a concomitant of the decline of the wholesale merchant as an economic intermediary. Before 1900, in a world in which most goods were produced by relatively small-scale producers, prices were set in markets dominated by merchants whose economic function it was to equate a demand and a supply the sources of which were equally beyond their control. Maximising their profits meant for them maximising their turnover. Hence they had to fix equilibrium prices reflecting every change in either supply or demand. Marshallian market equilibrium theory largely reflected this concrete situation which prevailed in the real world at the time when Marshall wrote. What matters for us is that this type of market required price flexibility in both directions if merchants were to maximise turnover. Producers and consumers alike had no choice in accepting these flexible market prices. The separation of the function of price setter from that of producer was thus the basis of price flexibility.

The modern consumer is still in the position of a price taker, but the modern producer is not. Having assumed the function of price setter left vacant by the demise of the wholesale merchant,[6] he naturally exercises it in such a fashion as to maximise his long-run profits rather than, as the merchant did, his short-run turnover. He will deal with an excess supply by reducing his output rather than by letting price drop. He can afford, as his forebear could not, to let his conduct at every moment be prompted by expectations largely reflecting rule-of-thumb interpretations of the contemporary world. He will avoid anything that might "spoil the market." And since he knows, as we all do, that he is living in a world of unidirectional long-run price change, and that any cost economy within his reach will sooner or later be swallowed up by wage demands, he will be loath to reduce his price even where he could gain an immediate market advantage. To reduce price when one knows very well that before long one will have to raise it again is not sound business strategy.

A cost increase, on the other hand, can be converted into a price increase by a stroke of the pen where producers are price setters. Of course, fear of "spoiling the market" may act here, too, as an obstacle. But long experience has by now taught our producer that in granting wage demands, where all his competitors are in the same position as he is, he need not hesitate to recoup himself by a price increase, and that so far as the relative price of his product to product prices outside his industry is concerned, the next round of wage increases in the country will soon rectify his position.

We now come to the third, and most important, cause of our inflation: the relentless nature of wage demands following upon one another, industry by industry, in what by now in most industrial countries has become a customary and well-established pattern. The subject is only too familiar.[7] We shall confine ourselves to three comments designed to set the phenomenon in historical perspective.

Our first two causes, while being necessary major conditions of inflation, are really only conditions. Neither the elastic nature of money supply nor the modern method of fixing industrial prices could by themselves have produced the phenomena we all know. As regards the "administered prices" in particular, there is little reason to doubt that modern industrialists would prefer stable prices and costs to unidirectional change in both. The really decisive force of our inflation has to be sought in the driving power of trade unions, and the environment, intellectual and institutional, within which they operate today.

The main original function of trade unions, as of cartels, was to prevent a movement of otherwise competitive prices which had taken place during a boom from being reversed during the subsequent slump; no wage rate must ever be allowed to fall. Once this had become an article of faith generally accepted in modern mass society, trade unions had to assume a new function to justify their continued existence. An economy with stable wage rates and prices gradually falling with higher productivity holds no attraction for trade unions. While it may present difficult problems to the setters of "administered" prices, it makes trade unions redundant. The option for an economy with steadily rising wage rates is therefore a natural option for a type of organization which otherwise would be left without any significant economic function.

But how were trade unions able to make their interests prevail above all others, including the social interest in a stable price level? How exactly did it come about that the annual creation of excessive claims on the social product became part of the accepted ritual of modern society, a social norm the more compelling for being an unwritten norm?

It seems to us that this process is unintelligible unless we pay some attention to the historical changes which the institutions of collective bargaining have undergone in the last half-century. When in the early 1920s most countries of the West followed the British example and set up such institutions, adding arbitration by an "impartial" arbiter in some cases, the prevailing climate of opinion was still such that the market economy with its autonomous and coherent price system was largely taken for granted. Sceptics were silenced by pointing out to them that "bargaining" is of the essence of market activity and that "collective bargaining" is a more sophisticated, perhaps a more civilised, method of attaining equilibrium wage rates. Few doubted that the existence of prices coordinated by the price system would set fairly narrow limits to the area of wage bargaining.

As we all know, the outcome has been a very different one. Instead of the price system containing the area of wage bargaining within narrow limits, the autonomous price system has been destroyed in the process. The wage level of each industry is no longer governed by an autonomous price system existing independently of it. On the contrary, the price system, if we still can speak of such, has become today the cumulative result of all the industrial wage bargains and consequent price adjustments which have taken place in time. Life on the "wage standard" means that the prices of industrial goods, at each moment in time, reflect, not the relative strength of the forces of demand and supply, but the relative bargaining power of the various trade unions at the moments when the last bargains were struck. Nobody expects the present set of prices to last beyond the date at which the next wage agreement is due for revision.

The institutions of collective bargaining which half a century ago were so confidently expected to add new luster to the market economy, have instead destroyed the autonomous price system on which this economy must rest.

4.

We must now turn to the consequences of our contemporary process of inflation. Some of these are so well known that we shall have to spend very little time on them. But certain others are less familiar. It would seem, in particular, that the effects of our contemporary mode of price increases (discontinuous rather than continuous) on relative prices, and the functioning of the economic system as a whole, have thus far received too little attention.

It goes without saying that monetary policy in a world of unidirectional price change presents problems that were unknown to our grandfathers.[8]

Formerly, when a central bank was slow in pulling the anti-inflationary brakes, so that prices had actually risen before it took action, it knew that the price rise could and would be reversed. An error in timing could be rectified in time. In our world a central banker must have the eye of an eagle and the perceptive qualities of a cat to detect new sources of inflationary pressure at once; otherwise it will be too late. In our world an error in timing is not rectifiable. In fact, the soundest rule of monetary policy today is probably that we can never do too much to check inflation, because whatever we are doing will not be enough.

It is also pretty clear that lenders are now becoming reluctant to deliver their fortunes into the hands of the wage bargaining parties. The "reverse yield gap" and the present level of interest rates are of course merely the first signs of the growing awareness of what is going on. No doubt in time a standard of deferred payment other than current money, a standard beyond the reach of wage bargainers and obliging bankers, will be devised. Borrowers will discover that they can borrow more readily and at lower interest rates if they are willing to shoulder the risk of debt depreciation.[9]

I have been asked to devote some attention, in this paper, to the effects of our contemporary inflation on the distribution of incomes, but frankly do not find this a rewarding subject. In the first place, we lack a standard of comparison. Since all countries which have a market economy have been affected by this inflation, none can serve as a measuring rod. I find myself unable to conjure up an image of what our world would be like without this inflation.

Secondly, it seems unlikely that the classical scheme of the theory of income distribution, couched as it is in terms of classes of income recipients, yields any interesting results in the circumstances of our age. Of course fixed-income recipients suffer, but whether wage earners or profit earners gain more at their expense it is hard to say.

In former times there may have been "profit inflations" in which wage earners suffered temporarily by the belated adjustment of wage rates. In our world, with the contemporary mode of price setting described above, profit recipients can recoup themselves partly at once by setting higher prices, but partly, so far as sales volume is concerned, only gradually as the new bout of inflation permeates the rest of the economy. As regards the distribution of real incomes, then, the most significant differences appear to exist not between wage earners and profit earners, but between people operating in different sectors of the economy. And these differences stem, not from the movement of absolute prices, but from the discontinuous mode of change of relative prices. This is most clearly seen in the case of the wage earners in any given industry. While they gain a relative advantage over all their fellow citizens every time their wage rates rise, they are on the losing side every time this happens in another industry. Nor is this a surprising result. Keynes, after all, showed that, except for the existence of fixed prices and incomes, changes in the wage unit will have no effect on the distribution of incomes. Of course, in our world there is no such thing as a "wage unit" and all the more interesting effects stem from relative wage and price changes.

We have to remember that far more important than these income changes are the capital changes concomitant with every inflation, the capital gains and losses made by debtors and creditors. With the hire-purchase system, workers may become debtors and thus benefit from inflation in a way for which no income statistics render an account, another reason why the analysis of inflationary processes in terms of real income changes seems so unrewarding. Perhaps I need to do no more than hint at the economic implications of the well-known fact that in an inflation the firms most heavily in debt will appear the most profitable, since the "return on the equity" here includes an element of capital gain. Such firms will naturally find it easier than their rivals to attract new capital for expansion. We may conclude that all inflation, quite apart from the effects on the relative price structure presently to be discussed, gives rise to a tendency towards a distortion of the capital structure. There is no longer an unambiguous criterion by which we could measure the relative performance of firms. Inflation offers another instructive example of how inseparable income and capital gains really are.

5.

Let me now draw your attention to a contemporary phenomenon which is not usually regarded as a consequence of the inflation of our age: the appearance of schemes of Economic Development Programming, promoted by governments, in countries whose economic systems conform to the pattern of the market economy; of what the French call "indicative planning" by government agencies.

I shall argue that a case can be made for such programmes as guideposts to entrepreneurial decision-making in a world in which relative prices, no longer responsive to market forces, no longer flexible in both directions, have largely lost their erstwhile function of guiding entrepreneurs in their actions.

There can of course be no doubt that, seen politically, Economic Programming is simply an extension of the principle of the full employment policy. The modern welfare state, having once taken responsibility for permanent full employment, is compelled, by the very nature of the forces inherent in modern mass society, to take the next step and make itself responsible for the maximum growth rate of incomes. But why should it be thought that the achievement of this aim cannot be left to the play of the market forces in what is, after all, a market economy?

The answer usually given to this question is, perhaps not surprisingly, couched in Keynesian terms. Economists advocating indicative planning will, as a rule, tell us that the market economy may not at all times make full use of all existing resources, and that to achieve this requires a coordination of the expectations of all entrepreneurs which market forces alone are unable to accomplish.

I regard this as an inadequate answer. Keynes was exclusively concerned with unemployment in industrial society. In Britain and France at least, the two countries which have in recent years been the protagonists of indicative planning, there has been no serious unemployment for almost three decades; hence their planning can hardly be justified in Keynesian terms. But if we are to include among our terms of reference resources other than labour, as well as extend them to malemployment, rather than unemployment, of labour, we are in any case unable to use the Keynesian tools.

A much stronger case for indicative planning can be made by simply asking how relative prices in our world, set in most cases by a "mark-up" on existing wage rates and material costs which nobody expects to last, can possibly act as guideposts to entrepreneurial action. Evidently they cannot. Prices, in a world in which they cannot fall, cannot reflect the forces of demand; they are not equilibrium prices. It is true that even disequilibrium prices may guide entrepreneurs, but they obviously can do this only where they are free to move in response to demand as well as supply, and it is precisely this which in our world they cannot do any more.

We simply no longer have a price "system" worthy of this name. The existing structure of relative prices reflects the history of past wage bargains and is thus nothing more than the cumulative result of a series of historical accidents. Of course it is governed by relative costs, but is no longer affected by disequilibrium of demand and supply. What does affect it are new wage bargains. A fall in demand for our product consequent upon a price rise may be safely disregarded for the good Keynesian reason that new wage bargains in other industries will in any case modify the demand for our product. Our price lasts as long as our wage bargain does. Everybody knows it and acts accordingly.

As I have pointed out elsewhere,[10] the opponents of Economic Programming have sometimes harmed their cause by claiming more for the price system of the market economy than can fairly be done. In particular, we must beware of confusing the general equilibrium system of Walras and Pareto, which assumes a stationary world, with the market economy of the real world. In the former all action is determined by present prices, while in the real world entrepreneurs will have to let themselves also be guided by expectations of future prices and sales. But while it is true that in an uncertain world present prices cannot offer entrepreneurs more than a basis of orientation for their plans, it is also true that the disappearance of this basis must constitute a serious loss. In the light of this fact it is easy to understand how the idea could gain ground that economic growth might be promoted by offering entrepreneurs another basis of orientation, in lieu of the vanished price system, couched this time in terms of coordinated expectations about future quantities of goods. The market economy, having lost its traditional steering-wheel, is to be offered another device for the coordination of expectations. If this account of the background of the idea of Economic Programming is accepted, it would also explain why in most programmes prices play such a minor part.

The question then arises whether it is really possible to estimate future output trends for a large number of goods while disregarding their relative prices. The programming of economic development will largely have to be guided by available resources. The aim must be to overcome shortages in some sectors coexisting with unused resources in others. Can this aim be achieved without a price system in which relative prices reflect the relative scarcity of goods? Is it likely that the planners can do better here than the market can?

We have to remember that the shortages and surpluses we are able to observe in our world are as likely to be the result of short-run price distortion as of long-run trends. A surplus in the supply of a certain good and the corresponding excess capacity in the industry producing it may be simply due to the fact that its price has recently risen ahead of other prices, while a shortage may be due to a wage level which has not been revised for a long time. The surplus will probably vanish once other prices start moving upward and the shortage disappear after the next wage rise. I do not deny that surpluses and shortages which are due to other causes, and therefore of a less ephemeral nature, exist in our world. Of course in a world of unexpected change many such causes exist. My point is that we are quite unable to distinguish surpluses and shortages indicative of long-run trends from those reflecting relative price distortion. At the moment of observation it is impossible to tell the one kind from the other. In this respect the economist-planners are no better off than the entrepreneurs. In a world in which quantities and prices are no longer coordinated by market forces neither can by itself any longer serve as a useful guide to action.

It seems therefore that the same event the existence of which appears to call for a new basis of orientation for the entrepreneurial assessment of long-run trends, viz. the disappearance of a coherent price system governed by demand and supply, must by the same token deprive this new basis of orientation of any economic significance it might have.

Professor H. M. Robertson, the first discussant, felt that the title of Professor Lachmann's paper was inadequate. Professor Lachmann had discussed "Causes and Consequences of the Inflation of Our Time," but he had also discussed causes and consequences of our ways of thinking about inflation in these times. He had thrown doubt on the usefulness of the currently fashionable macro-economic variables when discussing the phenomenon of inflation. But he had then assumed that a particular once-for-all change in attitudes and techniques had occurred in the last 30 years, and that henceforth, for all time, a maxim of policy would persist which had, historically speaking, only very recently become widely accepted, viz. that whenever there was any threat to the maintenance of full employment, action would be taken to increase the flow of money incomes sufficiently to take up the slack, wherever it appeared, and regardless of the labour shortages which would be caused elsewhere in the economy. Professor Robertson asked whether this recent revolution in thought was so complete that it had now come to a standstill and could be written into the macro-economic functions which would describe, explain, and govern all post-Keynesian economies, though any such variables, or rather, parameters, would have been absent from the functions appropriate to pre-Keynesian economies.

In his paper the author had fairly and squarely joined the ranks of the institutionalists, but he did not carry his institutionalism far enough. The institutions judged responsible ought to be described and analysed in some detail.

Undoubtedly there might be flashes of truth in the view that the really decisive force of our inflation had "to be sought in the driving power of trade unions, and the environment, intellectual and institutional, within which they operate to-day"; yet he (Robertson) believed that much more knowledge both of the actual pattern of wage changes and of the role of the trade unions in the processes of change had to be acquired before the decisive nature of this sort of explanation could be verified.

If the movements of wages and trends towards labour-cost-push inflation in South Africa were more thoroughly analysed on an institutional basis, the analysis would have to go much more deeply than any mere mention of the general role of trade unions in a world in which prices and wages could virtually never again move downwards. Such analysis should involve a deeper investigation not only into trade union structure but also into other elements in our political structure as well: elements which underlay much of the influence exerted by trade unionism itself upon the progress of inflation in this country, but elements which had perhaps contributed more strongly in other ways.

In regard to the emergence of Economic Development Programming as a consequence of inflation he felt that Prof. Lachmann had not derived economic development programming (and the forms which its "indicative planning" tended to take) from inflation itself. He really derived it as a further consequence of the same series of causes to which he ascribed the origins of the inflation of our times.

Professor D. Hobart Houghton, the second discussant, felt that he could not go the whole way with Prof. Lachmann in accepting the modern price structure as almost completely devoid of any competition. While it was true that prices, as a whole, tended to move upwards he was not sure whether it was true of all relative prices and questioned whether it took into account sufficiently the new techniques which replaced processes which had priced themselves out of existence in the modern world.

He endorsed Prof. Robertson's comments about the trade unions. Professor Lachmann had over-emphasized the upward pressure of trade union collective bargaining. Not merely the trade unions, but the whole population of democratic countries were essentially responsible for cost-push inflation. The main strength of the inflation of our time was that we expected it to continue but we as citizens of a democratic society were in one way or another making its continuance inevitable. One wondered whether democratic representative government, let alone the trade union movement, was compatible with the maintenance of the value of a currency unit, unless a powerful watchdog were set to uphold the currency status.

Dr. Holloway expressed the view that the discussants had not got down to the basic facts of inflation, for the reason that no attempt had been made to count the cost in terms of

(a) undermining the whole economic system; and

(b) undermining the freedom of the individual.

Inflation had, he said, turned the scale in favour of debtors and had brought about a quiet, relentless civil war between producers and authoritarian monetary managers. To avoid the collapse of the machinery of production they had no option but to load their prices. Inflation was disintegrating the economy. Monetary inflation had been the cause of all this. Cost inflation and demand inflation were merely symptoms, merely consequences. There could be no civilization without discipline. To expect this discipline to come from an army of bureaucrats was a vain hope. Whence this pathetic faith in bureaucrats? he asked. Bureaucrats were but a cross-section of the community; they were no supermen.

There was only one way of getting discipline into our economic relations and that was by having more money which had value on account of its intrinsic properties.

Mr. K. A. H. Adams, commenting on Lachmann's paper, said that another possible cause of inflation could be based on observations that Pareto's Law of Income Distribution had occurred in South Africa each year for the past 50 years. The Pareto index had increased from about 2 to 2.5 in this period and implied a certain concentration of incomes and people. In employee groups the income distribution was far more concentrated, principally because the top salaries in the Public Service had been limited to unnaturally low values.

The concentrated public service salary pattern set a model for the whole country and caused personnel migration, dissatisfaction and eventually an elevation of incomes in sub-groups, he said. With a more expanded income pattern in the public service the difficulties could be minimised, reaching negligible proportions probably when the pattern was twice as concentrated as the income distribution in the population. In this way inflation could be restrained.

J. Katzenellenbogen doubted whether there were many producers who had the resources to be their own price setters and who were able to ignore the market and able to let their prices withstand the elasticity of demand and supply. He felt that the South African system was still to a large extent based on a very competitive market and producers in the main used the price mechanism even in the short run. There were many small and medium-sized individual producers who had to face a competitive society and who could make inroads into it only by an attack from a price point of view.

R. L. Kraft stated that it was commonly held that wages went up and never came down. In a recent preliminary survey of wage costs in the various sectors of South African manufacturing industry he had discovered that the influence of collective bargaining on average wage cost per employee was not decisive. He also felt that wage costs per employee could and did fall in certain sectors. Wage behaviour reflected, among other things, the skills requirements of industries as well as the higher degree of automation and the mechanical complexity of these industries.

M. B. Dagut asked whether Prof. Lachmann, who believed that institutions were responsible for the continuing of inflation, did not also believe that there was some merit in the new type of institution tried abroad such as a prices and incomes board.

Dr. Timmerman said that as far as South Africa was concerned it might be the case that the unions were not so well organised as those overseas. Nevertheless they did exercise upward tendencies on prices. He also felt that technical workers, most of whom were not union members, had greatly influenced costs. He suggested increased productivity and longer hours of duty as the only remedy.

Prof. Lachmann replied in conclusion that while the only thing that he believed possible and socially acceptable was a combined price and wages policy, such a policy would require the introduction of a system of universal price control which we knew from experience was not a job to be well done.

In our world, he said, prices and wages were not flexible in the downward direction. He submitted that there had been some forces which had produced the downward inflexibility of wage rates and prices, which were also to be held responsible for the long-run upward trend of prices. There really could be no doubt about it. He would go further than Dr. Holloway and say that a society which was unable to control the creation of claims on its social product was a sick society. One of the evils of inflation was of course the capital losses of the savers which at the other end must correspond with certain capital gains. It seemed that some economists had acquired a view that those economic phenomena of which we had no record, and because capital gains and losses did not figure in our national income accounts, did not exist. Capital gains and losses did matter because a capitalistic economy was steered by them. There was also the view that the capital losses of the savers in an inflationary economy was a correctable thing and although this was not social justice it did not matter for the economy as a whole because what some lost others might gain. There was also the effect which such capital losses might have on price formation. He had no doubt that some of the wage increases which had been granted in the Western world for the last twenty years had partly been financed from such capital gains which, however, could not generally be maintained.

NOTES

1. John Hicks, *Capital and Growth* (Oxford: Oxford University Press, 1965), Ch. VII.

2. Ibid., p. 78.

3. Milton Friedman and A. J. Schwartz, *A Monetary History of the United States 1867–1960* (New York: National Bureau of Economic Research, 1963), p. 15.

4. Ibid., p. 37, Table 2.

5. Ibid., p. 35.

6. It is not impossible that in the future the modern chain store will come to assume the wholesale merchant's former role of a price setter. The extent to which this will happen must evidently depend on the degree of "countervailing power" these retail organizations contrive to acquire.

7. For a concise explanation of the implications of the "Labor Standard" see J. R. Hicks, "Economic Foundations of Wage Policy," *Economic Journal* 65 (September 1955):389–404.

8. The first to have pointed this out was, to my knowledge, the German economist Alfred Tismer in his book *Grenzen der Diskontpolitik* (Munich: Duncke & Humblot, 1932). See also J. K. Galbraith, "Market Structure and Stabilisation Policy," *Review of Economics and Statistics* 39 (May 1957):124–33.

9. Economists have thus far paid little attention to these possibilities, although we teach our first-year students that medium of exchange and unit of account need not coincide. For a notable exception see Joan Knox, "Index-Regulated Loan Contracts," *South African Journal of Economics* 32 (December 1964):237–52.

10. "Cultivated Growth and the Market Economy," *South African Journal of Economics* 31 (September 1963):165–74.

The Market Economy and the Distribution of Wealth

Everywhere today in the free world we find the opponents of the market economy at a loss for plausible arguments. Of late the "case for central planning" has shed much of its erstwhile luster. We have had too much experience of it. The facts of the last forty years are too eloquent.

Who can now doubt that, as Professor Mises pointed out thirty years ago, every intervention by a political authority entails a further intervention to prevent the inevitable economic repercussions of the first step from taking place? Who will deny that a command economy requires an atmosphere of inflation to operate at all, and who today does not know the baneful effects of "controlled inflation?" Even though some economists have now invented the eulogistic term "secular inflation" in order to describe the permanent inflation we all know so well, it is unlikely that anyone is deceived. It did not really require the recent German example to demonstrate to us that a market economy will create order out of "administratively controlled" chaos even in the most unfavorable circumstances. A form of economic organization based on voluntary cooperation and the universal exchange of knowledge is necessarily superior to any hierarchical structure, even if in the latter a rational test for the qualifications of those who give the word of command could exist. Those who are able to learn from reason and experience knew it before, and those who are not are unlikely to learn it even now.

Reprinted from Mary Sennholz, ed., *On Freedom and Free Enterprise: Essays in Honor of Ludwig von Mises* (New York: D. Van Nostrand, 1956).

Confronted with this situation, the opponents of the market economy have shifted their ground; they now oppose it on "social" rather than economic grounds. They accuse it of being unjust rather than inefficient. They now dwell on the "distorting effects" of the ownership of wealth and contend that "the plebiscite of the market is swayed by plural voting." They show that the distribution of wealth affects production and income distribution since the owners of wealth not merely receive an "unfair share" of the social income, but will also influence the composition of the social product: Luxuries are too many and necessities too few. Moreover, since these owners do most of the saving they also determine the rate of capital accumulation and thus of economic progress.

Some of these opponents would not altogether deny that there is a sense in which the distribution of wealth is the cumulative result of the play of economic forces, but would hold that this cumulation operates in such a fashion as to make the present a slave of the past, a bygone an arbitrary factor in the present. Today's income distribution is shaped by today's distribution of wealth, and even though today's wealth was partly accumulated yesterday, it was accumulated by processes reflecting the influence of the distribution of wealth on the day before yesterday. In the main this argument of the opponents of the market economy is based on the institution of Inheritance to which, even in a progressive society, we are told, a majority of the owners owe their wealth.

This argument appears to be widely accepted today, even by many who are genuinely in favor of economic freedom. Such people have come to believe that a "redistribution of wealth," for instance through death duties, would have socially desirable, but no unfavorable economic results. On the contrary, since such measures would help to free the present from the "dead hand" of the past they would also help to adjust present incomes to present needs. The distribution of wealth is a datum of the market, and by changing data we can change results without interfering with the market mechanism! It follows that only when accompanied by a policy designed continually to redistribute existing wealth, would the market process have "socially tolerable" results.

This view, as we said, is today held by many, even by some economists who understand the superiority of the market economy over the command economy and the frustrations of interventionism, but dislike what they regard as the social consequences of the market economy. They are prepared to accept the market economy only where its operation is accompanied by such a policy of redistribution.

The present paper is devoted to a criticism of the basis of this view.

In the first place, the whole argument rests logically on verbal confusion arising from the ambiguous meaning of the term "datum." In common usage as well as in most sciences, for instance in statistics, the word "datum" means something that is, at a moment of time, "given" to us as observers of the scene. In this sense it is, of course, a truism that the mode of the distribution of wealth is a datum at any given moment of time, simply in the trivial sense that it happens to exist and no other mode does. But in the equilibrium theories which, for better or worse, have come to mean so much for present-day economic thought and have so largely shaped its content, the word "datum" has acquired a second and very different meaning: Here a datum means a necessary condition of equilibrium, an independent variable, and "the data" collectively mean the total sum of necessary and sufficient conditions from which, once we know them all, we without further ado can deduce equilibrium price and quantity. In this second sense the distribution of wealth would thus, together with the other data, be a DETERMINANT, though not the only determinant, of the prices and quantities of the various services and products bought and sold.

It will, however, be our main task in the paper to show that the distribution of wealth is not a "datum" in this second sense. Far from being an "independent variable" of the market process, it is, on the contrary, continuously subject to modification by the market forces. Needless to say, this is not to deny that at any moment it is among the forces which shape the path of the market process in the immediate future, but *it is* to deny that the mode of distribution as such can have any permanent influence. Though wealth is always distributed in some definite way, the mode of this distribution is ever-changing.

Only if the mode of distribution remained the same in period after period, while individual pieces of wealth were being transferred by inheritance, could such a constant mode be said to be a permanent economic force. In reality this is not so. The distribution of wealth is being shaped by the forces of the market as an object, not an agent, and whatever its mode may be today will soon have become an irrelevant bygone.

The distribution of wealth, therefore, has no place among the data of equilibrium. What is, however, of great economic and social interest is not the mode of distribution of wealth at a moment of time, but its mode of change over time. Such change, we shall see, finds its true place among the events that happen on that problematical "path" which may, but rarely in reality does, lead to equilibrium. It is a typically "dynamic" phenomenon. It is a curious fact that at a time when so much is heard of the need for the pursuit and promotion of dynamic studies it should arouse so little interest.

Ownership is a legal concept which refers to concrete material objects. Wealth is an economic concept which refers to scarce resources. All valuable resources are, or reflect, or embody, material objects, but not all material objects are resources: Derelict houses and heaps of scrap are obvious examples, as are any objects which their owners would gladly give away if they could find somebody willing to remove them. Moreover, what is a resource today may cease to be one tomorrow, while what is a valueless object today may become valuable tomorrow. The resource status of material objects is therefore always problematical and depends to some extent on foresight. An object constitutes wealth only if it is a source of an income stream. The value of the object to the owner, actual or potential, reflects at any moment its expected income-yielding capacity. This, in its turn, will depend on the uses to which the object can be turned. The mere ownership of objects, therefore, does not necessarily confer wealth; it is their successful use which confers it. Not ownership but use of resources is the source of income and wealth. An ice-cream factory in New York may mean wealth to its owner; the same ice-cream factory in Greenland would scarcely be a resource.

In a world of unexpected change the maintenance of wealth is always problematical; and in the long run it may be said to be impossible. In order to be able to maintain a given amount of wealth which could be transferred by inheritance from one generation to the next, a family would have to own such resources as will yield a permanent net income stream, i.e., a stream of surplus of output value over the cost of factor services complementary to the resources owned. It seems that this would be possible only *either* in a stationary world, a world in which today is as yesterday and tomorrow like today, and in which thus, day after day, and year after year, the same income will accrue to the same owners or their heirs; *or* if all resource owners had perfect foresight. Since both cases are remote from reality we can safely ignore them. What, then, in reality happens to wealth in a world of unexpected change?

All wealth consists of capital assets which, in one way or another, embody or at least ultimately reflect the material resources of production, the sources of valuable output. All output is produced by human labor with the help of combinations of such resources. For this purpose resources have to be used in certain combinations; complementarity is of the essence of resource use. The modes of this complementarity are in no way "given" to the entrepreneurs who make, initiate, and carry out production plans. There is in reality no such thing as *A* production function. On the contrary, the task of the entrepreneur consists precisely in finding, in a world of perpetual change, which combination of resources will yield, in the conditions of today, a maximum surplus of output over input value, and in guessing which will do so in the probable conditions of tomorrow, when output values, cost of complementary input, and technology all will have changed.

If all capital resources were infinitely versatile the entrepreneurial problem would consist in no more than following the changes of external conditions by turning combinations of resources to a succession of uses made profitable by these changes. As it is, resources have, as a rule, a limited range of versatility, each is specific to a number of uses.[1] Hence, the need for adjustment to change will often entail the need for a change in the composition of the resource group, for "capital regrouping." But each change in the mode of complementarity will affect the value of the component resources by giving rise to capital gains and losses. Entrepreneurs will make higher bids for the services of those resources for which they have found more profitable uses, and lower bids for those which have to be turned to less profitable uses. In the limiting case where no (present or potential future) use can be found for a resource which has so far formed part of a profitable combination, this resource will lose its resource character altogether. But even in less drastic cases capital gains and losses made on durable assets are an inevitable concomitant of a world of unexpected change.

The market process is thus seen to be a leveling process. In a market economy a process of redistribution of wealth is taking place all the time before which those outwardly similar processes which modern politicians are in the habit of instituting, pale into comparative insignificance, if for no other reason than that the market gives wealth to those who can hold it, while politicians give it to their constituents who, as a rule, cannot.

This process of redistribution of wealth is not prompted by a concatenation of hazards. Those who participate in it are not playing a game of chance, but a game of skill. This process, like all real dynamic processes, reflects the transmission of knowledge from mind to mind. It is possible only because some people have knowledge that others have not yet acquired, because knowledge of change and its implications spread gradually and unevenly throughout society.

In this process he is successful who understands earlier than any one else that a certain resource which today can be produced when it is new, or bought, when it is an existing resource, at a certain price A, will tomorrow form part of a productive combination as a result of which it will be worth A'. Such capital gains or losses prompted by the chance of, or need for, turning resources from one use to another, superior or inferior to the first, form the economic substance of what wealth means in a changing world, and are the chief vehicle of the process of redistribution.

In this process it is most unlikely that the same man will continue to be right in his guesses about possible new uses for existing or potential resources time after time, unless he is really superior. And in the latter case his heirs are unlikely to show similar success—unless they are superior, too. In a world of unexpected change, capital losses are ultimately as inevitable as are capital gains. Competition between capital owners and the specific nature of durable resources, even though it be "multiple specificity," entail that gains are followed by losses as losses are followed by gains.

These economic facts have certain social consequences. As the critics of the market economy nowadays prefer to take their stand on "social" grounds, it may be not inappropriate here to elucidate the true social results of the market process. We have already spoken of it as a leveling process. More aptly, we may now describe these results as an instance of what Pareto called "the circulation of elites." Wealth is unlikely to stay for long in the same hands. It passes from hand to hand as unforeseen change confers value, now on this, now on that specific resource, engendering capital gains and losses. The owners of wealth, we might say with Schumpeter, are like the guests at a hotel or the passengers in a train: They are always there but are never for long the same people.

It may be objected that our argument applies in any case only to a small segment of society and that the circulation of elites does not eliminate social injustice. There may be such circulation among wealth owners, but what about the rest of society? What chance have those without wealth of even participating, let alone winning, in the game? This objection, however, would ignore the part played by managers and entrepreneurs in the market process, a part to which we shall soon have to return.

In a market economy, we have seen, all wealth is of a problematical nature. The more durable assets are and the more specific, the more restricted the range of uses to which they may be turned, the more clearly the problem becomes visible. But in a society with little fixed capital in which most accumulated wealth took the form of stocks of commodities, mainly agricultural and perishable, carried for periods of various lengths, a society in which durable consumer goods, except perhaps for houses and furniture, hardly existed, the problem was not so clearly visible. Such was, by and large, the society in which the classical economists were living and from which they naturally borrowed many traits. In the conditions of their time, therefore, the classical economists were justified, up to a point, in regarding all capital as virtually homogeneous and perfectly versatile, contrasting it with land, the only specific and irreproducible resource. But in our time there is little or no justification for such dichotomy. The more fixed capital there is, and the more durable it is, the greater the probability that such capital resources will, before they wear out, have to be used for purposes other than those for which they were originally designed. This means practically that in a modern market economy there can be no such thing as a source of permanent income. Durability and limited versatility make it impossible.

It may be asked whether in presenting our argument we have not confused the capital owner with the entrepreneur, ascribing to the former functions which properly belong to the latter. Is not the decision about the use of existing resources as well as the decision which specifies the concrete form of new capital resources, viz. the investment decision, a typical entrepreneurial task? Is it not for the entrepreneur to regroup and redeploy combinations of capital goods? Are we not claiming for capital owners the economic functions of the entrepreneur?

We are not primarily concerned with claiming functions for anybody. We are concerned with the effects of unexpected change on asset values and on the distribution of wealth. The effects of such change will fall upon the owners of wealth irrespective of where the change originates. If the distinction between capitalist and entrepreneur could always easily be made, it might be claimed that the continuous redistribution of wealth is the result of entrepreneurial action, a process in which capital owners play a merely passive part. But that the process really occurs, that wealth is being redistributed by the market, cannot be doubted, nor that the process is prompted by the transmission of knowledge from one center of entrepreneurial action to another. Where capital owners and entrepreneurs can be clearly distinguished, it is true that the owners of wealth take no active part in the process themselves, but passively have to accept its results.

Yet there are many cases in which such a clear-cut distinction cannot be made. In the modern world wealth typically takes the form of securities. The owner of wealth is typically a shareholder. Is the shareholder an entrepreneur? Professor Knight asserts that he is, but a succession of authors from Walter Rathenau[2] to Mr. Burnham have denied him that status. The answer depends, of course, on our definition of the entrepreneur. If we define him as an uncertainty-bearer, it is clear that the shareholder is an entrepreneur. But in recent years there seems to be a growing tendency to define the entrepreneur as the planner and decision-maker. If so, directors and managers are entrepreneurs, but shareholders, it seems, are not.

Yet we have to be careful in drawing our conclusions. One of the most important tasks of the entrepreneur is to specify the concrete form of capital resources, to say what buildings are to be erected, what stocks to be kept, etc. If we are clearly to distinguish between capitalist and entrepreneur we must assume that a "pure" entrepreneur, with no wealth of his own, borrows capital in money form, i.e., in a non-specific form, from "pure" capital owners.[3]

But do the directors and managers at the top of the organizational ladder really make all the specifying decisions? Are not many such decisions made "lower down" by works managers, supervisors, etc.? Is it really at all possible to indicate "the entrepreneur" in a world in which managerial functions are so widely spread?

On the other hand, the decision of a capital owner to buy new shares in company A rather than in company B is also a specifying decision. In fact this is the primary decision on which all the managerial decisions within the firm ultimately depend, since without capital there would be nothing for them to specify. We have to realize, it seems, that the specifying decisions of shareholders, directors, managers, etc., are in the end all mutually dependent upon each other, are but links in a chain. All are specifying decisions distinguished only by the degree of concreteness which increases as we are moving down the organizational ladder. Buying shares in company A is a decision which gives capital a form less concrete than does the decision of the workshop manager as to which tools are to be made, but it is a specifying decision all the same, and one which provides the material basis for the workshop manager's action. In this sense we may say that the capital owner makes the "highest" specifying decision.

The distinction between capital owner and entrepreneur is thus not always easily made. To this extent, then, the contrast between the active entrepreneurs, forming and redeploying combinations of capital resources, and the passive asset owners, who have to accept the verdict of the market forces on the success of "their" entrepreneurs, is much overdrawn. Shareholders, after all, are not quite defenseless in these matters. If they cannot persuade their directors to refrain from a certain step, there is one thing they can do: They can sell!

But what about bondholders? Shareholders may make capital gains and losses; their wealth is visibly affected by market forces. But bondholders seem to be in an altogether different position. Are they not owners of wealth who can claim immunity from the market forces we have described, and thus from the process of redistribution?

In the first place, of course, the difference is merely a matter of degree. Cases are not unknown in which, owing to failure of plans, inefficiency of management, or to external circumstances which had not been foreseen, bondholders had to take over an enterprise and thus became involuntary shareholders. It is true, however, that most bondholders are wealth owners who stand, as it were, at one remove from the scene we have endeavored to describe, from the source of changes which are bound to affect most asset values, though it is not true of all of them. Most of the repercussions radiating from this source will have been, as it were, intercepted by others before they reach the bondholders. The higher the "gear" of a company's capital, the thinner the protective layer of the equity, the more repercussions will reach the bondholders, and the more strongly they will be affected. It is thus quite wrong to cite the case of the bondholder in order to show that there are wealth owners exempt from the operation of the market forces we have described. Wealth owners as a class can never be so exempt, though some may be relatively more affected than others.

Furthermore, there are two cases of economic forces engendering capital gains and losses from which, in the nature of these cases, the bondholder cannot protect himself, however thick the protective armor of the equity may happen to be: the rate of interest and inflation. A rise in long-term rates of interest will depress bond values where equity holders may still hope to recoup themselves by higher profits, while a fall will have the opposite effect. Inflation transfers wealth from creditors to debtors, whereas deflation has the opposite effect. In both cases we have, of course, instances of that redistribution of wealth with which we have become acquainted. We may say that with a constant long-term rate of interest and with no change in the value of money, the susceptibility of bond holders' wealth to unexpected change will depend on their relative position as against equity holders, their "economic distance" from the center of disturbances; while interest changes and changes in the value of money will modify that relative position.

The holders of government bonds, of course, are exempt from many of the repercussions of unexpected change, but by no means from all of them. To be sure, they do not need the protective armor of the equity to shield them against the market forces which modify prices and costs. But interest changes and inflation are as much of a threat to them as to other bondholders.

In the world of permanent inflation in which we are now living, to regard wealth in the form of government securities as not liable to erosion by the forces of change would be ludicrous. But in any case the existence of a government debt is not a result of the operation of market forces. It is the result of the operation of politicians eager to save their constituents from the task of having to pay taxes they would otherwise have had to pay.

The main fact we have stressed in this paper, the redistribution of wealth caused by the forces of the market in a world of unexpected change, is a fact of common observation. Why, then, is it constantly being ignored? We could understand why the politicians choose to ignore it: After all, the large majority of their constituents are unlikely to be directly affected by it, and, as is amply shown in the case of inflation, would scarcely be able to understand it if they were. But why should economists choose to ignore it? That the mode of the distribution of wealth is a result of the operation of economic forces is the kind of proposition which, one would think, would appeal to them. Why, then, do so many economists continue to regard the distribution of wealth as a "datum" in the second sense mentioned above? We submit that the reason has to be sought in an excessive preoccupation with equilibrium problems.

We saw before that the successive modes of the distribution of wealth belong to the world of disequilibrium. Capital gains and losses arise in the main because durable resources have to be used in ways for which they were not planned, and because some men understand better and earlier than other men what the changing needs and resources of a world in motion imply. Equilibrium means consistency of plans, but the redistribution of wealth by the market is typically a result of inconsistent action. To those trained to think in equilibrium terms it is perhaps only natural that such processes as we have described should appear to be not quite "respectable." For them the "real" economic forces are those which tend to establish and maintain equilibrium. Forces only operating in disequilibrium are thus regarded as not really very interesting and are therefore all too often ignored. There may be two reasons for such neglect. No doubt a belief that a tendency towards equilibrium does exist in reality and that, in any conceivable situation, the forces tending towards equilibrium will always be stronger than the forces of resistance, plays a part in it.

But an equally strong reason, we may suspect, is the inability of economists preoccupied with equilibria to cope at all with the forces of disequilibrium. All theory has to make use of coherent models. If one has only one such model at one's disposal a good many phenomena that do not seem to fit into one's scheme are likely to remain unaccounted for. The neglect of the process of redistribution is thus not merely of far-reaching practical importance in political economy since it prevents us from understanding certain features of the world in which we are living. It is also of crucial methodological significance to the central area of economic thought.

We are not saying, of course, that the modern economist, so learned in the grammar of equilibrium, so ignorant of the facts of the market, is unable or unready to cope with economic change; that would be absurd. We are saying that he is well-equipped only to deal with types of change that happen to conform to a fairly rigid pattern. In most of the literature currently in fashion change is conceived as a transition from one equilibrium to another, i.e., in terms of comparative statics. There are even some economists who, having thoroughly misunderstood Cassel's idea of a "uniformly progressive economy," cannot conceive of economic progress in any other way![4] Such smooth transition from one equilibrium (long-run or short-run) to another virtually bars not only discussion of the process in which we are interested here, but of all true economic processes. For such smooth transition will only take place where the new equilibrium position is already generally known and anticipated before it is reached. Where this is not so, a process of trial and error (Walras' *"tâtonnements"*) will start which in the end may or may not lead to a new equilibrium position. But even where it does, the new equilibrium finally reached will not be that which would have been reached immediately had everybody anticipated it at the beginning, since it will be the cumulative result of the events which took place on the "path" leading to it. Among these events changes in the distribution of wealth occupy a prominent place.

Professor Lindahl[5] has recently shown to what extent Keynes's analytical model is vitiated by his apparent determination to squeeze a variety of economic forces into the Procrustean bed of short-period equilibrium analysis. Keynes, while he wished to describe the *modus operandi* of a number of dynamic forces, cast his model in the mold of a system of simultaneous equations, though the various forces studied by him clearly belonged to periods of different length. The lesson to be learned here is that once we allow ourselves to ignore fundamental facts about the market, such as differential knowledge, some people understanding the meaning of an event before others, and in general, the temporal pattern of events, we shall be tempted to express "immediate" effects in short-period equilibrium terms. And all too soon we shall also allow ourselves to forget that what is of real economic interest are not the equilibria, even if they exist, which is in any case doubtful, but what happens between them. "An auxiliary makeshift employed by the logical economists as a limiting notion"[6] can produce rather disastrous results when it is misemployed.

The preoccupation with equilibrium ultimately stems from a confusion between subject and object, between the mind of the observer and the minds of the actors observed. There can, of course, be no systematic science without a coherent frame of reference, but we can hardly expect to find such coherence as our frame of reference requires ready-made for us in the situations we observe. It is, on the contrary, our task to produce it by analytical effort. There are, in the social sciences, many situations which are interesting to us precisely because the human actions in them are inconsistent with each other, and in which coherence, if at all, is ultimately produced by the interplay of mind on mind. The present paper is devoted to the study of one such situation. We have endeavored to show that a social phenomenon of some importance can be understood if presented in terms of a process reflecting the interplay of mind on mind, but not otherwise. The model-builders, econometric and otherwise, naturally have to avoid such themes.

It is very much to be hoped that economists in the future will show themselves less inclined than they have been in the past to look for ready-made, but spurious, coherence, and that they will take a greater interest in the variety of ways in which the human mind in action produces coherence out of an initially incoherent situation.

NOTES

1. The argument presented in what follows owes a good deal to ideas first set forth by Professor Mises in "Das festangelegte Kapital," in *Grundprobleme der Nationalökonomie*, pp. 201–14. [English trans. in *Epistemological Problems of Economics* (New York: D. Van Nostrand, 1960), pp. 217–31.]

2. Vom Aktienwesen, 1917.

3. This definition has, of course, certain social implications. Those who accept it can hardly continue to regard entrepreneurs as a class access to which is impossible for those with no wealth of their own. Whatever degree of the "imperfection of the capital market" we choose to assume will not give us this result.

4. For a most effective criticism of this kind of model building see Joan Robinson, "The Model of an Expanding Economy," *Economic Journal* 62 (March 1952):42–53.

5. Erik Lindahl "On Keynes' Economic System," *Economic Record* 30 (May 1954): 19–32; 30 (November 1954):159–71.

6. Ludwig von Mises, *Human Action* (New Haven: Yale University Press, 1949), p. 352.

Cultivated Growth and the Market Economy

1.

In looking around for a suitable subject for this address I have been struck, once again, by the limited range of topics available to an academic economist on occasions such as this. In this age in which, the narrower the range of one's speciality the higher the reputation one is able to enjoy, there are few fields in which his knowledge can permit him to speak with competence and with the confidence that he has anything worthwhile to say. Moreover, where his own field of interests lies on a level of abstraction to which he cannot very well expect a "captive" audience to follow him willingly, and not merely for the sake of politeness, this field, too, is barred to him.

Last year I endeavoured to solve the problem by inviting my audience to follow me in an exploration of the deeper causes of the inflation of our time, which we found partly in certain characteristics of the economic institutions of modern society, and largely in the climate of opinion within which these institutions have to function. Alas, such themes, in which the topical impinges upon the abstract, and which permit the academic economist to display the practical relevance of supposedly esoteric issues, are rare.

Yet I have come to think that there is one kind of contribution such an academic economist might make that may be of wider interest, viz.: to clarify the terms in which controversial opinions on an economic issue are expressed. For we often find cases in which controversy on an economic issue is due not so much to

Presidential address delivered at the Thirty-sixth Annual General Meeting of the Economic Society of South Africa held in Pretoria on 16th August 1963. Reprinted from *South African Journal of Economics* 31 (September 1963).

different observations of facts, nor to differences in value judgements (in which latter case the economist as such can have nothing to say), but to the fact that different economists relate the facts observed and the practical issues in hand to different conceptual frameworks. In such cases we say that they "do not speak the same language" or "misunderstand each other's terms" because these belong to different conceptual structures. Here it is possible to feel that the economist whose chief interests lie in the field of theory may perhaps render a service by helping to make it clear where and how the conceptual frameworks of the contestants differ from each other, and by thus contributing towards the elucidation of the issues at stake.

In what follows I shall endeavour to make a contribution of this nature with regard to the controversy on *non-coercive Planning or Economic Budgeting* in the course of which some of my fellow-economists have of late expressed their views on the compatibility of certain forms of PLANNING with the principles and *modus operandi* of a Market Economy.

I have to make it clear at the outset that I shall not plead for or against this or that type of Planning. My task will be to find out whether or not a certain type of Planning would be possible within the framework of a Market Economy. Whether or not it is, or will be, possible in practice, and if so, whether it should be adopted in the present situation in this country, are entirely different questions on which I do not feel competent to pronounce. For, let me add that I lack all practical knowledge of the subject. My knowledge of it, such as it is, is all derived from reading books and articles on various forms of Planning in different countries and at different times. It is truly academic— in the worst of possible senses. But it may be just for this reason that I think I have been able to detect, in the controversy mentioned, certain differences in shades of meaning, in approach and conceptual structure, and in particular in what is implicitly taken for granted, that may seem of no interest to the man of action absorbed in his task, but are of interest to those concerned with the clarification of controversial issues.

In turning now to this task of elucidation I shall first deal with the fundamental concepts involved. Later on I shall have some-thing to say about certain economic problems likely to be en-countered by a policy of cultivating growth by concerted action.

2.

What are the essential characteristics of the new Planning? In the first place, it has nothing whatever to do with the kind of Central Planning typical of the countries under the domination of Communism. Private enterprise is safeguarded and all Plan-ning is private planning by entrepreneurs. Nor is it akin to the form of Planning we found, e.g., in Nazi Germany before 1939 (what Walter Euken called *Zentralverwaltungswirtschaft*) which so largely employed compulsion over what were otherwise still private producers. The new Planning uses no compulsion, it leaves the entrepreneurs the free choice of their resources—but it tries to persuade them to plan and act otherwise than they would have done, had they drawn up their respective plans in isolation from each other.

The essence of *Economic Budgeting*, this new non-coercive type of Planning, as I understand it, is, then, the continuous exchange of information among entrepreneurs about each other's inten-tions, which will enable every entrepreneur, in making his plan, to know what every one else plans to do. Also, since certain projections of expected future trends in the economic system are being shown to them, it is hoped and expected that they will take them into account. In other words, we find here a method, not of engineering growth by decree, but of *cultivating* it by creating the conditions, at least so far as entrepreneurial knowledge goes, which may give rise to it. The analogy of the gardener, as distinct from the engineer, naturally suggests itself.

How far all this is really feasible, or would produce results notably different from what would happen without such con-certing of plans, only experience can show. I would hesitate to draw too far-reaching conclusions from the French example. In the first place, the economic theorist must show some caution in interpreting economic history. We never know how much of what happened was due to the special circumstances of time and place, and how much to underlying economic forces. Secondly, French planning methods themselves have changed in seventeen years.

In any case, we are here concerned not with feasibility but with conditions and implications. When we ask how far such Planning is compatible with the existence of a Market Economy, we are really asking: Are the conditions which make the existence of a Market Economy possible such that better knowledge obtained by exchange of information is likely to cause faster growth?

What we have to deal with, then, is an endeavour to co-ordinate the plans of entrepreneurs, investment plans as well as plans about the use of existing resources, *ex ante*. It is true that in a Market Economy the market process would in any case produce co-ordination, but it would do so only *ex post*. Economic Budgeting means that the participants, entrepreneurs and economic planners, acting in concert, determine the *collective environment* within which each private planner carries out his own plan. The fact that he knows, or at least hopes to, what plans the others—be they customers or suppliers, or even potential rivals—will follow, offers him points of orientation which should reduce his uncertainty and, in favourable circumstances, enable him to make more definite plans. Individual plans are thus being *attuned* to each other. Each entrepreneur is able to carry out his plans with a greater assurance than he could do otherwise.

We must now take a closer look at the social and political background of the scheme. The modern State in its Western version, which promotes such schemes for faster economic growth, is what has come to be known as a Welfare State: it has taken over the responsibility for satisfying more and more needs. Already it has made itself responsible for Full Employment. It may be said that taking on the responsibility for growth is merely a further step along the same road. But it is a step which must be regarded with great misgivings, in general and not merely on economic grounds.

In the first place, we have to ask ourselves: Where and when is this process to end? Secondly, it means that more and more economic phenomena will become political issues—with all that this means in the age of the mass electorate! It is difficult to contemplate with equanimity a situation in which, whether a government can stay in power, will depend on its ability to persuade the electorate that the rate of growth of the national economy could not possibly have been higher, and in which the opposition will have to address itself to refuting this claim. Already it is possible to sense a certain note of hysteria in some discussions, even academic, on growth. Can we economists relish the prospect of an era in which the range of political jugglery with economic concepts is thus greatly extended, until one day perhaps the question whether a country's "actual growth" was what was "warranted," not to mention its "natural rate," becomes a favourite topic for comment in the columns of the daily press? Perhaps the pages adjacent to the sports columns would provide an appropriate place for such a feature.[1]

Let us remember two facts. First, "Economics is the study of mutual interference: any 'abnormal' movement cannot long continue without sooner or later bringing into play corrective movements."[2] Secondly, all policy consists in the simultaneous pursuit of a number of objectives, the relative significance of each of which has to be continuously weighed against that of the others. "Growth" cannot be pursued in isolation from other economic objectives.

We now have to confront our main question, viz. whether Economic Budgeting of the kind described above is compatible with the principles and *modus operandi* of the Market Economy.

A Market Economy is an economy in which all want-satisfying activities are carried out by individuals. Units of production are organised by individual entrepreneurs (who usually act in groups). The very essence of the Market Economy consists in the continuous *Market Process,* the never-ending course of entrepreneurial action set in train by price-cost differences, actual or expected. In exploiting these profitable opportunities entrepreneurs adjust supply to demand thus reducing existing disequilibria. If their activity is unhampered, and if no new changes supervened, their action should in the end wipe out the very price-cost differences which originally motivated it. Of course this never happens. In the real world equilibrium does not exist.

We therefore have to distinguish sharply between this "ideal type" of a Market Economy and what is often now called the *neoclassical* model, as it has emerged from the work of Walras, Pareto and Cassel. This model denotes a *closed system* in which equilibrium prices and equilibrium quantities produced and exchanged are all mutually determined. The Market Economy, on the contrary, is an open system. Its prices and quantities are not equilibrium prices and quantities; hence they are not determinate. The very possibility of making profits stems from the absence of equilibrium. The Market Economy essentially rests on a mechanism of adjustment, but of adjustment to everchanging circumstances. To put one's trust in the Market Economy is not to assert a faith in the final attainment of equilibrium, nor even in the efficacy of the equilibrating forces, which might be hampered or deflected before attaining their goal. It is to assert a faith in the beneficial results of the continuous Market Process the *modus operandi* of which I have tried to sketch.

There is another important difference between the neoclassical equilibrium system and the Market Economy which lies behind the dichotomy "closed system—open system." This difference concerns the kind of knowledge assumed. In the former case we have to assume that all those who participate in market action leading towards equilibrium actually know the equilibrium position before it is reached. Otherwise it is hard to see how it can be attained. But it has been pointed out that equilibrium theory, for all its sophistication and ostensible precision, fails to explain where entrepreneurs derive such knowledge from.[3] Equilibrium theory has to assume a state of knowledge shared by all participants as a datum the origin of which is left in the dark.

In the Market Economy, on the other hand, we can assume no such state of knowledge. Each entrepreneur, at each moment, has to make the most profitable use of the resources at his disposal, including his knowledge. Naturally he will do his best to improve the latter. Entrepreneurial action is a good example of "learning by doing." But there is here no such thing as a common state of knowledge shared by all which we could regard as a datum. On the contrary, it is knowledge superior to that of others which brings success. A common state of knowledge may emerge, perhaps, in the end, as the net result of these diverse actions. It would then last only until circumstances change again.

From the fact that in a Market Economy everybody is engaged in the exploitation of profitable opportunities inherent in price-cost differences, actual or expected, it does not follow that all such opportunities in existence at any moment will actually be exploited. There may well be "gaps" due to that incomplete knowledge which is a feature of reality, as distinct from the neo-classical model. Some profitable opportunities will be neglected. We cannot even say that these will be the least profitable. It all depends on the distribution of knowledge among entrepreneurs, and this is a matter about which we can say nothing in general.

In the light of these circumstances, the conclusion that a scheme for the exchange of information and subsequent action based upon it is incompatible with the principles and *modus operandi* of the Market Economy does not appear to be warranted. The Market Economy is an open system. We cannot say what concrete action an entrepreneur confronted with a given situation will actually take. It depends on his interpretation of it. Hence, we are unable to say that Economic Budgeting will deflect the course of his action from what it would be otherwise, since we simply do not know what that might have been. A closed system, like the Walrasian, would permit us to say that. But it has no counterpart in reality, as equilibrium is merely a figment of the imagination of the model-builders.

Similar reasoning applies to the question of the effect on entrepreneurial knowledge. Economic Budgeting certainly will change the distribution of knowledge among entrepreneurs in the direction of greater similarity. But, as we saw, no assumption about the mode of distribution of this knowledge is included among the fundamental postulates of the Market Economy. In it changes in knowledge happen every day. The Market Economy is neutral with respect to the knowledge required of its actors.

Again, it would be different in a general equilibrium model in which a certain state of knowledge has to be assumed. But for the reasons given no such model can serve as a standard of comparison for anything that happens in the real world.

3.

We now have to address ourselves to the question, in what way Economic Budgeting by the co-ordination of entrepreneurial plans can lead to a higher rate of growth than would otherwise exist. In general, our answer has to be, by widening knowledge about the possible use of resources and its consequences. But what specific results might be achieved in this way? What are the plants we are thus enabled to cultivate in our garden?

There are in general, so far as I can see, three methods of promoting faster growth:

(1) By increasing investment at the expense of consumption. But, whether this takes place in the form of demand inflation or otherwise, e.g., by taxation, this method could hardly be called non-coercive. I shall therefore ignore it.

(2) By making full use of resources that would otherwise not be used, or not fully used. This is of course the essence of Keynesian teaching. As regards labour, I have nothing new to say. But as regards capital and natural wealth I shall have something to say later on.

(3) By reducing the amount of *malinvestment*. I trust you will forgive me as one who has, for some time, taken a special interest in problems of capital structure, if I not merely find this a congenial theme, but also if I see in the possible reduction of malinvestment the most promising avenue for cultivating growth by means of the co-ordination of plans within a Market Economy.

Every capital good exists in a specific form which limits the range of its possible uses: it has limited versatility. Each capital good therefore depends for its efficient use on the support of other capital goods complementary to it. Malinvestment may arise in many ways through faulty expectations, but failure of complementary capital goods to become available is one of them.

The market process tends to produce a coherent complementarity pattern throughout the economic system *ex post,* but it does its work by compelling the scrapping of those capital goods which do not fit into this pattern, or at least their removal to other spheres of production where a pigeon-hole can be found for them, usually with a concomitant capital loss. The market process tends to eliminate the results of malinvestment but cannot prevent its occurrence.

The question now before us is, whether it is possible by co-ordinating investment plans of many entrepreneurs *ex ante* to prevent such a waste of resources. If we succeed in this we can make a given amount of investment yield more output; we obtain a higher rate of growth per unit of investment input. To illustrate this possibility let me give you two well-known examples of malinvestment which might be prevented by co-ordination of plans.

There is, firstly, the case, often mentioned by critics of the Market Economy,[4] where, owing to the market structure, an increase in demand for the product leads to excess capacity. Let us assume that the demand for a certain product rises by m. If the marginal capital output ratio in the industry is 3, an investment of $3m$ in the industry is required. But if the industry consists of ten firms each of which hopes to attract the additional demand entirely to itself, $30m$ will actually be invested with the result we can all imagine. It is possible to see the primary function of Economic Budgeting in the prevention of this kind of excess capacity.

There is, secondly, the case where capital investment in an industry cannot be profitably used for lack of complementary capital resources at other stages of production. This may result either from weakness of what has come to be known as the *infra structure* or from what we shall have to call "weakness of the *super structure*." The latter happens where, e.g., the possibilities opened up by a new capital good are not exploited by the consumption goods industries, or where lack of an adequate sales organization hampers the sale of a new consumption good. Even in such cases we need not doubt that the market process will ultimately lead to the growth of such complementary resources, in infra structure and super structure, as will be required. The question before us is whether by co-ordination of plans and concerted action such a result can be brought about earlier, or without the temporary waste of resources.

I see the chief importance of *growth point planning* in the possibility of anticipating the effects of growth in some industries on the composition of output and the capital structure of others. And I see the significance of input-output tables in that they enable us, I will not say to "forecast," but to form an idea about the changes in the composition of the flow of circulating capital between earlier and later stages of production which a given change in output is likely to entail. It is to be hoped that in assessing the effects of output changes on capital requirements it will become possible to extend this type of analysis to fixed capital which does not enter the input-output streams.

So far I have spoken of the prevention of excess capacity. But there are also interesting problems resulting from the existence of excess capacity the occurrence of which could not be prevented. It may be the result of malinvestment of the past, or of sudden changes in demand or in technique of production. Of the numerous problems we meet here I shall confine myself to two.

(1) The problem of how to use excess capacity, i.e., capital resources which are excessive in the industry in which they happen to be, is really a problem of making the best use of what has turned out to be unsuccessful investment of the past. The question before us here is really, how to draw from these resources an output stream different from the one for which they were originally planned, but the value of which still exceeds direct costs. The problem here is that there can be few entrepreneurs with that comprehensive knowledge of the whole economy required for a successful shifting of such resources. No doubt a Market Economy would after a time produce a specialist in such capital regrouping operations, perhaps from the ranks of industrial bankers. On the other hand, the comprehensive knowledge at the disposal of growth point planners might enable them to do it more expeditiously.

An example of what I have in mind is what would happen in a mining district in which the mines are exhausted and in which the infra structure (houses, transport, power, etc.) complementary to mining resources is still physically intact now that it has lost its complements. The infra structure is specific to the area but not specific to the economic activities taking place in it. There is here evidently a case for the centralised collection and subsequent diffusion of information about such alternative activities in order to increase the range of possible uses of these temporarily complementless capital resources.

(2) On the other hand, all unexploited mineral and other natural wealth is also a kind of complementless excess capacity provided by Nature. This case is the exact opposite of the one just discussed, since here it is precisely the lack of complementary capital in the form of the infra structure, as well as of more specific capital resources like mining equipment, etc., which prevents us from exploiting all this wealth at one and the same time. Here location in space presents the greatest problem. If the infra structure were not specific to an area we could move it about to meet the changing needs of the areas presently to be exploited. The hard fact of its specificity compels the making of economic decisions about the exploitation of such wealth, which calls again for the application of comprehensive knowledge about the likely effects of changes in the mode of exploitation of such resources on the rest of the economy. Here, too, we can see scope for concerted action.

4.

Lastly, I come to the question, whether the practice of Economic Budgeting is at all compatible with the principles of competition. Does not competition require the competitors to act in ignorance of one another's intentions, with their minds directed solely to market prices, actual or expected? Will these business men, exchanging information, learning about one another's plans, agreeing among one another to avoid excess capacity, not end up by constituting a super-cartel—with the benevolent connivance of the planners?

This is a serious and difficult question. It is a question I dare not shirk since I did promise to devote myself to the clarification of concepts in this controversial issue. At the same time it is a question which has been raised in the controversy. It might even be said that it is the central question.

Now the main difficulty in answering it can be stated briefly. At bottom it is the same difficulty we encountered before. The only concept of competition we could use as our criterion exists only within the framework of an equilibrium model. It is the well-known notion of *pure* or *perfect competition*. But in the real world it does not exist. The Market Economy, on the other hand, certainly requires competitive markets. But in spite of valiant attempts to work out a concept of *"workable competition"* to serve as a criterion for a Market Economy, we have not succeeded (yet?) in finding one that would be suitable. We are unable to say how competitive a Market Economy has to be.

Moreover, in reality it would be quite impossible for all markets within a Market Economy to be equally competitive. Hence, whatever our criterion is to be, some might fall within it, others not. How, then, do we determine the permissible scope of the Market Economy? What range of dispersion of market conditions do we have to use as our criterion, and how is this range to be defined? This is of some importance for our problem since Economic Budgeting, as we saw, concerns not merely relationships between producers for the same market but also between suppliers and customers at different stages of production. In practice we often find that the problems arising in such inter-industrial relations are solved by means of *vertical integration*, e.g., coal-iron-steel, or by similar devices. It seems that they are hardly compatible with the competitive character of a Market Economy. But in the absence of a clearly defined criterion of such competition as is required by the principles of the Market Economy, how are we to judge them? The same applies to Economic Budgeting.

But I do not think we should rest content with the negative conclusion that the case against the compatibility between Economic Budgeting and the Market Economy cannot be proved as long as we do not know how much competition the latter requires. I think we should go a step further.

I said earlier on that in a Market Economy there is no such thing as a common state of knowledge, but that everybody acts on his own individual knowledge. But is it not one of the purposes of Economic Budgeting, perhaps the most important, to produce just such a common state of knowledge? It seems to me that here we have to consider the social function of competition.

In a Market Economy, everybody, producer and consumer, is continuously engaged in acquiring new knowledge, testing and diffusing it. The very fact, e.g., that successful innovations will be imitated, illustrates this. The Market Economy as it were, sends out its agents in various directions on reconnaissance duties. What they bring back is then tested, in workshop and market-place, and the consumer ultimately decides what he likes best. Technical progress requires experiments in various directions, and this entails product differentiation.

But this is not the only way in which new knowledge can be acquired, tested and diffused. Sometimes this task is delegated to a special agency, say a research institute, which then puts the new knowledge at the disposal of all by direct communication.

It now seems to me that the knowledge to be diffused by means of Economic Budgeting may be such as to lend itself to this second method of diffusion. Or, to put this distinction in another way: Competition is an excellent method of reducing our ignorance in those cases in which division of labour will be most useful. But there are other cases in which the best results will be obtained by close cooperation of specialists in a narrow field and the subsequent direct communication of their results to those who can make use of them. The knowledge conveyed by input-output tables, for instance, appears to be of this second kind. In other words, in those cases where we can obtain knowledge otherwise than through the market process, competition is not a necessary requirement either.

We need not doubt that, in the absence of a scheme such as the one under discussion, wherever the exchange of information is of mutual profit to entrepreneurs, the Market Economy would still evolve institutions which serve this end. European economic history in the age of free enterprise offers many examples of this. I find this view perfectly compatible with a belief that a public agency, guided by competent economists, could do it more expeditiously and perhaps more thoroughly. I should not care to say, however, which way fewer mistakes are likely to be made.

Earlier on I promised you not to plead for or against this or that type of Planning, but to confine myself to the elucidation of conceptual differences. In so doing I drew attention, in particular, to what appear to me to be important differences between the "ideal type" of the Market Economy and the neo-classical equilibrium model. In this regard we found that different assumptions about distribution of knowledge among entrepreneurs and its diffusion between them called for special notice.

I believe it to be no accident that thus, in probing a practical problem of economic organization, we have found ourselves at last confronted with a problem concerning knowledge. This fact in my view should serve us as a warning against a narrowly materialistic interpretation of the subject of our discipline.

"Economics is not about goods and services; it is about human choice and action," Ludwig von Mises has said. To which I would add, if you will permit me such an *obiter dictum* as a concluding remark, that the knowledge we gain from economic study is not knowledge about things but knowledge about knowledge. This is the strongest reason I can think of why the study of our discipline must not be pursued as though it were a natural science.

NOTES

1. The effect of the current obsession with growth on the quality of economic theorizing has been no less disastrous. "In tackling the problems of economic growth, economists in the last decade or so appear to have adopted the custom of discarding their habitual apparel and

instead donning that of the planner or technocrat. Indeed the recent cataract of journal articles and books on this obsessive subject have set a deplorable standard in economic writing. It would seem that the ability to manipulate a second order difference equation—plus, perhaps some passing reference to holy works—is the only qualification required of the writer. At any rate, it is often the only one displayed." E. J. Mishan, *Economica* 29 (February 1962):88.

2. See previous footnote.

3. G. B. Richardson, *Information and Investment* (London: Oxford University Press, 1960), Chapter I.

4. See, e.g., Joan Robinson, *Economic Philosophy* (London: C. A. Watts & Co., 1962), p. 136.

APPENDIX
Economic Writings of Ludwig M. Lachmann

Books and Monographs

Economics as a Social Science: Inaugural Lecture. Johannesburg: University of the Witwatersrand, 1950.

Capital and Its Structure. London: London School of Economics and Political Science, 1956. Reprint edition. Kansas City: Sheed Andrews & McMeel, forthcoming.

The Legacy of Max Weber. Berkeley, California: Glendessary Press, 1971.

Macro-economic Thinking and the Market Economy: An Essay on the Neglect of the Micro-Foundations and Its Consequences. London. Institute of Economic Affairs, 1973.

Articles

"Commodity Stocks and Equilibrium." *Review of Economic Statistics* 3(June 1936):230–34.

"Uncertainty and Liquidity Preference." *Economica* 4(August 1937):295–308.

"Investment and Costs of Production." *American Economic Review* 28(September 1938):469–81.

"Commodity Stocks in the Trade Cycle." Jointly with F. Snapper. *Economica* 5(November 1938):435–54.

"On Crisis and Adjustment." *Review of Economics and Statistics* 21(May 1939):62–68.

"A Reconsideration of the Austrian Theory of Industrial Fluctuations." *Economica* 7(May 1940):179–96.*

"On the Measurement of Capital." *Economica* 8(November 1941):361–77.

"The Role of Expectations in Economics as a Social Science." *Economica* 14(February 1943):108–19.*

"Finance Capitalism?" *Economica* 11(May 1944):64–73.

"Notes on the Proposals for International Currency Stabilization." *Review of Economics and Statistics* 26(November 1944):184–91.

---

*Indicates that the article is included in this volume.

"A Note on the Elasticity of Expectations." *Economica* 12(November 1945):248–53.

"Complementarity and Substitution in the Theory of Capital." *Economica* 14(May 1947):108–19.*

"Investment Repercussions." *Quarterly Journal of Economics* 62(November 1948):698–713. "Reply." *Quarterly Journal Economics* 63(August 1949):432–34.

"Joseph A. Schumpeter, 1883–1950." *South African Journal of Economics* 18(June 1950):215–18.

"Economics as a Social Science." *South African Journal of Economics* 18(September 1950):233–41.*

"The Science of Human Action." *Economica* 18(November 1951):412–27.*

"Some Notes on Economic Thought, 1933–1953." *South African Journal of Economics* 22(March 1954):22–31.*

"The Velocity of Circulation as a Predictor." *South African Journal of Economics* 24(March 1956):17–24.

"The Market Economy and the Distribution of Wealth." In *On Freedom and Free Enterprise: Essays in Honor of Ludwig von Mises*, edited by Mary Sennholz. New York. D. Van Nostrand, 1956.*

"Mrs. Robinson on the Accumulation of Capital." *South African Journal of Economics* 26(June 1958):87–100.*

"Professor Shackle on the Economic Significance of Time." *Metroeconomica* 11(September 1959):64–73.*

"Cost Inflation and Economic Institutions." *South African Journal of Economics* 30(September 1962):177–89.

"Cultivated Growth and the Market Economy." *South African Journal of Economics* 31(September 1963):165–74.*

"Sir John Hicks on Capital and Growth." *South African Journal of Economics* 34(June 1966):113–23.*

"The Significance of the Austrian School of Economics in the History of Ideas." Translation of "Die geistesgeschichtliche Bedeutung der österreichischen Schule in der Volkswirtschaftslehre." *Zeitschrift für Nationalökonomie* 26(January 1966):152–67.*

"Model Constructions and the Market Economy." Translation of "Marktwirtschaft und Modellkonstruktionen." *Ordo* 17(1966):261–79.*

"Causes and Consequences of the Inflation of Our Time." *South African Journal of Economics* 35(December 1967):281–91.*

"Methodological Individualism and the Market Economy." In *Roads to Freedom: Essays in Honour of Friedrich A. von Hayek*, edited by Erich Streissler et al. London: Routledge & Kegan Paul, 1969.*

"The Rationale for Economic Development Programming and the Market Economy." *South African Journal of Economics* 39(December 1971):319–32.

"Ludwig von Mises and the Market Process." In *Toward Liberty: Essays in Honor of Ludwig von Mises,* edited by Friedrich A. Hayek. 2 vols. Menlo Park, Calif.: Institute for Humane Studies, 1971.*

"Sir John Hicks as a Neo-Austrian." *South African Journal of Economics* 41(September 1973):195–207.*

"From Mises to Shackle: An Essay." *Journal of Economic Literature* 14(March 1976):54–62.

"On the Central Concept of Austrian Economics: Market Process." "On Austrian Capital Theory." "Toward a Critique of Macroeconomics." "Austrian Economics in the Age of the Neo-Ricardian Counterrevolution." In *The Foundations of Modern Austrian Economics,* edited by Edwin G. Dolan. Kansas City: Sheed Andrews & McMeel, 1976.

INDEX

341

Untersuchungen (Menger), 47-49, 57
User cost, 30-31
Utility concept, 4, 5, 55, 156

Value and Capital (Hicks), 6, 143, 239, 241, 251, 252, 263
Value judgments, 166
Value theory, 11, 16, 50-53, 156, 198, 215, 223, 225
Verstehende, 9, 16, 47, 49, 55, 59, 60, 154, 155; *see also* Understanding
Vertical integration, 334

Wage and price controls, 22
Wage fund theory, 253, 256
Wage level, 281
Wage theory, 22, 28, 31, 32, 216-217, 219, 220, 253, 255, 258, 270, 274-275, 278, 280-282, 296-302, 304, 306
Wage unit, 300
Walras, Léon, 46, 47, 54-56, 92, 122, 150, 186, 244, 245, 261, 263, 264, 268, 269, 302, 320, 328, 329;

equilibrium theory, 189, 192-193; marginalism of, 4, 5
Walras-Paretian general equilibrium theory, 29
Wealth, 315
Wealth distribution, 17, 124, 163, 308-322
Wealth redistribution, 309-310, 313, 314, 316, 319, 321
Weber, Max, 7, 9, 15, 16, 23, 53; on methodology, 95; subjectivism of, 4
Welfare economics, 134-135, 301, 326
Wicksell, Knut, 7, 29, 268; on expectations, 92, 141; interest theory, 78-79
Wicksteed, Philip, 5
Wieser, F. von, 48, 52, 53, 57, 59
Wilson, Thomas, 76-77
Wirtschaftsrechnung (Schönfeld), 193
World War II, 15, 135

Zentralverwaltungswirtschaft, 325